# 100 THINGS METS FANS
## SHOULD KNOW & DO
## BEFORE THEY DIE

Matthew Silverman

TRIUMPH
BOOKS

*To Shea Stadium and all who've kept the faith,*
*but mostly to my trio of Mets fans,*
*fleeter than birds: Debbie to Tyler to Jan.*

Copyright © 2008, 2010 by Matthew Silverman

No part of this publication may be reproduced, stored in a retrieval system, or trans-mitted in any form by any means, electronic, mechanical, photocopying, or otherwise, without the prior written permission of the publisher, Triumph Books, 542 South Dearborn Street, Suite 750, Chicago, Illinois 60605.

Triumph Books and colophon are registered trademarks of Random House, Inc.

Library of Congress Cataloging-in-Publication Data

Silverman, Matthew, 1965–
  100 things Mets fans should know and do before they die / Matt Silverman.
    p. cm.
  Includes bibliographical references.
  ISBN 978-1-60078-424-8
  1. New York Mets (Baseball team)—Anecdotes. 2. New York Mets (Baseball team)—Miscellanea. I. Title. II. Title: One hundred things Mets fans should know and do before they die.
  GV875.N37S55 2010
  796.357'64097471—dc22

                              2010002147

This book is available in quantity at special discounts for your group or organization. For further information, contact:
    **Triumph Books**
    542 South Dearborn Street
    Suite 750
    Chicago, Illinois 60605
    (312) 939-3330
    Fax (312) 663-3557
    www.triumphbooks.com

Printed in U.S.A.
ISBN: 978-1-60078-424-8
Design by Patricia Frey
All photos courtesy of Getty Images unless otherwise indicated.

# Contents

# Acknowledgments

When the hardcover version of this book was published in the spring of 2008, Shea Stadium was preparing for its final year. The 2010 paperback version of *100 Things Mets Fans Should Know & Do Before They Die* finds the Mets in Year Two of Citi Field. There are incessant injury bugs, ever-present pitching woes, front office foolishness, exorbitant ticket prices…in other words, the same old stuff. This book takes the long view of the Mets, which means that no team can likely be as bad as the first club in 1962 and no team will probably be as good as the 1969 squad. If you doubt that argument, then flip ahead and start reading—though you'll note the book begins with the quintessential 1986 moment.

Mets history has endured a tumultuous couple of years and that is reflected in this edition. There are also a few things that got left out because the original book had numerous entries detailing how to get around Shea Stadium before the shelf life of that advice expired. Well, they paved paradise, put up a parking lot…and we now have Lee Mazzilli, not to mention profiles of Carlos Beltran, Al Leiter, David Cone, Johan Santana, and the person I still think of when I hear the words "Shea Stadium" and "home run" in the same sentence: Dave Kingman. Additions include the tale of the Home Run Apple and the last day at Shea Stadium. Citi Field has a new entry and has moved up 11 places in two years—if the Mets could move up that far that fast, they'd be tied for second-best record in the National League by 2012. Some say that '12 also marks either the start of a new era of mankind or the end of the planet. I can only guess which one Mets fans think it will be. If you're standing by someone in a Mets hat at Armageddon, the last words you ever hear may be: "Great, just when we started winning…"

Most of the 100 items in this book (plus sidebars) are filtered through the perspective of how a Mets fan would look at them…or at least one that shares my views and values on the team. To shed a little more light on a subject dear to all our hearts, I asked a few others to share their perceptions on the franchise. The feedback from my previous book, *Mets Essential,* and the stories people relayed to me at various appearances made me think these stories should be chronicled in some way. You'll find many of these "Fan's View" tidbits scattered throughout *100 Things Mets Fans Should Know & Do Before They Die.* In the case of one fan's journey north to see the '86 World Series, I even participated. The stories are intended to ring a bell, touch a chord, and provide different perspectives on key moments in Mets history.

Some facts are repeated in *100 Things Mets Fans Should Know & Do Before They Die,* as happens a lot with good stories. But scratch the surface of the items herein and you'll find more than just a ranked list. If a favorite memory is missing, read on and you'll likely find it.

My genuine gratitude goes to those who eagerly shared their Mets memories with me: John and Laura Booth, Liam Butler, Dan Carubia, Bill Earl, Lou Longobardi, Paul Lovetere, Mike Meserole, Robert Pizzella, and Jim Starr. While there are many Mets websites and blogs out there, these people were chosen because this book is pretty much their outlet beyond Citi Field to communicate their thoughts and experiences as Mets fans. Their feelings are genuine, and I'm honored they allowed me to present them. Thanks.

I also want to express my appreciation for Mets-related help from Ralph Kiner, Shannon Forde, Roberto Beltramini, and Victoria Estevez. Thanks to Adam Motin, Tom Bast, Natalie King, and Mitch Rogatz at Triumph Books. Also thanks to Authentic Writing Workshop in Woodstock for their help in finding a voice, as well as Bruce Markusen, Jon Springer, Brad Smith, Alec Dawson, and Linc Wonham. And thanks to Josh Leventhal, Mark Weinstein, Greg Prince, Greg Spira, Jim Walsh, Andy Esposito, Stanley Cohen, and Dana Brand, as well as my agents Anne Marie O'Farrell and

Chris Morehouse. Plus Keith Hernandez, who dialed in at a very solid #14 in the first edition of this book months before we met to team up as improbable co-authors for *Shea Good-Bye*. His skills as an editor put me on point, got me to dig deep, made me a better writer, and showed me that book signings can rock. Thanks to Kai and Duncan for their patience. As always, thanks to my parents for the opportunity to see the team often, and to siblings Marie, Michael, and Mark for listening to me go on and on about the Mets (and not just when we were kids).

Books that have been of help are listed in the Notes section. Number 81 in *100 Things Mets Fans Should Know & Do Before They Die* contains a list of other helpful Mets books and websites. Two sites that deserve mention specifically are retrosheet.com and baseball-reference.com, both of which make this type of work less arduous and more fun. A special thanks to my cousin and friend Blair Rafuse, who patiently and expertly helped get metsilverman.com off the ground and made it work better than I could have hoped. Comments and observations are always welcome.

Two books deserving specific mention were written by the late Leonard Koppett and Jack Lang, newspapermen there at the beginning of the Mets. Their team histories, very different yet both outstanding, shared the same title: *The New York Mets*. I felt remarkably disillusioned and shortchanged when Tom Seaver was traded in 1977, but Jack Lang kept writing about the team in the *Daily News,* so I kept on reading. That Lang, who died in 2007, made that listless, Seaver-less team worth reading about is proof enough of his ability. Leonard Koppett's analysis of the club is still among the best ever written. These men were as significant in the telling of Mets history as Gil Hodges and Tom Seaver were in making it.

# Introduction

If you had to come up with a list of the 100 quintessential things about the Mets that you needed to know, what would they be? You could take the best 100 of the 800-plus players in franchise history, and weave in the managers. You could take the 100 most important games the team has played, but you'd be grasping toward the end. You could take 100 experiences from a Mets fan's perspective and arrange them from top to bottom. You could take the top 100 key moments from a historical perspective. Or you could throw them all together and dive right in.

Picking these moments takes a thorough knowledge of baseball history, a floor strewn with books and printouts, an electronic spreadsheet that allows for constant resorting, and a pressing deadline. One thing that wasn't agonized over was the understanding that rooting for the Mets is the greatest test of a sports fan's soul in New York. The sweeping highs and lows, the inferiority complex that comes from living in the shadow of Big Brother's Evil Empire, the legacy that not one but *two* baseball teams had to abandon New York for you to even exist, and the underlying feeling that things can't possibly get any worse. Well, sometimes they do. And sometimes you're on top of the world.

*100 Things Mets Fans Should Know & Do Before They Die* is about history, both of the team and those who follow it. Now that the book is done, let the kibitzing begin. In a city that argues about everything, and with a team whose fans stay up nights fretting over every decision, it's only fair that someone who writes about the ups and downs of others' careers has his hand put to the fire by ranking every great moment, player, and manager, not to mention concepts, stadiums, and even the club's primary media outlets. There is much to be said about all these things, but in the end it comes down to an individual choice, a right to root in a town that doesn't like fence-sitters. The question seems simple.

"Yankees or Mets?" In fourth grade I had an idea that those were baseball teams, but I wasn't 100 percent positive. "Mets or Yankees?" my teacher, Mr. Walker, asked again, transposing the names. I noticed everyone looking at me, expecting a decision. I had been daydreaming, about what I'm not sure, but it wasn't baseball. I didn't follow baseball and had never given it much thought, to be quite honest. It was like waking up and having no idea what you'd dreamt. I was awake after 10 years of peaceful slumber.

The boys around me at Iona Grammar School explained that both the Yankees' and the Mets' season openers were on television, and Mr. Walker was letting us spend the last hour of the day watching one game or the other—the vote was up to us. The tally was dead even, 15–15. (A couple years later it would be 25–5.)

Everyone was waiting and some were starting to get impatient. They were the Yankees fans, apparently accustomed—even at the age of 10 and a decade removed from the World Series—of getting what they wanted. They pressed me with threats of "Yankees." Friends on the other side quietly urged "Mets." It never occurred to me that our New Rochelle school was just 15 miles from Yankee Stadium (being rebuilt just then); or that my brothers and sister had been crazy about the Mets during the 1969 and 1973 pennant furies; or that my great-grandmother, about to turn 100, had been a rabid Yankees ticket holder in the days of Ruth and Gehrig. At that time, the question was like someone asking if I wanted my eggs fried or scrambled.

"Mets," I said. And Mr. Walker turned on the black-and-white set in the classroom, heretofore used exclusively for the weekly student-run program and the updates of the top sellers of the Emerald Isle Sweepstakes tickets we were all forced to sell. As the set quickly warmed up, Mr. Walker switched the knob to Channel 9, a station I would be glued to for seasons to come. The Mets won.

Others have come about their Mets obsession through heredity, proximity, or even via milk carton. Interspersed in this book among the 100 things every Mets fan needs to know in this lifetime are stories from other Mets fans from all over the New York area about their lives and devotion to the team. Some fans have lost the fire over time, and some are just igniting it, but each one has their own story to tell about the franchise that brought us Casey, Kranepool, Al Jackson, Yogi, Ron Hunt, Ron Swoboda, Ron Taylor, Cleon, Tug, Bud Tom Terrific, Grote, Gil, Agee, Kooz, Kong, Rusty, Matlack, Maz, Mookie, Keith, Straw, Doc, Darling, El Sid, HoJo, Kid, Dykstra, McDowell, Coney, Fonzie, Bobby V., Mike, Leiter, David, Carlos, Johan, and Jose, with the word picture painted ever so perfectly by Ralph, Lindsey, and Murph, plus those who have followed.

The Mets make summer last longer or pass more swiftly, depending on the kind of season the team is enjoying/enduring. The Mets teach us about suffering and humility, not to mention joy and living in the moment, as well as retrospection and an appreciation of history. Even when the team is 10 games out and records a bottom-of-the-ninth victory, it's only after the mind compartmentalizes and rationalizes the standings that the moment is trivialized or elevated. Then we move on with our lives; the players go on with theirs. It quickly transforms into history. But neither side seems complete without the cheering, whether it's in a player's ear or in our throats.

Maybe life would be a little different if there had been different Yankees fans back in fourth grade. If it had been a year or two later, they would not have needed my vote at all, and maybe I would have continued oblivious to the pulsing of baseball for a while longer. Such would have been the pity. Because when you're in that stadium and the man is rounding third and the left fielder makes ready that throw home, there is nothing in the world but that ball in the air. The waiting is what keeps a fan alive. The knowing is what makes us appreciate it.

# 1 First Off, Bill Buckner

Bill Buckner killed the Mets. After he became a Cub in 1977, Billy Buck hit .332 with 43 RBIs against the Mets over his first six years in Chicago, with four homers and 18 knocked in during 1982 alone. He petered out a little the next year against New York and was traded to the American League for Dennis Eckersley. Mets fans may have wondered, whatever happened to Bill Buckner?

With Buckner batting third in a veteran lineup, the Red Sox took the first two World Series games at Shea Stadium in 1986. The Mets powered back to win the next two at Fenway Park. Boston won Game 5 to reach the brink of its first world championship since 1918. The Red Sox beat New York's ace, Dwight Gooden, and that was Doc's last start of the Series…and his second loss.

Bob Ojeda, hated by his Red Sox teammates (and vice versa) prior to his off-season trade to New York, was on the mound for his second Game 6 in 10 days. With the Mets having to win in the NLCS or else face nemesis Mike Scott in Game 7, Ojeda started at the Astrodome…and promptly gave up three runs in the first inning. The Mets won in an epic 16-inning marathon. This time he looked in for the sign with Buckner at the plate in the first inning when every eye at Shea suddenly turned skyward. Michael Sergio, an actor from the soap opera *Loving*, parachuted onto the field near first base. A couple of policemen matter-of-factly collected Sergio, his parachute, plus his "Go Mets" banner, and led him off the field. Pitcher Ron Darling gave Sergio a high five on his way through the dugout. Buckner flied out, but a single, a walk, and then a double by Dwight Evans made it 1–0. Boston added another run in the second.

1

# Fan's VIEW

## Bill Earl
## (Stone Ridge, NY)

### Nobody Move or It's All Over

That the 1986 Mets were going to win the National League East wasn't news—even after a four-game losing streak, they still led by 18—but that it had taken five days longer than expected made it must-see baseball. Bill Earl, a senior at Francis Lewis High School next door in Fresh Meadows, bought distant upper-deck seats at Shea the night of September 17 with a few classmates. "You walked into the stadium knowing it was the night, you just knew," Earl recalled. "Gooden was on the mound. It was a party from the first inning. It was definitely a party in the upper deck."

Earl and several thousand others worked their way down to the field level for the ninth inning. "When the last out was made, it was like the whole stadium emptied onto the field," he said. While he watched fans tear up the grass, Earl, a future high school baseball coach, thought about the field: "I kept thinking, they have another game tomorrow."

The field was in fine shape by Game 6 of the World Series. "A friend of mine who worked there over the summer sort of knew someone who knew someone who helped lift a gate open and we went in. I don't think you could do that now with all the security," he said. "We sort of floated around, hit or miss, and when we got to the field level, first-base side, we didn't want to leave because we weren't sure we'd get back down there."

Just when it looked like it was all going to be for naught, Gary Carter's single kept the Series alive. "At the same time my friend and I both said, 'Don't move.' The third guy we were with didn't know what we were talking about. There was no time to explain baseball super-stition, but we told him he couldn't move because the whole World Series could change if he did. Keith Hernandez was sitting in the club-house smoking a cigarette; he didn't move either."

Three stiff bodies and a reliever later, Mookie Wilson lined a ball just foul. "In my heart, I thought, 'Crap, that was the one.' And then you get the wild pitch and the place went absolutely bananas and you never heard anything...well, I can't say that because when the

> ball went through Buckner's legs, that was the loudest sound I can ever remember."
>
> He was in the upper deck for the Game 7 comeback and culmination, but that almost felt anticlimactic. "It's weird to say, but to me it felt like the World Series ended in Game 6. There was no way they could lose Game 7," he said. "It was either the curse of the Red Sox or someone steering the Mets' fate. One thing or another."
>
> Or maybe it was someone sitting very still. Waiting. And Orosco's pitch to Barrett...

The Mets tied it against Boston's ace, Roger Clemens. Ray Knight had an RBI single, and Danny Heep, batting for shortstop Rafael Santana in the fifth inning, brought in the equalizer on a double-play ball. Knight's error in the seventh allowed Boston to take the lead. It stayed a one-run game when Jesse Orosco replaced Roger McDowell with the bases loaded in the eighth and retired Buckner on a fly out to center.

The Red Sox made a pitching change of their own in the bottom of the eighth, replacing Clemens with Calvin Schiraldi, Boston's key figure in the Ojeda deal with the Mets the previous winter. The pitcher made a bad throw to second on a sacrifice, and the Mets had two men on with none out, instead of one on and one out. The Mets tied the game on Gary Carter's sacrifice fly on a 3–0 pitch.

The tense game passed through the ninth and into the tenth inning with New York's bullpen and bench taxed. The Mets were on their third shortstop of the night, Howard Johnson (a third baseman by trade), and had gone through their top two relievers. Rick Aguilera, a starter during the season, allowed a home run to Dave Henderson to snap the tie, and then a two-out single by Marty Barrett made it a two-run lead. Buckner was hit by a pitch, presenting manager John McNamara a chance to replace the hobbled veteran with Dave Stapleton as he'd done throughout the postseason

*The most memorable moment in Mets history—and perhaps the worst moment in the lives of Bill Buckner and millions of Boston Red Sox fans.*

in games Boston led. But Buckner remained at first base and stayed there for the bottom of the inning. He wanted to be on the field for the celebration.

The Mets had had everything go their way all season and now this. Shea Stadium grew despondent as Wally Backman and then Keith Hernandez flew out against Schiraldi. Gary Carter was the last hope. Brought over from Montreal in an effort to finally win the World Series, Kid pulled a single into left field to keep the game alive. Rookie Kevin Mitchell, who would have a long and interesting career, carved his name into Mets lore by reaching base with a line single. Knight followed with a single to center to make it 5–4 with Mitchell going to third and Schiraldi out of the game.

Bob Stanley came in to face Mookie Wilson. Wilson had played for Mets teams that finished an average of 23 games out of first place his first four years as a major leaguer. Now here he was facing

Bob Stanley, who'd pitched in Boston's 1978 one-game playoff loss against the Yankees. Something had to give.

Wilson fouled off Stanley's best stuff and watched two pitches off the plate for balls. Stanley made one bad pitch, a darting palm-ball at Wilson's feet, but Mookie jackknifed out of the way and, as catcher Rich Gedman chased it, Mitchell scored the tying run. Shea was deafening. And it wasn't over yet.

Knight led off second base and headed for third mechanically when Wilson rolled a grounder right at Buckner. The first baseman bent down for it and was ready to do what he did as well as anybody in baseball: flip the ball to the pitcher covering. Bothered by ankle problems, especially in 1986, he had led his league in assists four of the past five years. Only this time the ball missed his glove completely and kept rolling until it stopped several feet behind him on the grass. Right through his legs. He started after it and then stopped. Knight, on the other side of the field, threw his hands up and danced home in disbelief. Mets fans have seen the replay and have heard the radio call countless times. It never gets old. It never will.

# 2 Standing the World on Its Ear

The 1969 season began like all others before it: with a Mets loss. This time they lost to a team that had never even played a game before. The Montreal Expos won their inaugural game over the Mets, 11–10. Tom Seaver allowed a home run to pitcher Dan McGinn. Relief ace Ron Taylor surrendered a three-run home run to the first batter he faced in '69: Coco Laboy. It was the first major league hit for both Expos.

Yet from early on, there was something different about these Mets. When Seaver blanked Atlanta's Phil Niekro to put the Mets at 18–18 on May 21, eager writers cooed about it being the latest the Mets had ever been .500. The club refused the bait. "What's .500?" Seaver replied. "Let us reach first place. That'll mean something. We're looking far beyond .500."

On the distant horizon sat the Cubs. They came into Shea Stadium on July 8 with a 5½-game lead and the best record in the National League. Chicago had won five of the first six meetings between the clubs. The Mets had, however, swept a doubleheader in their last visit to Wrigley Field and were 34–20 since then. Jerry Koosman, who'd missed a few starts with an arm problem early in the year, was right as rain as he beat Fergie Jenkins. The next night Seaver was perfect—or as perfect as a Met was ever going to get— retiring the first 25 batters before Jimmy Qualls spoiled it with a single. Even after Chicago's Bill Hands won the third game at Shea and the opener at Wrigley the next week, the Mets took both series. As the Mets headed back home for the All-Star break five games behind, they watched a man walk on the moon on television at the Montreal airport. Stars would be in their eyes the whole second half.

It was a little cloudy for the first few weeks though. Second baseman Ken Boswell fulfilled his military service while Bud Harrelson returned and was a little off. The Mets played like a team that had never been in contention before, going 9–12, including sweeps both home and away by the Astros. The low point came when manager Gil Hodges walked out to left field and removed Cleon Jones, who'd been the All-Star starter and was contending for the batting title, in the middle of an inning when he did not hustle after a ball during a rout.

On August 13 the deficit was 10 games. The Mets weren't even in second place anymore. In truth, the Mets had the league—and especially Chicago manager Leo Durocher—right where they wanted them.

The Cubs, playing .632 ball at the time, went 18–27 down the stretch while the Mets were 38–11, a .776 clip. Using the Hodges platoon system at three infield positions and right field, plus Rube Walker's five-man pitching rotation, the Mets were rested and unbeatable. Durocher's veteran-laden Cubs used a four-man rotation and the same lineup day in and day out. Catcher Randy Hundley caught 30 out of 31 games in a 34-day span. Ernie Banks and Ron Santo missed two starts each in that period, right fielder Jim Hickman missed one, while Glenn Beckert and Billy Williams, who would set the National League record with 1,117 consecutive games, played every day. After averaging 4.7 runs per game through the first 117 games, the Cubs averaged 3.6 after that. Chicago's ERA was 4.16 over the final 45 games. It had been 3.08 up to that point.

New York's offense was inconsistent yet opportunistic. The Mets set a still-standing franchise mark for wins in a month, with 23 in September 1969, even though they scored fewer runs than they had in July or August. And their batting average was the lowest of any month all year (the Mets were even no-hit by Pittsburgh's Bob Moose on September 20). The thing was, the pitching staff surrendered just 70 runs all month, only 65 of which were earned, for a 2.15 ERA. The staff allowed three home runs in 30 games, something you might've expected in the Dead Ball Era 50 years earlier. And the mound had actually been lowered in '69.

Seaver won 25 games, including his last 10 decisions, allowing just 14 earned runs over those 11 starts. The Mets tossed 21 complete games out of their last 48 starts. On those rare occasions the starters needed a little help, the bullpen did not disappoint. Southpaw Tug McGraw allowed two earned runs over his last 19 appearances (38 innings), while Taylor, the righty, surrendered five in his last 18 outings (25 innings). The pair combined to go 7–2 with 11 saves and a combined ERA of 1.00 down the stretch.

Even after Chicago's collapse was official and newspapermen tried to come up with new adjectives and superlatives to describe what was happening, the Mets kicked it up another notch and put the thing away. Following three straight losses to the Pirates—the third being Moose's no-hitter—the Mets won nine in a row, including the division clincher. This was on top of a 10-game winning streak earlier in the month. The Mets finished with 100 wins. Amazin'.

More amazin' was the ease with which they dispatched the Braves in the first NLCS. The opener saw the Mets take an early lead, fall behind, tie it in the eighth, and take the lead when two Atlanta errors accounted for four unearned runs. The Mets took a big early lead the next day, but Koosman couldn't get through the fifth; New York pulled away, 11–6. With no off day, Game 3 in New York saw the best pitching of the series by the Mets, but it wasn't by starter Gary Gentry. The rookie was knocked out in the third inning, and Nolan Ryan entered with men on second and third, none out, and the Mets trailing 2–0. Atlanta didn't score. The Mets, meanwhile, took the lead on homers by Tommie Agee and Boswell. Ryan allowed a two-run home run by Orlando Cepeda in the fifth, but he singled to start a rally in the bottom of the inning. Rookie Wayne Garrett, snagged from the Braves in that year's Rule 5 draft, hit a two-run homer for the lead, and Ryan finished off Atlanta. Fans destroyed the field again, but by then everyone wanted a piece of this 100–1 shot that was now in the World Series.

This was where the story would end; the glass slipper wouldn't fit. That was the feeling after Baltimore spanked Seaver and the Mets in the opener 4–1. But New York would hold the Orioles to just five runs—and two extra base hits—over the final 39 innings of the Series. Koosman allowed two hits in Game 2, Gentry and Ryan permitted four hits in Game 3, Seaver surrendered six hits the following afternoon, and Koosman allowed five hits in what turned out to be the Series finale. Of course, it took legendary catches by Agee and Ron Swoboda to deprive Baltimore of three extra base hits and perhaps six runs. Shoe polish, a stray wrist, and some good old-fashioned home runs—three by Series MVP Donn Clendenon, one apiece by Agee and Ed Kranepool, and an unlikely game-tying blast by Al Weis in Game 5—and the mighty 108-win Orioles, virtually the same team that rolled the Dodgers for the 1966 world championship, were done. Seems that slipper was a perfect fit after all, colored orange and blue.

# 3 Tom Seaver

In typical Mets fashion, the franchise's greatest pitcher was acquired by pure luck. USC star pitcher Tom Seaver had been signed a few days after the 1966 college season had begun by the relocated Atlanta Braves. Commissioner William Eckert, who did little else in his brief and inconsequential reign, ruled that the Braves had acted improperly and Seaver could go to a team chosen at random if they matched the $50,000 promised in Atlanta's voided contract. The Mets—one of only three teams that bothered to enter the special lottery—beat out the Phillies and Indians. "The Franchise" changed the franchise quicker than anybody would have ever imagined.

George Thomas Seaver was National League Rookie of the Year just 18 months after signing with the Mets. Two years after that he had a Cy Young Award, the first of three he'd win in a seven-season span. But adding up the wins (198) and the accolades ("He's the kind of man you'd want your kids to grow up to be like," said Cleon Jones) never came close to measuring what Seaver meant to the club and to the fans.

Tom Terrific was completely in control of every situation. No opponent could rile him and no one could tell him he was coming out of a ballgame unless he agreed. At age 24 he was a 25-game winner and leader of the most unlikely world champion anyone could remember. He was brash and brave, a leader by example. He told his catcher, acerbic Jerry Grote, what he wanted to throw. Only once in his first 10 years was he not picked for the All-Star Game. He fanned 200 batters a record nine years in a row. In short, he was as close to Ted Williams as the Mets would ever get. And when Williams came to Shea Stadium for a ceremony in June 1999, a month before his poignant All-Star Game appearance, who other than Seaver was qualified to drive Teddy Ballgame to the mound?

Columnist Dick Young, who'd helped promote the term "new breed" for the early 1960s Mets, turned out not to really like the breed itself. With a few angry words on his typewriter, he helped send Seaver to Cincinnati on June 15, 1977—the day that it officially became a chore to be a Mets fan. When No. 41 returned to Shea on April 5, 1983, the cloud was officially lifted. The team wouldn't be good for another year—after Seaver was inexplicably let go in a compensation snafu—but fans could finally come out of hiding. It was as if the fans had the vote when Seaver was elected to the Hall of Fame with the highest percentage in history in 1992. But it was the writers saluting the king of the new breed. Seaver, not yet 30, had once said, "If you don't think baseball is a big deal, don't do it. But if you do, do it right."

**TRIVIA**
**Question**

It's pretty well known that future Mets manager Davey Johnson made the final out in the 1969 World Series, but what future Mets manager grounded into a double play to clinch the NL East title that year?

Trivia answers on page 256

Seaver came back as the club's announcer for seven seasons, until 2005. Everyone leaned a little closer to the set when he gave a critique of a young Mets pitcher. And everyone silently wished the years could pass away and he'd step back on that mound, shake off the catcher, go into his perfect motion, drag his knee across the dirt, and fire an unhittable pitch on the black.

# 4 Messy Jesse's Sweet 16 in Houston

This was supposed to be easy. The 1986 Mets, winners of 108 games and clearly the best team in baseball—just ask their fans—were supposed to march right over anyone they faced in the postseason. The Houston Astros? That franchise once named after a gun? The franchise that had entered the National League the same year as the Mets and hadn't even gotten to a World Series? The franchise that had trouble selling out their dome for the playoffs? Please.

Houston had their number. It was No. 33: Mike Scott. Scott, who actually came up through the Mets system, hadn't been considered worth much more than spare outfielder Danny Heep (the return from Houston in the 1982 trade). Then Roger Craig spent a winter showing him the split-fingered fastball. Add that to Scott's perceived ability to scuff the ball—he sure had the Mets looking and lunging—and New York's dreams of easy conquest were out the window. With Scott going the distance in Games 1 and 4 and ready to go again in Game 7, the only way it seemed the Mets could conquer Houston at all was to make sure they didn't face Scott a third time.

Thing was, every Houston pitcher had given the Mets trouble. Nolan Ryan had been off in Game 2 against Bob Ojeda, but Ryan was brilliant in Game 5, fanning 12 Mets. But a line drive by Darryl Strawberry that just carried over the fence was one of two hits he allowed in nine innings. Two more New York hits and an error by Houston in the bottom of the twelfth off Charlie

## Pain in the Schneck

Outfielder Dave Schneck set the Mets record by batting 11 times in one game on September 11, 1974. He had two hits in the 25-inning marathon with St. Louis, the longest game at Shea Stadium and the longest game played to a conclusion in National League history. (The Mets lost on an error.) Schneck managed the feat by being the only starter not to draw a walk in the game, and his subsequent 3-for-22 finish earned him a ticket to Philly as a throw-in in the lamentable Tug McGraw deal. Schneck never played in the majors again after his rough September in '74.

Kerfeld—with Gary Carter snapping a series-long slump to be the hero—provided the deciding run and gave the Mets the series lead.

Bob Knepper had one bad inning in his first start in the series yet still left Game 3 with the lead before the Mets pulled it out in the bottom of the ninth against Dave Smith. Knepper had the lead quickly in Game 6 as well, as Houston peppered Ojeda in the bottom of the first to take a 3–0 lead. The Astros were held off the scoreboard thereafter, but it seemed of little difference as Knepper allowed the Mets just two hits and a walk through eight innings.

Lenny Dykstra, whose homer had stolen Knepper's win in Game 3, pinch-hit in the ninth, lefty against lefty. Dykstra hit the hardest ball yet off Knepper for a leadoff triple. Mookie Wilson singled to right to make it 3–1. Knepper got Kevin Mitchell to ground out as Wilson reached second. Keith Hernandez came through with a double to make it a one-run game and knock out Knepper. In came Smith. He walked Carter and then Strawberry. Ray Knight lifted a long fly to right that plated Hernandez and tied the game.

Roger McDowell, who to this point had appeared in just one NLCS game, threw five scoreless innings while the Astros bullpen threw four. Finally, in the fourteenth inning, Wally Backman singled in Strawberry to make it 4–3. Jesse Orosco, who'd set the Mets career saves record earlier in the season and had earned the win the previous afternoon, came in to finish it. Orosco got the first out, but Billy Hatcher lifted a drive down the left-field line that hit the screen. Tied once more.

The Mets scored three times in the sixteenth on RBI hits by Knight and Dykstra, plus a wild pitch. It seemed like that should be enough. But at this point it was clear that nothing in this series happened as expected. Three straight Astros reached base. Glenn Davis kept the game alive with a two-out single to make it 7–6. Orosco was exhausted, everyone watching was spent, and nerves on the field were frayed.

With Kevin Bass at the plate and the tying and winning runs on base, Hernandez came over to the mound from first base. "I thought Jesse needed a little pumping up, and we couldn't throw Bass another fastball at that point," Hernandez recalled. "Then I waited for Gary to get there. I was looking at Jesse, but I was talking to Kid. I want to loosen him up. So I just looked at him and said, 'If you call one more fastball, we're going to fight.'"

Bass saw nothing but sliders and found nothing but air to set off a mad celebration by the Mets at the Astrodome. It carried into the locker room and all the way back to New York as the Mets trashed the airplane's interior. A book the next spring about that game by noted sportswriter Jerry Izenberg was called *The Greatest Game Ever Played*. No one on the Mets' side could argue about the title.

# 5 Mike Piazza

Since the arrival of Tom Seaver, the Mets have been considered a pitching club first with hitting secondary. Housed in a stadium that proved hard to hit in, the big free-agent boppers usually said no to

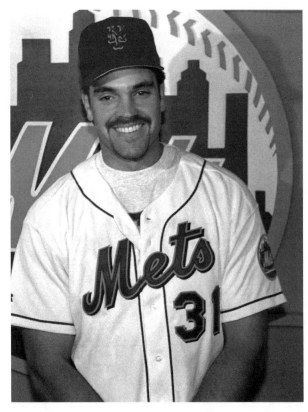

*After being traded to the Mets in 1998, catcher Mike Piazza quickly became the face of the franchise.*

Flushing. Mike Piazza became available in a deal that would disturb Los Angeles the way the Seaver trade had New York. Except the Dodgers didn't trade Piazza to the Mets, they sent him to the Marlins. Florida, the defending world champion, had dealt nearly every player of value since the previous fall's World Series, and there was little doubt Piazza would go in the next clearinghouse deal. Memorial Day weekend he was sent to the Mets for three young players, with only one (Preston Wilson) going on to a decent career.

Piazza was cheered, booed, and then cheered again in his four-month stay in New York before he became a free agent. The Mets had missed the postseason on the final weekend, but it certainly wasn't because of their new All-Star catcher. For the second time in six months, a Piazza transaction had fans honking their car horns as they sat in traffic. The team gave him seven years, $91 million, and he gave back a few numbers of his own: 220 home runs, 655 RBIs, and a .296 average (the next catcher on the club's career list, John Stearns, hit .259 with 46 home runs; Jerry Grote knocked in 298 fewer runs than Piazza in 263 more games).

Beyond stats, Piazza provided pizzazz. In a market dominated by the Yankees—who won the world championship in each of his first three seasons as a Met—Piazza was the face of the franchise, a national star. He led the Mets to the postseason in consecutive seasons, a first in club history. He was voted to start the All-Star Game all seven of his seasons with the Mets, missing the 2000 game with an injury. His feud with Roger Clemens, begun when he was hit in the head by a fastball and exacerbated when the Yankee threw a bat shard at Piazza during the 2000 World Series, became a national issue discussed ad nauseam for two years. Piazza earned a measure of revenge by homering when Clemens finally pitched at Shea. The press and the fans still wouldn't let it go.

Piazza let his actions speak, never more so than in the first outdoor sporting event after the attack on New York on September 11, 2001. His majestic home run at a key point in an important—a relative term in lieu of what had happened in the city—game helped give people reason to forget their problems, if only for a few moments.

Piazza's skills behind the plate, though never on par with his offensive capabilities, declined with age. Not long after he broke Carlton Fisk's career record of 351 home runs, the long-rumored switch to first base became official. It wasn't pretty, but in the long line of Mets first basemen, there have been worse (see Kingman, Dave). Manager Willie Randolph replaced Art Howe and switched him back to catcher the next year. Piazza played his last game as a Met in 2005 with a raucous sendoff rarely seen at Shea Stadium. It was repeated when he returned in 2006 as a Padre. And it will probably happen again someday when his No. 31 is hoisted up next to Seaver's 41 at Citi Field.

# 6 The Shoe Polish Incident

All the bad luck and tough breaks the Mets had accrued in their first seven seasons turned around in one year: 1969. The year that man landed on the moon, the Mets landed in first place. Hits found holes, opponents' liners found gloves, young pitchers found their mark, and the Mets found the Cubs in their sights and overtook them. New York City held on tight to their new heroes. Mayor John Lindsay, hip deep in the Mets bandwagon, went on to be reelected in a stunning political development. Even New York's infamous crime rate went down in 1969. Everyone was tuned into the Mets as they brought the Miracle into October.

The National League Championship Series, the first in history, was a bizarrely offensive affair. The Mets outscored the Braves in a three-game sweep, 27–15. The World Series started with a dose of reality, as the 108-win Orioles took the opener from Tom Seaver 4–1. The Mets held Baltimore to just two runs over the next three games thanks to great pitching, brilliant catches in the outfield by Tommie Agee and Ron Swoboda, and a throw that hit Met J.C. Martin's wrist and bounced away to put the Mets a win away from a world championship. It all happened that quickly.

The Orioles awoke in the third inning of Game 5. Pitcher Dave McNally and slugger Frank Robinson slammed home runs off Jerry Koosman for a 3–0 lead. It was the same score in the sixth inning when a McNally pitch near Cleon Jones's foot ricocheted toward the Mets' dugout. Umpire Lou DiMuro immediately threw a new ball in play, but Gil Hodges emerged from the dugout holding a ball, showing DiMuro a spot with shoe polish on it. Impressed, the ump sent Jones to first, even though an even closer pitch had gone against Frank Robinson in the top half of the inning (DiMuro said the ball hit the bat before it hit Robinson's thigh).

The next man up, Donn Clendenon, homered off the auxiliary scoreboard in left, and it was a 3–2 game. The next inning was light-hitting Al Weis's turn. He had never homered at Shea and he picked the seventh inning of Game 5 to do it. In the eighth Hodges chose to stick with his right-handed platoon players against righty Eddie Watt, and it worked. With first base open, Ron Swoboda lined a double down the line and Jones came around to score the go-ahead run. Two Orioles errors on Jerry Grote's grounder brought in Swoboda for a 5–3 lead.

To tease fate a little, Koosman walked the leadoff hitter and then mowed through Boog Powell, Brooks Robinson, and, finally, Davey Johnson on a fly to left. At 3:17 PM on October 16, 1969, a Thursday afternoon, the impossible came true. Everyone shine those shoes for the parade. It would be even bigger than the one the astronauts got just a few months earlier.

# 7 Gil Hodges

The reorganized Mets minor league system of the late 1960s produced unbelievable arms and a few good bats, the franchise had good scouting and acquired just enough hitting, but without the deal for the manager, the Amazin' Mets may have just been the Average Joes. Gil Hodges was the Miracle Man.

A coalminer's son from Indiana, a Marine sergeant and Bronze Star recipient in World War II, and a slugging first baseman with trusting hands who was so beloved in Brooklyn that a borough's prayers went out to him during a famous slump, Hodges could best

# Fan's VIEW
## Mike Meserole
## (Waterbury, Connecticut)

### Turning Point

Mike Meserole grew up watching National League baseball in the 1950s and was drawn to the Mets when they were formed. A lot of Meserole's enthusiasm was reserved for the team's first baseman, Gil Hodges. The Brooklyn legend was sent to Washington to try his hand at managing the new Senators. Hodges returned via trade in 1968 to take on the seemingly impossible task of making the Mets into a reputable franchise.

"Gil was my guy, from the first time I saw him play at Ebbets Field when I was seven, to his return from L.A. in 1962, to his return from Washington in 1968," Meserole says. With sophomore classes not yet started at Union College in September 1969, Meserole drove from his home in Englewood, New Jersey, to Shea every day the week the Mets took over first place in mid-September. He attended the pennant-clincher against the Braves with his brother who'd just been mustered out of the navy. Meserole made it back for one more Mets moment that year.

"I was standing on top of a phone booth during the '69 Series parade when Gil and Joan [Hodges] came by in the first or second convertible," he says. "I yelled out and pointed at him and got a laugh, a wave, and the coveted point from him in return. Thinking about it now gives me goose bumps."

Meserole's passion for the team dropped to detached interest in the years that followed Hodges's fatal heart attack in spring training 1972. "I'd forgotten what a big Mets fan I was in the '60s and…how much my love for the team died with Gil Hodges years ago," he admits.

Hodges had a lot of clout in the organization and the region, and things may have turned out much differently for the Mets in the 1970s if he had lived. But Mets fans—and Dodgers fans, too—are eternally grateful they had Gil Hodges for as long as they did.

be summed up by three simple words on a pin the Mets distributed 28 years after his death: "A Quiet Hero." Actions spoke loudly with Hodges. He made every man in his charge rely on the other. He told them individually before the 1969 season that he wanted just a little bit more out of each of them, and that would make the whole better. The result was a team no one could've imagined, except for Hodges.

As the first baseman on the expansion Mets, he played along with the promotional photos, jumping in the air before the first Mets game in 1962. Yet when Cubs third baseman Ron Santo clicked his heels three times after every Cubs win at Wrigley Field in 1969, Hodges called him on it and walked away at home plate during the exchange of lineup cards in July. Santo kept clicking, but with Hodges's club on their tail, Santo had fewer opportunities to jump and less reason to do so. The Mets went from 10 games down to eight games up over the last month and a half of the season.

The Mets had traded Hodges in 1963 so he could manage in Washington, but he returned to New York to manage the Mets after the 1967 season. He made recommendations on which players to get and which to get rid of, and probably would have eventually moved on to be general manager if he'd lived.

Hodges suffered a heart attack in 1968, but he was in good health when the Mets took the field the following spring. The Mets were in great shape, too. Tom Seaver, Jerry Koosman, Gary Gentry, and Nolan Ryan were at his disposal, along with Tug McGraw, whom he'd switched to the bullpen and approved the use of his screwball. Hodges made the most of veterans Ron Taylor, Cal Koonce, and Don Cardwell. He used a strict platoon at four positions, but he wasn't afraid to go with his instincts, despite the book's logic, even if the book was his own. He let Ron Swoboda bat against right-hander Eddie Watt in the eighth inning with Game 5 of the 1969 World Series tied 3–3. Rocky knocked in the run that capped the Miracle.

There was some good fortune that year, certainly, and Hodges found some himself when a baseball with shoe polish rolled to him and started a crucial Mets rally in the World Series. But Hodges had worked hard instilling confidence and installing his guys in the right situation. That it didn't work in 1970 or 1971 was frustrating, but '72 looked like a great team.

Rube Walker, Joe Pignatano, and Eddie Yost, coaches who'd followed Hodges from Washington and probably would have followed him through a wall, watched Hodges fatally drop from a heart attack in a parking lot after playing golf together on April 2, 1972. New York was grief-stricken. Hodges had helped take Brooklyn to its lone world championship in 1955. Then he made the whole country take notice of the next generation of National League baseball in New York. They've never had a finer leader.

# 8 Dykstra Nails It

Shea Stadium had been packed throughout 1986. The traffic for the U.S. Open and West Coast homestand at Shea on Labor Day weekend had been excruciating. Now tennis was long done and school was in its second month. It was October. The NLCS was tied. For many Mets fans with tickets for Game 3—and for every man on the roster—this was the first postseason game they'd ever seen at Shea. And after two innings the Mets were down, 4–0.

Manager Davey Johnson had experienced October at Shea. He'd made the last out in the 1969 World Series for Baltimore, flying out against Jerry Koosman, who now threw out the first pitch for Game 3 against Houston. Johnson and the Mets didn't panic, even as Bob Knepper kept the score unchanged into the bottom of

## Rallies, Indoors and Out

The 1972 season started with the death of Gil Hodges. His replacement, Yogi Berra, had the Mets at 31–12 on June 3. Injuries, slumps, and a listless offense undermined the team until the Mets were just four games over .500 following an 8–0 loss in the Astrodome on September 1. The next night they trailed by that same score when they came to bat in the eighth against Don Wilson.

Ken Boswell's three-run home run put the Mets back in the game as they scored seven times on eight hits. Tommie Agee led off the ninth with a walk and the Mets down by a run. A single, an error, and an intentional walk set up Cleon Jones to be the hero, and he singled in the tying and go-ahead runs. The Mets batted around in both the eighth and ninth to win 11–8.

A little less than 28 years later, a 10-run eighth-inning rally from an 8–1 deficit, culminated by a tiebreaking three-run shot by Mike Piazza, would beat Atlanta by the same 11–8 score on Fireworks Night in 2000. It was witnessed by a packed stadium because of the promised postgame fireworks display by the Grucci family; otherwise thousands would have left when the Mets fell way behind early. It wasn't as big a comeback as in the Astrodome, but it was one instance where the fireworks went off a little early, due to Piazza—not Grucci.

the sixth. New York took advantage of an error by Craig Reynolds to get on the scoreboard. Darryl Strawberry followed with a three-run homer off the southpaw, and the game was tied.

It didn't stay tied long. Houston got an unearned run in the top of the seventh to regain the lead, and the Mets went down quietly the next two innings. Wally Backman led off the bottom of the ninth with a bunt up the first-base line and skidded out of the baseline to avoid the tag. The Astros raged in vain that he should have been ruled out. Moments after Houston manager Hal Lanier went back to the dugout, Backman took second on a passed ball. He could not advance to third on a fly to short center. Up stepped Lenny Dykstra, who hadn't started the game and fanned earlier as a pinch-hitter, to face Houston relief ace Dave Smith. Bob Murphy called the action:

"Lenny Dykstra, the man they call 'Nails' on the Mets ballclub is waiting. Now the pitch…and a high fly ball hit to right field, it's fairly deep, it's way back, by the wall…"

"He did it!" radio partner Gary Thorne jumped in. Who could blame Thorne for not waiting? The Mets had waited since 1973 for a postseason game, and what a finish!

The team mobbed the unlikely slugger who'd hit almost as many triples as home runs during the year (seven and eight, respectively). The Mets led the series, a crucial turnabout given that unhittable Mike Scott was to pitch the next night. While Scott still tied the Mets in knots—and drove them to distraction as they collected scuffed balls—New York would beat Houston's bullpen three times in the series. Dykstra's homer marked the first of three NLCS wins in the Mets' last at-bat. The time for waiting was over.

# 9 All-Star Announcing Trio

At the start the Mets had little talent, a patchwork farm system, and a reliance on too many people whose best days in the game had already passed. What they did have from the very first day, however, was a great announcing team.

Lindsey Nelson, Bob Murphy, and Ralph Kiner earned their own individual places in Mets history, but it's significant that they also be thought of as a team. No announcing trio has ever been together for 17 seasons, much less the first 17 seasons of a team's existence. They could have broken up in the 1970s. Kiner could have gone to the Dodgers when Nelson left, and M. Donald Grant wasn't a huge fan of Murph's because he thought the man who made "happy recap" part of the Mets vernacular was too critical (as if Grant, the C. Montgomery Burns of the Mets, didn't come off as enough of a villain). While Nelson escaped the sinking ship, Murphy and Kiner stayed the course, and their names tug at the memories and emotions of two generations of Mets fans.

Lindsey Nelson was the big name, the one the team and sponsors needed, the pro's pro. He was a national name, giving up his spot on NBC's *Game of the Week* to cover the Mets in 1962. Why? "No network can give me what the Mets do," he said after his fourth year with the team. "A baseball broadcaster has the best showcase in the city. During the season he's on the air almost every day, at prime time in the evening, on Sunday afternoons, anywhere from two hours to five at a stretch. His identification with the ballclub is absolute. He is as well known to the fans as their brightest star, and, since he doesn't have to depend on his pitching arm, his batting eye, or his legs, the chances are he'll last much longer."

Nelson lasted 17 seasons with the Mets before joining the San Francisco Giants. He wasn't afraid to try new things. He broadcasted Mets games suspended from the roof of the Astrodome and from the Goodyear blimp (he watched the action on a monitor); Nelson was notorious for his collection of gaudy striped jackets that clashed with both the set in the booth and color TV sets in viewers' homes. Nelson often left on weekends during football season, lending his honeyed Tennessee voice to football, while leaving Murphy and Kiner to cover both radio and TV. There were no replacements, just three in the booth. It was a magic number.

Bob Murphy started in the major leagues with the Boston Red Sox covering Ted Williams with partner Curt Gowdy. He went to Baltimore in 1960 and called Roger Maris's 60th home run the following year. That was on the tape he sent the Mets for his audition.

Murphy did other sports, including football—he broadcast games for the New York Titans, forerunners of the Jets—and hosted the New York version of *Bowling for Dollars,* but Murph was so synonymous with the Mets it was a shock to hear his voice on anything else. The Oklahoman with a fondness for cloud description was on hand for the greatest—and worst—moments in Mets history. It is hard to picture 1986 without thinking of his jubilant calls of Jesse Orosco's strikeouts that won both the pennant and the world championship. His call of Bill Buckner's error, starting with a routine "And a ground ball trickling..." and reaching a crescendo moments later, is probably the most beloved call in franchise history.

Murphy initially thought of his full-time switch to radio in 1982 as a demotion, but it became his signature. While the TV booth was crowded with a half dozen or more different people doing cable or over-the-air broadcasts, Murphy and his partners—Steve LaMar (1982–1984), Gary Thorne (1985–1988), and Gary Cohen (1989–2003), plus others filling in—could be found on the same spot on the dial every night. Murphy's brother, Jack, had been an influential sports editor in San Diego with the stadium there named in his honor, but Bob was just as indispensable on the other coast. The Mets named the radio booth in his honor and had a night for him when he did his final broadcast from Shea Stadium in 2003. He received the Ford C. Frick Award in Cooperstown for his broadcasting contributions in 1994 (Nelson had received the award six years earlier).

The three men generally worked solo: one did TV, the other radio, and the third took a three-inning break. Kiner usually spent the late innings getting ready for his postgame show, *Kiner's Korner,* sometimes waiting endlessly as games went long into the night. A Mets win wasn't complete without seeing Kiner's show, and people tuning in late to Channel 9 could tell immediately who'd won based on the uniform of the player he was interviewing.

Kiner had a couple of years of broadcasting experience before joining the Mets, but he was the ballplayer portion of the triumvirate. He hit 369 home runs in just 10 years in the majors before severe back problems forced him to retire. He earned or shared the National League home-run crown a record seven consecutive times and was inducted into the National Baseball Hall of Fame in 1975.

While his malapropisms became legend—"If Casey Stengel were alive today, he'd be spinning in his grave"—he could also be memorably poetic, as he was in describing Philadelphia's Gold Glove center fielder: "Two-thirds of the earth is covered by water. The other third is covered by Garry Maddox." He battled through Bell's Palsy in 1998 to return to the booth and was still broadcasting selected games from Citi Field at age 86. The Mets had a night in his honor in 2007.

Nelson, Murphy, and Kiner all were inducted into the Mets Hall of Fame in 1984. Nelson died in 1995 and Murphy in 2004. In the hearts of Mets fans, their voices will always be tuned in.

# 10 The Grand-Slam Single

Because details get lost and meaning sometimes runs together as time goes by, let's just state the facts up front. Robin Ventura's drive over the right-field fence in Game 5 of the 1999 NLCS was not a home run; it was an RBI single. The hit did not clinch a series; it merely staved off elimination. It was not the greatest win in Mets history; it just felt like it.

The Mets, ecstatic to be in the postseason after a wrenching near-miss the year before and a near-fatal case of the yips at the end of the regular season, looked like they were going to get swept. This was just a week after Todd Pratt's home run eliminated the Diamondbacks in the Division Series to put the Mets in the NLCS against archnemesis Atlanta. John Olerud knocked in the tying and go-ahead runs in the eighth inning of Game 4 against the Braves, inconveniencing Atlanta's travel schedule and making more than a few Mets fans pick between their baseball team and the NFL on a Sunday afternoon. Take the Mets and the over.

The Mets scored on their first drive, a two-run blast by Olerud against Greg Maddux before many had even found their seats. They'd be sitting in those seats a long time before they saw another Met cross home plate. The teams played 15 innings over 5 hours, 46 minutes. They used 45 players: 22 by Atlanta and 23 by the Mets. Cox kept his three remaining starting pitchers out of the game. Bobby Valentine used three starting pitchers in relief and had two other starters, the previous day's hurler (Rick Reed) and the next game's (Al Leiter), loosening up in case a sixteenth inning was needed.

Orel Hershiser, who before the 1999 postseason hadn't relieved in a game in a decade, replaced Masato Yoshii in the fourth inning after the Braves tied the game. The Bulldog fought his way out of that jam and remained on the mound until he hit the second batter in the seventh. Turk Wendell came on and struck out Andruw Jones, but pinch-runner Otis Nixon stole second. Wendell fell behind Brian Jordan and was replaced by Dennis Cook with a 2–0 count. Cook then walked Jordan intentionally (though it was charged to Wendell). With the lefty on the mound, Cox sent up Brian Hunter to bat for Ryan Klesko. Now that the dangerous Klesko was out of the game and Cook had fulfilled the rule stating a pitcher must pitch to at least one batter, Valentine made another move. He called for righty Pat Mahomes, who'd danced through raindrops all season while going 8–0. That rain dodging was key because it had been falling for several innings and wouldn't stop all night. Mahomes also got out of the jam.

John Franco got the final out in the eighth and retired the Braves in the ninth. Armando Benitez labored through an inning and was done. In came Kenny Rogers, New York's Game 2 starter, for the night shift. Octavio Dotel, who'd spent his rookie season mostly as a Mets starter, came out of the bullpen for the thirteenth inning. He was the ninth Mets pitcher of the night.

Dotel had last pitched an ugly third of an inning in the Division Series 11 days earlier. Now he gave up a two-out double to Chipper Jones that Melvin Mora corralled and threw to Mike Piazza who tagged Keith Lockhart for the third out. Even fans in wet Braves hats and carrying soggy foam tomahawks had to say, "Man, this is a great game." For Mets fans, this was the season.

It moved on. The fourteenth inning saw the Mets get their first runner to second base since a bases-loaded chance had been wasted in the sixth. They couldn't cash in this opportunity either. The Braves broke through the next inning with an RBI triple by Lockhart.

Shawon Dunston battled Braves rookie Kevin McGlinchy in an epic 12-pitch battle before Dunston singled to lead off the bottom of the fifteenth. Valentine had no nonemergency pitchers left, but he did have two bench players. Matt Franco, who'd set an obscure record during the season by drawing 20 walks as a pinch-hitter, batted for Dotel and earned another base on balls. After Edgardo Alfonzo sacrificed the runners over, Roger Cedeno, who'd set a club record with 66 steals during the year, ran for Franco, representing the winning run at second.

With first base open, Cox walked Olerud. Todd Pratt, who'd replaced Piazza after the catcher's last at-bat, drew New York's third walk of the inning. The game was tied. Again. The Mets had drawn one walk in 13 innings before McGlinchy entered and had four bases on balls since he came in. Up came Ventura. With the problems bases-loaded walks would be in this series, McGlinchy made sure his 2–1 pitch was a strike. Ventura crushed it through the soggy mist and somehow made it disappear over the fence. As the fans and players jumped up and down, Pratt was the first to make contact, turning and starting the dog-pile on Ventura. The Mets won the game, but

Pratt was ruled to have passed Ventura on the bases and the grand slam became just a single. Neither Pratt nor Ventura ever got near home plate and after a few minutes the scoreboard reversed from 7–3 to 4–3. No one much cared at the time, but it was a once-in-a-lifetime occurrence for a singular postseason moment in Shea history.

Ventura was a virtuoso of the grand slam. He'd hit three in just his first year as a Met—and five in his career with the club—including one in each game of a doubleheader, a baseball first. The 18 he would hit in his career would be more than slammin' immortals Ted Williams, Jimmie Foxx, Hank Aaron, Babe Ruth, and, yes, Dave Kingman. But the one that didn't count became far more famous than any of the others. And while the series would have a sour ending, it had more thrills and memorable moments than a few others that the team won.

# 11 1986: Of Cruise Control and Comebacks

The 1985 season had ended in heartbreak. From the outset of 1986 the Mets told anyone with a pen or tape recorder that they were better than anyone else and weren't settling for second place this time.

Second place had sounded good when the Mets finished either fifth or sixth for seven straight seasons, but since Davey Johnson arrived in 1984, there was a different dynamic to the team: a young, talented vibe bordering on arrogance. The Cubs and Cardinals had beaten them out in tight races the previous two years, but that made no difference to the Mets. They would take no prisoners in '86.

The Cardinals beat the Mets in the home opener, dropping New York to 2–3, tied for fourth place, and the pitching staff had allowed more runs than all but one National League team. The Mets won their next 11 games to tie the club record, including a four-game sweep in St. Louis that put up a white flag over Busch Stadium. When that winning streak ended in Atlanta, the Mets won their next seven. By May 12 the Mets had a 21–5 record and a five-game lead. By the time school let out in mid-June, the Mets had completed another seven-game streak and had 44 wins in their first 60 games. The lead was 11½ games over the Expos, 15½ over the Phillies, and 19 ahead of the Cubs, Pirates, and Cardinals. The Mets rolled into July with an eight-game winning streak.

The Mets weren't just beating the competition, they were beating them up as well. Fights with the Dodgers, Braves, and Reds kept people's attention. The brawl in Cincinnati after a stolen base in the tenth inning on July 22 resulted in Ray Knight and rookie Kevin Mitchell being ejected and, along with Darryl Strawberry's getting kicked out earlier for arguing balls and strikes, forced the Mets to play catcher Gary Carter at third base and alternate pitchers Jesse Orosco and Roger McDowell between the outfield and the mound, depending on the batter. The Mets won the five-hour game in 14 innings. In Houston, just after the All-Star break, they'd gotten into a fight in a bar instead of on the field.

It was obvious this was a playoff team, but general manager Frank Cashen continued making changes. Bob Ojeda had been a brilliant addition to the pitching staff, one of six Mets who wound up winning in double figures. George Foster was released in August amid complaints that it was a racial issue. Although former Met Lee Mazzilli was added, Mitchell and Mookie Wilson, who got the lion's share of time at Foster's former left-field position, were African Americans.

The Mets had their best August on record at 21–11. They hit September with a bigger lead (19 games!) than the other three divisions in baseball combined…and none of those races were that close. A four-game losing streak prolonged their clinching, but it also

## Twin Tag

The news is shocking. The Mets' perceived top postseason starter, Orlando Hernandez, injures his hamstring in a workout the day before the 2006 Division Series. Rookie John Maine will now open the first Mets postseason game in six years. If he can only get to the fifth…

Maine retires the Dodgers in the first inning, but Jeff Kent and J.D. Drew single to open the second at Shea. Russ Martin follows with a shot off the right-field wall. Shawn Green fires to relay man Jose Valentin, whose perfect strike to catcher Paul Lo Duca nails Kent. Three ex-Dodgers gun down a former Met. Beautiful!

Suddenly, Drew runs the stop sign and emerges within diving distance of the plate. Lo Duca looks up in time to tag out the prone Drew. He pumps his fist while the crowd doles out high fives like it's 1999. There's even a delayed reaction by those blocked from view, slow on the uptake, or just coming back from the bathroom asking, "Anything happen?"

Once and future Met Marlon Anderson spoils it with an RBI double, but Maine escapes with just the one run allowed, pitches into the fifth, and despite a bullpen tightrope walk, the Pedro-less, Duque-free Mets are on their way to a sweep.

enabled them to do it at home. The fans destroyed the field in what turned out to be the fifth and final sacking of Shea Stadium. From here on, police would make sure no one tore up the field. The fans took it in stride; they just wanted something to celebrate peacefully.

The postseason started with a shock: other teams were good too! Mike Scott and Houston gave the Mets all they could handle in the NLCS. Scott, a former Met, allowed just eight hits while throwing two complete games and fanning 19. The Mets were convinced they couldn't beat him and became preoccupied with complaining to the league office about Scott's scuffing of the ball. It did no good. Neither did the Houston bullpen. While the Mets hit just .189 as a team, they pummeled closer Dave Smith. Lenny Dykstra's two-run homer off him in the ninth inning won Game 3 and changed the series. In Game 6, with the Astros two outs away from Scott pitching a deciding game, Smith came in and walked two batters and allowed the tying run on a sacrifice fly.

Jesse Orosco, who'd won the previous day—and had gotten the victory on Dykstra's blast in Game 3—had New York pulling out its collective hair as he surrendered a game-tying home run to Billy Hatcher in the fourteenth inning and allowed two runs in the bottom of the sixteenth after the Mets had scored three in the top of the inning. It all became part of Mets lore when Orosco fanned Kevin Bass; New York was back in the World Series.

Like Houston, the underdog Red Sox had plenty in store for the Mets. Boston took the opener on an error at frigid Shea and pounded Dwight Gooden in Game 2. Lenny Dykstra, never a power hitter before October 1986, admitted he tried for one leading off Game 3 at Fenway Park. He connected. The Mets scored four times in the first inning, and the swagger was back. Carter homered twice the next night, and Dykstra went deep again. Yet a Boston win in Game 5 put the Red Sox in position for their first world championship in 68 years.

The Red Sox held leads of 2–0 in the fifth, 3–2 in the eighth, and 5–3 with two outs in the tenth. The Mets came back each time. The last time they got three singles to score one run, a wild pitch to plate the tying run, and an unforgettable error brought home the winning run. The 13 years between World Series at Shea seemed to be providing positive mojo.

Even after a rainout allowed the Red Sox to start Bruce Hurst for the third time, and Boston pounded Ron Darling for a 3–0 lead, the Mets bided their time—thanks to Sid Fernandez's brilliant relief—until they could push three across in the sixth. Two scored on a Keith Hernandez single and the other came home on Carter's RBI. Ray Knight snapped the tie with a home run. The Mets tacked on runs and survived a Boston comeback until they were an out away from a world championship. Jesse Orosco fanned Marty Barrett. It was all over. No second place this time.

# 12 Zeroing In on a Miracle

The third-place Mets trailed the Cubs by 10 games on August 13, 1969. Yet by September 10 New York had taken over first place and by September 24 the Mets had clinched the first National League East title. They finished eight games up in the standings. How did this happen? Easy. They didn't let the opposition score.

The Mets set a club record with 36 straight scoreless innings between September 10 and 13. Nolan Ryan started it by holding Montreal scoreless after the second inning and putting the Mets in first place. Gary Gentry blanked Montreal, Jerry Koosman and Don Cardwell shut out Pittsburgh the same night (more on this later), and Tom Seaver blanked the Pirates into the third inning the next afternoon. Mets nemesis Willie Stargell singled in Fred Patek to finally snap the string, but Seaver still went the distance for the win.

That club record lasted just over two weeks.

The still-standing Mets mark of 42 consecutive scoreless innings began with six shutout innings on September 23 against St. Louis: two by Jim McAndrew and four by Tug McGraw in an 11-inning win. Gentry went the distance the next night to clinch the division title. Luckily they were scheduled to hit the road, because the ecstatic fans had trashed Shea Stadium. New York blanked the Phillies over the entire weekend behind Koosman, Seaver (earning his franchise-record 25th win), and Gentry. That also gave the Mets a club-record 23 wins in September, not to mention a staff ERA for the month of 2.15, with 15 complete games and 10 shutouts. The team's ERA over August and September was 2.23, with 24 complete games, 17 shutouts, and a 44–17 record. "Miracle" they called it, but it was the pitching that was truly miraculous.

## Twin 1–0 Wins

Rosh Hashanah arrived during a doubleheader, with the Mets in first place, without their hard-hitting left fielder or left-handed right fielder. So the Mets did the logical thing—they had their pitchers do double duty.

With Art Shamsky sitting in the hotel in observance of the Jewish holiday and Cleon Jones on the bench with a strained muscle in his lower back, the Mets had their hands full against the Pirates, who would match Cincinnati as the best-hitting team in baseball in 1969. Bob Moose, who would throw a no-hitter against the Mets the following weekend, allowed just one hit through four innings in the opener of the twin bill. But Bobby Pfeil and Duffy Dyer put together consecutive singles with one down in the fifth. Koosman, batting .044 coming into the contest, singled in Pfeil with what turned out to be the only run of the game.

Don Cardwell stepped up to the plate in the second inning of the nightcap with a robust .171 batting average, and he hadn't knocked in a run in three months until he banged a Dock Ellis pitch through the hole to left to bring in Bud Harrelson, who'd doubled with two out. Pittsburgh's best scoring chance came in the bottom of the eighth when Cardwell's wild pitch pushed Manny Sanguillen to third with one out. Cardwell then struck out Jose Pagan and pinch-hitter Roberto Clemente. Tug McGraw retired the Pirates in the ninth and—even with the Cubs ending their eight-game losing streak—the two pitcher-driven 1–0 wins increased the Mets' lead to 2½ games. Amazin'.

The Cubs ended the Mets' scoreless streak at 42 in the first inning at Wrigley Field on October 1 against Koosman, but the Mets still won their 100th game. Chicago stopped the Mets' nine-game winning streak on the last day of the season, when New York was looking ahead to what was to come.

# 13 The Seaver Deal

June 15, 1977, a Wednesday, began with the Mets in Atlanta. The club wound up winning that night, but Tom Seaver wasn't there. He left in the first inning for New York, his No. 41 jersey in his locker. Seaver had last worn it in a game three days earlier in Houston. When his turn came up in the rotation again, No. 40 was on the hill: Pat Zachry.

What happened in between was both a long time in coming and should never have happened. The 1977 team had seven players who had been All-Stars during their Mets careers, and none of them were happy. Jon Matlack and Dave Kingman openly groused about the team's parsimonious ways, especially in light of the Mets coming up empty during the first winter of free agency. The others watched as the team's poor start led to Joe Torre going from backup infielder to rookie manager. Seaver, on the other hand, was working on a contract extension to remain a Met.

A discussed deal with owner Linda de Roulet, who'd taken over ownership of the team following the 1975 death of her mother, Joan Payson, called for an extension of three years—worth a total of $1 million—that would have kept Seaver at Shea through 1981. Negotiations went on even as he feuded with Mets board chairman M. Donald Grant. Grant, who tended to treat players like ungrateful serfs who should take what they're offered and say thank you, was ill equipped to deal with the modern athlete. Seaver, a well-spoken, smart leader who'd commanded respect even as a rookie on a 100-loss club, was not Grant's kind. Further, Seaver was the team's player representative, and Grant believed the pitcher was behind Kingman's spring training holdout. Seaver and Grant squabbled almost daily in the

*Tom Seaver cleaned out his locker after being sent to the Reds in one of the Mets'*
*all-time worst trades.*

papers. Seaver went directly to the owner about the contract, giving Grant more to resent.

Grant's mouthpiece, *Daily News* columnist Dick Young, had been a trailblazer in his field but now firmly sided with Grant. Young's son-in-law, Thornton Geary, was in the team's communications department (at the columnist's request). Young compared Seaver to Walter O'Malley, the Dodgers' owner still despised in New York for moving the club. "Both are very good at what they do," Young said in his comparison. "Both are very deceptive in what they say. Both are very greedy."

**TRIVIA**
**Question**

**Who handed Tom Seaver his first loss against the Mets?**

Trivia answers on page 256

Jack Lang, who'd been hired by the *Daily News* just a few months earlier after the *Long Island Press* folded, covered the Seaver side. Lang had eaten breakfast with the pitcher and was with him when he heard about Young's column in that morning's *Daily News*.

"When he sat with reporters and television men at poolside later, Seaver learned of a Dick Young *Daily News* column alleging that Nancy Seaver was jealous of Ruth Ryan because Nolan Ryan had signed a much bigger contract with the California Angels. Seaver pondered the allegations, then suddenly bolted from his chair. He strode briskly to his hotel room and called Arthur Richman, the club's public relations director.

"'Get me out of here,' he yelled to Richman over the phone. 'Get me out of here.'"

Seaver was traded to the Reds for a package of Steve Henderson, Doug Flynn, Dan Norman, and Zachry. Mets fans were devastated. Another Grant-inspired deal sent Kingman to San Diego for Bobby Valentine and Paul Siebert. Trading Joel Youngblood to St. Louis for Mike Phillips actually worked out pretty well, but the three deals at the deadline were forever dubbed the "Midnight Massacre." The next day wasn't any better.

Seaver had stayed in Manhattan and appeared on the network television shows the next morning. He cleaned out his locker at Shea and then met the media. He spoke matter-of-factly about the situation, having repeated the details several times by now, but when he was asked about the New York fans, Seaver's calm demeanor crumbled. He left for nearly 10 minutes before he regained his composure. When he started talking about the fans again, he could not go on. Lang was there:

"Seaver's voice broke off and he began to sob. He tried to continue but could not. His head bowed again, he asked for a reporter's notebook and scribbled a few words. He asked the reporter to read it and sat and quietly listened to what he had written: 'And the ovation I got the other night after passing Sandy Koufax [on the career strikeout list], that will be one of the most memorable and warmest moments of my life.'"

The red-eyed Seaver went to his locker and collected his belongings. In a minute he was gone.

# 14 Keith Hernandez

Keith Hernandez brought both elegance and grit to Shea Stadium, not to mention a Gold Glove. When he arrived in New York in 1983, three Mets had won Gold Gloves. Hernandez won six in as many years as a Met. Hernandez, who was the National League co-MVP in 1979 as a Cardinal, in 1984 became the first Met to be runner-up since Tom Seaver in 1969. And, like Seaver, Hernandez was a leader on a Mets world championship team.

Hernandez was traded in June 1983 from defending world champ St. Louis to a team in the midst of a youth movement (featuring heralded rookie Darryl Strawberry), nostalgia tour (Seaver, 38, back from exile), and management change (George Bamberger resigned a week before the trade). Hernandez thought long and hard about whether he wanted to remain in a city he wasn't fond of, in a place he felt was "the Siberia of Baseball." Hernandez stayed and was glad he did. So were the Mets.

Hernandez was smack in the middle of the Mets' renaissance. New manager Davey Johnson, promoted from Class AAA Tidewater, knew the young Mets were good and let them play. If the infield defense was shaky with a revolving door at shortstop, you never knew it the way Hernandez handled every throw. Mex—everyone called him that even though his family ancestry dated back to Spain—told it like it was to writers who hadn't bothered covering the Mets in years. He smoked cigarettes (he later quit), did crossword puzzles at his locker, and provided big hits as needed. While his RBI totals seem somewhat modest by current standards—his

*In addition to his All-Star appearances, Gold Gloves, and MVP Award, Mets first baseman Keith Hernandez was forever immortalized in a classic episode of the NBC series* Seinfeld.

high as a Met was 94 in 1984—he was the all-time career leader in the short-lived statistic of game-winning RBIs with 129.

His sordid past with cocaine as a Cardinal—leading to his one-sided trade to the Mets—came to light in the 1985 Pittsburgh drug trials, but he didn't let that or his ugly divorce affect his play. He got off with a hefty fine in spring of '86 for his past sins and then batted .310, his sixth and final career .300 season. On a team without much postseason experience, Mex's leadership proved invaluable as the Mets fought off the Astros in the NLCS. (Hernandez famously said he'd fight catcher Gary Carter if the catcher called any more fastballs for Jesse Orosco in the sixteenth inning of Game 6.) Hernandez choked up on the bat and knocked in two runs against tough Boston lefty Bruce Hurst in New York's sixth-inning comeback in Game 7 of the World Series, just as he'd done four years earlier for St. Louis in the deciding game against Milwaukee southpaw Bob McClure. His sacrifice fly in the seventh inning of the deciding game at Shea proved to be crucial when the Red Sox mounted a comeback the next inning. Less than an hour later the Mets were mobbing each other on the mound.

Hernandez was named the first captain in club history in 1987; Carter was named cocaptain a year later. Mex remained a fiery leader, but injuries marred his last two years as a Met. Hernandez and Carter left after the '89 season. Mex finished his career in Cleveland.

He gained lasting popularity for his part in a *Seinfeld* episode. "They told me it was going to be minimal lines," Hernandez recalled, "but when I got the script, obviously there was a lot more to it, and I immediately panicked." For his part, Jerry Seinfeld, a lifetime Mets fan, was so nervous being around the Mets great he could hardly speak. It wound up working out pretty well. Hernandez remains on TV as an outspoken and entertaining Mets commentator.

# 15 1999 Division Series

When a postseason ballclub has an established catcher, the backup sees about as much playing time as a reserve goalie in the NHL playoffs. They wait for an injury or a blowout, but otherwise it's a lot of sitting. All that time for analysis makes catchers a good source for future coaches, managers, and broadcasters. Todd Pratt was one of those backup catchers, and a cheerleader, too.

He had backed up Darren Daulton during Philadelphia's pennant run in 1993, riding the bench for the NLCS and World Series and getting exactly one at-bat (he struck out). As a 1999 Met, Pratt was backup to Mike Piazza, a sure-fire future Hall of Famer. With the Mets needing to win every day the last two weeks of the season, Piazza caught each of the last 12 games. Pratt had caught exactly one inning and batted twice in that span.

A thumb injury incurred a couple of weeks earlier by Piazza was aggravated on a tag play in Game 2 of the Division Series. The Mets lost the game and, as it turned out, their All-Star catcher for the series. Piazza couldn't bend his left thumb, and a catcher who can't bend his thumb, well, can't catch. Fans who hadn't tuned in to pregame reports were shocked to see Benny Agbayani batting cleanup and Pratt catching and residing in the seven spot in the Game 3 lineup against the Diamondbacks. Pratt, known as "Tank" for his build and subtlety, walked twice in a 9–2 Friday night win as the Mets moved a game away from taking the series.

Al Leiter had a two-hitter and a 2–1 lead Saturday afternoon with two outs and none on in the eighth. A walk and a mishandled grounder that went for a hit brought in Armando Benitez. Jay Bell's two-run double made it a 3–2 Arizona lead, but Melvin Mora's throw to Pratt nailed Bell to keep a fourth run off the board. That turned out to be key because, in the bottom of the inning, Tony Womack's dropped fly ball in right field enabled the Mets to tie the game on Roger Cedeno's sacrifice fly. Diamondbacks closer Matt Mantei came in to face Pratt and got him out on a fielder's choice. The game remained tied into the bottom of the tenth.

With one out, Pratt faced Mantei again. Pratt, a .293 hitter during the season with three homers in 140 at-bats, was 0-for-7 in the series. With Darryl Hamilton to follow, fans couldn't be faulted for thinking about the thumpers Arizona had coming up in the eleventh. A loss meant a cross-country flight to Phoenix and a date with Randy Johnson Sunday night. New York's starter looked to be Masato Yoshii. Suddenly, Saturday afternoon shifted back into focus as Pratt took a wicked cut.

Gold Glove center fielder Steve Finley seemed to have the ball tracked all the way. Finley got to the center-field fence, but he didn't jump high enough, and the ball ticked off his glove. Finley, Pratt, and the fans all thought he had it until the outfielder slapped his glove and put his hands on his hips. The "Mojo Risin'" refrain from the Doors' "L.A. Woman," the de facto theme song for the '99 Mets' surreal stumble/run in the closing weeks of the season, blared as fireworks went off. The Mets mobbed Pratt as he reached the plate, and Shea shook for the first postseason series victory by the club since the 1986 World Series.

Only four players had ever ended a postseason series on a home run: Bill Mazeroski, Chris Chambliss, Joe Carter, and now Todd Pratt. Pratt, who'd been working as a Domino's Pizza manager just a couple years earlier, who'd been in the minor leagues pre-Piazza while the Mets auditioned the likes of Tim Spehr and Alberto Castillo behind the plate, and who'd be sitting on the bench when the NLCS started as Piazza returned. But on October 9, 1999, Pratt was "walking off" before it was even a generally used term, and taking the Mets to another round of playoffs when a week earlier it was doubtful they'd be involved in anything at all. That's why teams carry an extra catcher and that's why every spot in the lineup gets to take their hacks. Just in case.

# 16 Davey Johnson

Davey Johnson's 2010 election into the Mets Hall of Fame was well deserved and long overdue. He managed more games than anyone in club history, won more times, and his .588 winning percentage is by far the highest of any Mets manager.

It was Johnson's fly to left as an Oriole that clinched the 1969 championship for the Mets, but Johnson's playing career was more substantial than that. He hit .257 as a rookie second baseman as the 1966 Orioles claimed the franchise's first world championship (dating back two cities to 1901). He went to Atlanta in 1972 and joined Hank Aaron and Darrell Evans as the first trio of teammates in history with 40 home runs apiece. He played in Japan and was one of the first players to return and contribute on the major league level.

Influenced by Orioles managers Paul Richards and Earl Weaver and willing to integrate computer-generated numbers with his own gut instincts, Johnson was talked out of real estate to join the Mets' minor league system. He almost left for the Cardinals after a disagreement with the front office in 1983, but he was convinced to stay by baseball operations VP Lou Gorman. The next year Mets general manager Frank Cashen, who had overseen both his Baltimore signing and departure, hired him to manage in New York.

With working knowledge of the Mets' young players as manager at Jackson and Tidewater, plus a stint as roving instructor, Johnson plugged the young arms in and let them play. The team had veteran Keith Hernandez to help show them the ropes and Jesse Orosco to make the kids' leads stand up. The club's 90 wins in 1984 were the most since Gil Hodges won a franchise-high 100 in 1969. In '85 the Mets won 98 and just missed the NL East title in a battle to the wire with the Cardinals.

Johnson challenged the '86 Mets from the beginning, and they responded. The Mets won 108 games, producing a winning record

## The Mets Hall of Fame

The Mets Hall of Fame honors individuals who have meant the most to the team. After years of confounding dormancy, the honor roll of the greatest Mets increased by four names at Citi Field in 2010.

| Person | Position | Year Inducted |
| --- | --- | --- |
| Joan Payson | Owner | 1981 |
| Casey Stengel | Manager | 1981 |
| Gil Hodges | Manager | 1982 |
| George M. Weiss | President | 1982 |
| William A. Shea | Mover and Shaker | 1983 |
| Johnny Murphy | General Manager | 1983 |
| Ralph Kiner | Announcer | 1984 |
| Bob Murphy | Announcer | 1984 |
| Lindsey Nelson | Announcer | 1984 |
| Bud Harrelson | Shortstop | 1986 |
| Rusty Staub | Outfielder | 1986 |
| Tom Seaver | Pitcher | 1988 |
| Jerry Koosman | Pitcher | 1989 |
| Ed Kranepool | First Baseman | 1990 |
| Cleon Jones | Outfielder | 1991 |
| Jerry Grote | Catcher | 1992 |
| Tug McGraw | Pitcher | 1993 |
| Mookie Wilson | Outfielder | 1996 |
| Keith Hernandez | First Baseman | 1997 |
| Gary Carter | Catcher | 2001 |
| Tommie Agee | Outfielder | 2002 |
| Frank Cashen | General Manager | 2010 |
| Dwight Gooden | Pitcher | 2010 |
| Davey Johnson | Manager | 2010 |
| Darryl Strawberry | Outfielder | 2010 |

against every team except Philadelphia (8–10), while going 12–6 against St. Louis and beating Pittsburgh 17 of 18 games. The club's cocksure style annoyed some opponents, and fights were not uncommon, but the team rallied at key moments and, most importantly, pitched superbly. The Mets won three times in the final at-bat against Houston in the NLCS. Their two-out, nobody-on comeback from two runs down against the Red Sox in Game 6 of the World Series is something that will be talked about as long as the Mets exist.

The scrappy, crazy bunch that had quickly turned the team from perennial loser to solid contender to world champion did not get lectures from their manager. When they trashed a plane after winning the pennant in Houston, Johnson took care of it. After the Mets lost the first two games in the World Series, he gave the team the day off instead of going to a workout in Boston. The Mets won four of the last five games in the Series. But in 1987 the Mets sustained numerous injuries, especially to pitchers, and lost ace Dwight Gooden for the first two months while he underwent drug rehabilitation.

The Mets didn't repeat in 1987, and 100-win 1988 was marred by losing the NLCS to Orel Hershiser and a Dodgers team they'd dominated during the year. The 1989 Mets failed to win 90 games for the first time since Johnson took over. Johnson was retained after much debate, but he was fired with the team at 20–22 in May. Despite a 595–417 record as manager of the Mets, it took three years until Johnson was hired again. He took the Reds and Orioles to the postseason, winning a Manager of the Year Award with Baltimore in 1997, but was fired by Cincinnati and quit his Baltimore job because of disagreements with ownership. He managed the Dodgers for two seasons with an overall winning mark before being let go after the 2000 season. He has since served as manager for Team USA baseball and as a consultant for the Washington Nationals.

# 17 Casey Stengel

Could the Mets have come into being without Casey Stengel? Certainly. Could anyone other than Stengel have bought as much time or brought as much excitement to a team that bad? Certainly not.

Charles Dillon Stengel, nicknamed "Casey" for his Kansas City hometown, debuted as a major league outfielder in 1912, a year after the building of the concrete-and-steel Polo Grounds. That he was still in uniform in 1965, a year after the place was torn down, shows the kind of staying power he had. Stengel had a brilliant baseball mind; he was also acerbic, a clown, and a tireless booster of the game. He won more pennants (10) than any American League manager, matching the major league record set by his mentor, John McGraw, with the New York Giants. Stengel's seven world championships are also the most ever, tied with Yankees predecessor Joe McCarthy. When Casey's 10th pennant did not translate into his eighth world championship, he was told he was too old and sent packing after the bitter loss to Pittsburgh in the 1960 World Series.

The Mets convinced him to take the job. From his home in Glendale, California, he declared, "It's a great honor for me to be taking over the Knickerbockers." Casey wasn't great with names, especially those of his new players—they came and went so fast and were so forgettable, who could blame him?—yet he put the focus on the fans, which was brilliant. The Mets were bad, historically bad, and a man who'd seen as much baseball as Stengel knew that early on. The Ol' Perfessor talked about the banners in the stands, the young players, families in the crowd, anything to take people's minds off what they were watching on the field.

## Stengel-ese Decoded

It's been almost 50 years since Casey Stengel first started talking about the Mets. He didn't always make sense, but the team hardly made a lick of sense with their over-the-hill hitters and shouldn't-be-on-the-hill pitchers. And the fielding…the Mets were the first team since World War II to commit 200 errors in a season, and no one's matched them since.

So why have people always followed them so passionately? Casey had his pulse on the Mets fan from the start:

> I want to say that the Mets fans has been marvelous. And they come out and done better than we have on the field and I'm glad we got 'em. If we could do as well as them it'd be better and we're tryin' 'cause in supportin' us the attendance has got trimmed. You'd think we'd do better and without all these people turnin' out to help us we wouldn't but they come out with the banners and cheers and it's 'Metsie, Metsie, Metsie.' When the little children first start to speak they once said 'Mamma' and 'Papa,' but with the fans we got they say the first thing, 'Metsie, Metsie, Metsie.' I'm glad we got so many of the ladies turnin' out to see our team 'cause it proves that we got effeminate appeal which is the result of my charm school which I run as chief instructor in effeminate appeal and we got 'em turnin' out with their dates, the young 'uns and the old 'uns and I wish we could do it better on the field….

Translation: "Mets fans are great. Wish the team could win more for them."
The language is different, but the sentiment remains the same: "Metsie, Metsie, Metsie!"

His 1962 Mets lost their first nine games. They then won 12 of their next 22. An arduous trip from Milwaukee to Houston had the exhausted Stengel not arriving at his hotel room until 8:00 AM. The manager turned to traveling secretary Lou Niss and told him, "If any of the writers come looking for me, tell them I'm being embalmed." That night the Mets embarked on a 17-game losing streak.

August 7 was a milestone day. Not only was the club officially eliminated from pennant contention, but their 29–82 mark assured that they would not even finish .500. They reached 100 losses on August 29. The losses kept on coming until they reached 120, the most in the 20th century.

Delays with Shea Stadium construction kept the Mets at the Polo Grounds for another year, and Casey tried to keep things lively even if his team was not. As he'd done in spring training, he started his two best pitchers in the first Mayor's Trophy Game in front of 50,000 boisterous and mostly Mets fans at Yankee Stadium. Stengel wasn't one to forget a slight—he never warmed to clownish Met Jimmy Piersall, who ran the bases backward at the Polo Grounds after his 100th career home run, because of comments he'd made years earlier—and Casey reveled in tweaking the team that fired him, even if the exhibition game didn't count.

The Mets improved their second year—they had to!—but 120 losses to 111 and then to 109 at Shea Stadium in 1964 did not seem like progress to many. There were questions about whether Stengel should continue, and if he could really get the most out of the young players that were the club's only hope. On the eve of his 75th birthday, Stengel broke his hip during the celebration. He'd survived a broken wrist slipping in a dressing room at an exhibition game at West Point in May, but this was far more serious. He chose Wes Westrum, whom he'd met in a bar during the 1963 All-Star break, over his "assistant manager" Yogi Berra to succeed him as he convalesced. The appointment soon became permanent.

The Mets retired Stengel's No. 37 that September, and the following summer he was inducted into the Hall of Fame with

Ted Williams. He remained an ambassador for the club, and in 1969 was a symbol for the Amazin' Mets—his term—showing how far they'd come from their humble beginnings. Stengel was in the locker room when they won that year and he remained the grand master at Old Timers' events, even coming into Shea via chariot the last year of his life, ravaged by cancer. He died a week apart from Mets employer Joan Payson in autumn 1975. The Mets wore a black armband for the pair throughout the 1976 season. They were fittingly the first two inductees into the Mets Hall of Fame in 1981.

# 18 Jerry Koosman

In Mets lore—and in the record books—Jerry Koosman was always second to Tom Seaver. When it came to the biggest games in franchise history, though, Kooz took second fiddle to no one.

Signed out of the army based on a recommendation from a Shea Stadium usher's son, the Mets kept Koosman around in the minor leagues because he owed them money. By the time the southpaw could pay the club back, the Mets' interest in him was more than just as his lender. He arrived in New York to stay in 1968 and just missed 20 wins and the Rookie of the Year Award. He even got the last out in the All-Star Game.

The next year he missed a few early starts with arm trouble, but he rebounded well and was a major force as the Mets overtook the Cubs. He stumbled in the NLCS, but with the Mets down a game in the World Series against heavily favored Baltimore, Kooz took a no-hitter into the seventh inning at Memorial Stadium. Ron Taylor got the last out of the two-hit, 2–1 win.

## Frank Viola Forever?

Given that the 20-game winner is a vanishing breed in baseball, is it preposterous to think that the last 20-game winner in Mets history will be Frank Viola? "Sweet Music" won 20 for the 1990 Mets, becoming the fifth pitcher in club history to do so. He beat the Pirates on the last day of the season, scoring the go-ahead run himself when Pat Tabler, "Mr. Bases Loaded," was hit by a pitch to force him in. Since then, Al Leiter has come the closest to that total with 17 for the 1998 Mets. Given the reliance on pitch counts and relievers, betcha $20 it won't happen again for a while.

**Mets All-Time 20-Game Winners**

| 1969 | Tom Seaver | 25–7 |
|------|------------|------|
| 1971 | Tom Seaver | 20–10 |
| 1972 | Tom Seaver | 21–12 |
| 1975 | Tom Seaver | 22–9 |
| 1976 | Jerry Koosman | 21–10 |
| 1985 | Dwight Gooden | 24–4 |
| 1988 | David Cone | 20–3 |
| 1990 | Frank Viola | 20–12 |

By the time Koosman took the mound again, brilliant catches and strange bounces had the Mets a win away from the world championship. Koosman was roughed up early in Game 5, but he settled down, and the Mets rallied. He retired Davey Johnson on a fly to left for the last out, and Kooz hopped into catcher Jerry Grote's arms.

In his first two full seasons, Koosman won 36 times with 33 complete games, 13 shutouts, 504⅔ innings, and an ERA of 2.18. Because of injuries and inconsistency, it took Kooz three and a half seasons to earn his next 36 wins. Yet when the Mets needed him most for their unlikely "Ya Gotta Believe" run, Kooz led the way. After dropping five straight starts, he threw a club-record 31⅔ consecutive scoreless innings. He won four straight, including a 10-inning shutout of the Giants, as the Mets quickly climbed from

## 20 the Hard Way

A bet with higher odds may be the next 20-game loser in Mets history. Jerry Koosman was the fifth and last to turn the trick, while also becoming the last major league pitcher to go from 20-game winner to 20-game loser in successive seasons. (He can thank M. Donald Grant for help with that one.) Only one major league pitcher (Mike Maroth with Detroit in 2003) has lost 20 games since 1980. It's a tough mark to reach because of the old saying, "You have to be good to lose 20 games," and most managers help make sure their pitchers don't reach the hideous plateau. If someone does reach the dubious feat as a Met, they'll certainly have company.

### Mets All-Time 20-Game Losers

| 1962 | Roger Craig     | 10–24 |
|------|-----------------|-------|
| 1962 | Al Jackson      | 8–20  |
| 1963 | Roger Craig     | 5–22  |
| 1964 | Tracy Stallard  | 10–20 |
| 1965 | Jack Fisher     | 8–24  |
| 1965 | Al Jackson      | 8–20  |
| 1977 | Jerry Koosman   | 8–20  |

the bottom to the top of the NL East. Kooz earned the victory on September 30 when the Mets gained a tie for the division. Seaver clinched it the next day.

Koosman threw a complete game in his only NLCS start (the afternoon Pete Rose and Bud Harrelson had at it). In Game 2 of the World Series he had his only poor postseason outing as a Met, although New York wound up winning in 12 innings (they won all six of his career postseason starts). Koosman and Tug McGraw combined on a three-hitter in Game 5 to put the Mets a win away from a world championship, but that win never came. Kooz's World Series record was 3–0 with a 2.39 ERA, with more Series wins and starts than anyone in franchise history.

Despite a lousy 1974 by the club, Koosman had his first winning season since 1970 at 15–11. He followed that with 14 wins. In 1976 Koosman had his best season since his rookie year, becoming the first Met besides Seaver to win 20 or fan 200. He placed second to Randy Jones in the Cy Young voting. Then came 1977—Seaver was traded, the team fell apart, and Koosman lost 20, including one to Seaver the Red. After a 3–15 season that saw him finish the year in the bullpen, Koosman, by now saddled with more losses than any Met (137), threatened to retire if the Mets didn't trade him to his native Minnesota. The Mets acquiesced and got a lefty in return who would one day follow Koosman as the man on the mound for a world championship at Shea: Jesse Orosco.

Koosman won 20 his first year as a Twin and wound up pitching until age 42, racking up 222 wins (140 as a Met). He and Seaver were White Sox teammates on paper in the winter of 1984, but Kooz was sent to the Phillies a few weeks later. Koosman, who spent some time in the Mets organization as a minor league pitching coach, joined Seaver in the Mets Hall of Fame in 1989.

# 19 4:00 AM Wake-Up Call

Fans tuning in for the start of the Mets game in Atlanta on July 4, 1985, saw the tarp on the field. It looked like a washout for the fourth-place Mets, but the game started 90 minutes late and was delayed again in the third inning, bringing an end to the night for starters Dwight Gooden and Rick Mahler. The Mets went to rookie Roger McDowell. Terry Leach followed with four solid innings and was in line for the win with relief ace Jesse Orosco in to protect a 7–4 lead in the eighth. And Orosco got clobbered.

Now up 8–7, the Braves brought in Bruce Sutter, Hall of Fame closer to be, but in this game he played the role of spear carrier.

Rookie Lenny Dykstra singled off Sutter to tie the game. The game grew more bizarre. Keith Hernandez hit for the cycle and still made six outs in the game. Maligned Doug Sisk, who'd allowed the tying and go-ahead runs in the eighth, then threw 4⅓ scoreless innings. Tom Gorman tossed six innings in relief and also pitched well…as long as the game stayed tied.

After Howard Johnson's two-run homer gave the Mets the lead in the thirteenth, Gorman allowed Terry Harper's game-tying homer. When Dykstra's sacrifice fly gave the Mets an 11–10 lead in the eighteenth, Gorman surrendered a two-out, two-strike home run to Rick Camp. The pitcher. With a career .060 average coming in and no hits all year.

Then Camp couldn't get anyone out. Mets manager Davey Johnson, ejected along with Darryl Strawberry for arguing in the seventeenth inning, had sent word to win no matter what—pitching coach Mel Stottlemyre had considered using outfielder Danny Heep to pitch so they could avoid dipping into the starting rotation—and Rusty Staub batted for Gorman. Ray Knight doubled in the tie-breaking run, and Heep, freed from having to worry about pitching, singled with the bases loaded to break it open.

Starter Ron Darling made his first career relief appearance in the nineteenth. He allowed two unearned runs and then faced the slugging Camp, again representing the tying run. Darling fanned Camp, earning congratulations from Gary Carter, who'd caught all 19 innings and scored the go-ahead run. The *real* go-ahead run this time. Happy recap: Mets 16, Braves 13 in 6 hours, 10 minutes. The 3:55 AM finish was the latest in major league history.

Since it was Fireworks Night, the Braves kept their word to those who'd stayed. They fired up the display at 4:01 AM. Those who'd gone to bed hours earlier thought the city was under attack.

What's generally forgotten is that the win in Atlanta started a four-game sweep of the Braves, part of a nine-game winning streak, and a string of 15 wins in 17 games. The Mets wound up just short of the Cardinals for the division title, but they certainly showed they could go the distance.

# 24–4

Looking back, the hardest thing to comprehend about Dwight Gooden's 24–4 season is that he actually lost two in a row. He lost successive starts at Shea Stadium the last week of May 1985 against past Cy Young winners LaMarr Hoyt of the Padres and Fernando Valenzuela of the Dodgers. Heading into Memorial Day weekend he stood at 6–3 with a 1.89 ERA. That was as bad as it got for Doc that year.

From that point forward, he went 18–1 with a 1.39 ERA over his last 200 innings. He did not lose a game in the months of June, July, or September. He allowed no earned runs in 44 September innings. He won his only start in October, beating the Cardinals at Busch Stadium in a must-win series the final week. He went 2–1 with a 1.72 ERA against St. Louis, but he had three no-decisions against the Cardinals, more than he had against any other team. The Mets beat the Cards on Opening Day in 10 innings with Doc out of the game, but they lost the other two in extra innings by scores of 2–1 and 1–0, Jesse Orosco losing both.

Too bad it wasn't the Cubs the Mets were chasing. Gooden smoked the 1984 NL East champs, beating them all five times he faced them in complete-game efforts to an ERA of 1.00. He had a 0.00 ERA against the Pirates, but he somehow faced them only once and left after eight innings. He went 4–0 against Houston (1.89), and 3–0 against Cincinnati (1.50) and Philadelphia (1.45). The Braves hit him the hardest, to a 3.24 ERA. He beat them at

# Fan's VIEW **John and Laura Booth** (Greenwich, Connecticut)

## Purple Cow Milks Mets

John Booth is a Mets fan today courtesy of Dairylea Milk. Growing up in Farmingdale, Long Island, in the 1970s, he collected enough Dairylea cartons to earn free tickets to see the Mets. His father was a Yankees fan, and the younger Booth pulled for them, but his parents were leery of several 14 year olds going from Long Island all the way to the Bronx to see the Yankees. So with the Dairylea coupons and $7 or $8 from his mom, Booth and a few friends made it to several Shea matinees in 1979.

"I'd take the Long Island railroad into Woodside," he recalled. "We hopped on the subway and took the 7 train. When we got to the ballpark, there was no one there. We'd go down and hand ushers $5 each and we'd be sitting on the first-base line behind the dugout. The slogan was 'Catch a Rising Star' and they had Lee Mazzilli. Everyone else stunk, and we hoped he would be that one Met to play in the All-Star Game. Mazzilli and John Stearns both made it that year."

Booth was soon hooked. He met his future wife, Laura Cook, a Peekskill native and a fan of the Big Red Machine from the 1970s, at Williams College. Pretty soon the Mets were her team, too.

"She was a ball fan...and 1985 was the year she fell in love with the Mets," he said. "Three down with three to go in St. Louis in September. I remember listening to those games in our dorm room with my roommate, a huge Mets fan."

Radio reception for Mets games has never been good in western Massachusetts, but it was better than the reception they got at nearby Purple Pub a year later for the 1986 World Series against the Red Sox. One of the couple's proudest possessions is a signed ball from that year's world championship Mets team. "I'm looking at it right now," he said during a phone interview. "That will always be in our family."

With their two daughters, Julia and Amy, well indoctrinated into the Mets life, the ball is in good hands. The kids watched one parent or the other attend every postseason game at Shea in 2006, going in to work bleary-eyed the next day, and then getting ready for another game that night. And with Booth's college roommate, Alec Dawson, living with his family next door, reception for the Mets has never been better.

Shea Stadium in late July, but he went just 2⅓ innings in Atlanta on July 4, his shortest outing of the year. The reason wasn't the Braves; it was the weather. A 41-minute rain delay—after a 90-minute delay at the outset—got Gooden out of there early. The game continued until almost 4:00 AM before the Mets won in 19 innings. That 16–13 marathon win was as strange as Doc's season was dominating.

Gooden, in just his second year in the majors, took the mound for a Sunday game against San Diego—going for his 20th win—on August 25. It was his 14th consecutive win in '85, but two earned runs in six innings actually raised his ERA to 1.78. Although Gooden lost his next start in San Francisco, he did not lose again, going nine innings in five of his last six starts to finish with a 1.53 ERA, the lowest in franchise history. Oh, and he was 20 years old.

It was like watching an incarnation of someone from another era—1968, or 1908 for that matter—with opponents unable to touch the kid's stuff. Tom Seaver's 1969 season may be the best comparison across most categories. Seaver, 24, in his third major league season, went 25–7 with 18 complete games and five shutouts, compared with Gooden's 16 complete games (plus a nine-inning no decision) and club-record eight shutouts. While Seaver fanned 208, his second of a record nine straight years with 200 or more Ks, his total wasn't close to Doc's 268. Gooden's 276⅔ innings—the most by a Met since Seaver 10 years earlier—was almost six innings above Seaver's 1969 total. ERA was a major difference. Seaver's 2.21 ERA was 1.39 below the league average, while Gooden's was 2.06 below. Adjusting for era, linear weights, or substituting Seaver's 1.76 in 1971, and it's still all Gooden. Looking at every angle, Doc also hit .226 with his first major league home run; Seaver, though not a bad hitter generally, batted .121. The comparison is not a clean sweep, however; Seaver's Mets won the World Series, while Gooden and his teammates would have to wait 'til next year.

Like Seaver in 1969, Gooden walked away with the Cy Young, easily topping a career year from St. Louis southpaw John Tudor (21–8, 1.93). It was as good as any Mets pitcher before or since, and it was Doc Gooden's pinnacle. While Seaver won three Cy Young Awards, two pennants, and was elected to the Hall of Fame in a vote as close to unanimous as anyone has achieved, Gooden is a distant second in franchise history in wins (198–157) and is a few Mets down the list in numerous other Seaver-dominated categories. Gooden got involved in cocaine after the '85 season. He wasn't nearly as dominant in 1986, entered drug rehabilitation for the first time in 1987, and 20 years later is still plagued by personal problems. The way the

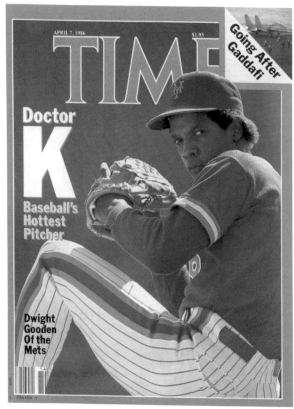

*Dwight Gooden's incomparable 1985 season landed him on the cover of* Time *magazine in 1986.*

game has changed in those intervening two decades, another season like Gooden's '85 may never be repeated. Here's hoping Gooden can avoid repeating the same mistakes away from the diamond.

# 21 Tug McGraw

Tug McGraw was arguably the best reliever in Mets history. There can be no argument, however, that he was the most colorful player the club has ever had. Not just colorful—Willie Montanez was, after all, pretty colorful—but McGraw backed his words up with deeds. If Tug said "Ya Gotta Believe," ya hadda believe. And he was right.

Frank Edwin McGraw was a sunny-eyed Californian signed on the recommendation of his bonus-baby brother (Hank McGraw crossed even more lines than Tug and never made the major leagues). Tug was a starter during Casey Stengel's time—he was the first Met to beat Sandy Koufax—before Gil Hodges, who allowed him to throw the screwball, finally moved the southpaw to the bullpen at age 24. Tug was one of just three Mets (Ed Kranepool and Cleon Jones were the others) to serve under the first five managers in Mets history; he was instrumental in helping two of them win unlikely pennants.

McGraw went 9–3 with a 2.24 ERA and 12 saves in 100⅓ innings in 1969, although the Mets amazingly didn't need his services to win the World Series. He became a two-time All-Star (once for the Mets), beloved by fans and the media alike for his attitude. (Of a new contract he famously said, "Ninety percent of my salary I'll spend on good times, women, and Irish whiskey. The other 10 percent I'll probably waste.") But Tug was one of the main reasons the 1973 team couldn't get out of last place.

After successive seasons with a 1.70 ERA, McGraw was at 6.17 on July 17 after a disastrous starting assignment (his first start in two years). On August 22, after going 0–6, Tug finally got his first win of the year. He went 5–0 from that day on, saved 12, and had a 0.88 ERA over 41 innings. Having adopted "Ya Gotta Believe" as the city's mantra—and yelling it repeatedly to cut off speechifying board chairman M. Donald Grant—Tug made the National League East believe. He slapped his glove against his thigh while locking down wins to push the Mets from last to first in the final month of the season. Then he made believers out of the Big Red Machine, throwing five innings in relief over the last two games after the Mets had complete games in the first three. McGraw's heavy use continued in the World Series. He threw 13⅔ innings against the A's, including six innings out of the pen to earn the win in Game 2. The Mets lost to a superior A's team, but New York made Oakland sweat through seven games.

The next year McGraw's shoulder was shot. He suffered through a terrible season and was traded to the Phillies in a deal that returned Del Unser and highly touted catching prospect John Stearns. McGraw had his shoulder examined in Philadelphia—the Mets had ignored his complaints—and after a simple procedure he became a vital member of the Phillies...for a decade.

He retired at age 40, trying everything from broadcaster to pitchman to orator of "Casey at the Bat." Along the way he picked up a famous son, country singer Tim McGraw, whom he had fathered out of wedlock as a Mets minor leaguer and denied as his son for years afterward. They eventually reconciled and became very close. Tug died of brain cancer in Tim and wife Faith Hill's cabin in Nashville in 2004. The Mets honored him that year with a simple phrase on their sleeve: "Ya Gotta Believe." Amen.

# 22 The Black Cat

The skeptics said the 1969 Mets knew nothing about first place. Well, what did the Cubs know?

Chicago's last pennant had come 24 seasons earlier, with teams still making do with 4-F ballplayers while able-bodied major leaguers made their way stateside from the service in World War II. Because travel restrictions were still in place, the 1945 World Series had the first three games in Detroit followed by the last four at Wrigley Field. The Tigers won in seven. The Cubs, apparently, had cursed themselves but good when ushers refused to let a tavern owner's goat sit in the stands for Game 4. Really.

So with the Cubs leading the Mets by 10 games (eight in the loss column) on August 13, 1969, there should have been nothing to worry about. The Mets cut the lead in half over the next three weeks, and when the Cubs dropped four straight before arriving at Shea Stadium on Monday night, September 8, blood was in the water.

Chicago was up now by 2½ games, but it was just one in the loss column because the Cubs had played four more games. Jerry Koosman fanned 13 to beat Bill Hands with rookie Wayne Garrett's run-scoring single snapping a tie in the sixth. While the teams each had 57 losses, the Cubs held first place because of the extra games played. But their lead was melting fast.

Tom Seaver was set to pitch to Billy Williams in the top of the first on September 9 when one of the most bizarre sights in Shea Stadium history occurred. A black cat emerged from the stands, sprinted over to the batter's box, stared at Williams, skulked past Ron Santo in the on-deck circle, and headed towards the visitor's dugout. It hissed at Cubs manager Leo Durocher and disappeared.

## Revenge of the Expansion Team

The expansion 1962 Mets set the 20th century mark for most losses, with 120. Seven years later they were no longer the new kid on the block. The Montreal Expos and San Diego Padres joined the league in 1969. They lost 110 games each—not enough to threaten the expansion record, but enough to help the Mets on their new and sudden quest to become the best team in baseball.

The Mets lost their first game of the 1969 season to the Expos, but won 13 of the remaining 17 games with Montreal, including a sweep of a doubleheader on September 10 that put New York in first place for the first time. The Mets won their last six against *les Expos*. Plus Montreal provided Donn Clendenon, the slugger the Mets needed, at the trade deadline. The Mets won 11 of 12 games against San Diego, including all six on the road. They went 5–1 against the Padres at Shea, despite averaging just 2.2 runs per game.

The Cubs also went 11–1 against San Diego, but they were just 10–8 against Montreal, including 2–2 in September. The Cubs were playing the Expos the day the Mets clinched the division.

(Shea's feral cat colony has even moved to Citi Field, but feline-opponent relations have not reached such a public level of animosity since the '69 incident.)

The spooked Cubs went down in order in the first while Ken Boswell's double plated two Mets in the bottom of the inning. Donn Clendenon, making a rare start against a right-hander, hit an opposite-field, two-run homer off Ferguson Jenkins in the third. Jenkins was pitching on two days' rest because Rosh Hashanah was on Saturday, and if Ken Holtzman had pitched against the Mets Tuesday, his next turn would come up on a day he wasn't available. Everything in heaven and earth seemed against the Cubs.

Late in Tuesday's game, many of the 51,448 fans at Shea waved handkerchiefs—everyone still carried handkerchiefs then—and sang an impromptu version of "Goodbye, Leo" to the Cubs and their manager. Seaver's 7–1 win not only put the Mets a mere half game out of first place, but it was New York's 82$^{nd}$ win, assuring the club of its first-ever winning season. When they swept the Expos in a doubleheader the next night—and the Phillies beat the Cubs—the Mets were officially in first place. And no goats, cats, or Cubs could budge them.

# 23 The Carom

There were a dozen or more moments that gave faith to the Mets faithful in 1969; if there was one moment that made believers in the "Ya Gotta Believe" season of 1973, it was an impossible bounce. "The Carom" helped put a team that had been in last place at the end of August a win away from first place three weeks later. It seemed all part of a divine plan, but it was a classic reminder that if a team hangs around long enough, they just might steal the pennant.

While the 1969 "Miracle Mets" remained fresh in everyone's mind, fresher still was the image of the Pirates as the division's best team. Pittsburgh had won three straight NL East titles, including a world championship. Both the Mets and Pirates had lost leaders tragically: New York manager Gil Hodges died of a heart attack in April 1972, and Pittsburgh's Roberto Clemente was killed in a plane crash on a humanitarian mission on the last day of that year. Both teams endured long, sluggish periods in 1973, but the first-place Pirates (74–72) and the fourth-place Mets (73–76) met for a five-game, home-and-home series a couple of weeks before the season was scheduled to close.

The Mets had lost the first game in Pittsburgh and were about to drop 4½ games behind in this wild scramble of mediocre teams.

New York rallied from a 4–1 deficit in the ninth and took the lead on a two-run single by Don Hahn. Although Bob Apodaca and Buzz Capra walked four men in the bottom of the ninth at Three Rivers Stadium, the Mets hung on to win. Then they won the next night behind George Stone and two home runs by Cleon Jones, his first homers at Shea Stadium since Opening Day.

# TRIVIA
## Question

**Who was the first Met to homer in his first career at-bat?**

Trivia answers on page 256

Thursday, September 20, 1973, was an emotional day. Willie Mays announced his retirement that afternoon. Mays had been a rookie in 1951, when the New York Giants rallied to beat the Brooklyn Dodgers in a legendary pennant race; now he was calling it quits as the Mets tried to do the same thing for a new generation of fans. He vowed he'd help the team if they reached the World Series. Let's not get carried away, Willie….

That night the Pirates took a 2–1 lead on Jerry Koosman and the Mets, but New York tied it in the eighth. The Bucs went ahead in the ninth, but the Mets knotted the score again. The game stretched into the thirteenth when Pirates rookie Dave Augustine belted a two-out drive to left field that seemed destined for the bullpen. It fell short by an inch, maybe less. The ball hit the top of the fence. By all rights it should have hopped over for a home run, but the ball instead bounced right back to Cleon Jones. Jones, who'd debuted as a Met at the Polo Grounds a decade earlier, whose shoe polish ignited a rally in the 1969 World Series, and who'd caught the championship-ending out near the same spot where he now stood four years later, took the carom off the wall, turned, and fired. Wayne Garrett grabbed the relay and threw to Ron Hodges at the plate. Richie Zisk, running from first, arrived a split-second later, and Hodges tagged him for the third out. Shea Stadium was exuberant and stunned all at the same time. The game went on.

But not for long. Hodges, a rookie who'd filled in for the injured Jerry Grote during the summer and who was in this game after Grote was replaced in a double-switch, singled in the winning run in the bottom of the thirteenth. The moment know as "The Ball on the Wall" put the Mets just a half-game out of first. Was this another Miracle? The renewed faithful clamored for a glimpse.

The Mets had their first crowd of 50,000 the next night as Tom Seaver bested the Bucs and the Mets were in first place for the first time. The Mets wound up on top in a five-team battle to claim the division with 82 wins—the lowest number ever for a team that went on to win a pennant over a full season—and beat the heavily favored Reds in the NLCS. The Mets eventually lost the World Series, but so had the Giants in '51 after the "Shot Heard 'Round the World" in Mays's rookie year. The National League in New York had seemingly come full circle. When pressed about his team's seemingly fading chances in July, Mets manager Yogi Berra had said, "It ain't over 'til it's over." The Carom confirmed it.

# 24 Mora Touches Down

**The History:**

September 22, 1998: Mets lead the wild-card by one game.

September 27, 1998: Mets lose their fifth straight and are eliminated from contention.

September 28, 1998: Cubs and Giants play a one-game wild-card playoff.

**The Repeat:**

September 21, 1999: Mets lead the wild-card by four games over the Reds; play in Atlanta for first place in the NL East.

September 28, 1999: Mets lose their seventh straight; trail wild-card by one.

September 30, 1999: Mets trail wild-card by two games with three games remaining.

Fans file out of Shea Stadium on September 30, the last Thursday night of the year. It is as if they are leaving a friend's funeral. The Mets, once a mortal lock for the wild-card, are now down by two with three games to play following an 11-inning loss to the Braves. The Braves. They had already clinched the division title, and the Mets still can't beat Atlanta. Again! Two straight years of blowing it at the end? (That indignity would catch up to the Mets and their fans eventually.)

Friday night, Pittsburgh in to end the season; Mets blow a late lead. In Milwaukee the Reds do the same thing. The Astros give an added twist. If there is a three-way tie between Houston, Cincinnati, and New York, the Mets get the wild-card and the other two would have to have a playoff for the NL Central. Doesn't seem fair, but it doesn't seem likely either. But wait, Robin Ventura singles in the winning run in the eleventh inning. A half hour later in Milwaukee, the Brewers knock off the Reds in 10.

Both the Reds and Astros play during the day on Saturday. Houston wins—21-game winner Jose Lima and Billy Wagner combine on a shutout—but the Brew Crew hammers Cincy. That means if the Mets win their last two, there will be a one-game playoff or, in case of two wins and one more Cincinnati loss, the Mets win the wild-card outright. It's hard to even ponder as the Mets and Pirates are scoreless in the sixth inning. But the Mets break the deadlock, and Rick Reed goes the distance for a shutout in front of 36,878 fans, about 7,000 more than Friday night.

Sunday arrives and there's not an empty seat in the house. There's no good news from Houston as Dodgers manager Davey Johnson lets prima donna Kevin Brown get away with missing his turn on the final day of the year with three other teams' destinies on the line. The Astros pound the Dodgers to take the NL Central. But you can't think bad thoughts about Davey Johnson, the man who guided the Mets out of the desert in the 1980s. Not today. Think about the karma. Think about Kris Benson.

Imagine having a young stud like the rookie Benson on the Mets? The Mets have Orel Hershiser, who just turned 41 and is looking for his 2,000th career K today, getting by on nothing but

## One-Game Playoff? Two-Hit Shutout

Al Leiter pitched seven postseason games as a Met. While he never got a win in any of those games, he was outstanding in six of them while suffering various degrees of snakebite. But his biggest start as a Met? That would be the 1999 one-game playoff, the unscheduled regular-season game, game number 163. Win and you're in the postseason, lose and you're essentially the ninth-best team in baseball, no matter what your record said. Thanks for playing. Good-bye.

The 1999 NL wild-card marked the 10th time in major league history—and the first time in Mets annals—that two teams were tied for a postseason berth at the end of the season. The Reds won an earlier coin flip to determine home field. The Mets, who slumped at the worst time and had to sweep their final series and pray that the Reds lost two of three in theirs, were lucky just to be at Cinergy Field.

The Reds had endured an almost six-hour rain delay to play, and win, their season finale in Milwaukee. Al Leiter took it from there the next night. He made the winner-take-all match in Cincinnati as stress-free as possible. Edgardo Alfonzo followed Rickey Henderson's leadoff single with a two-run home run off Steve Parris. Henderson added a homer later, and the Mets put together two more runs. It was more than enough for Leiter. He threw 135 pitches, the last one was lined at Alfonzo, and the 11-year postseason drought was over. The 5–0 win—and the season—had been put in the books. Despite some classic highs over the next two weeks, it would end in a stupefying low. Still, it was sure better than watching at home for another year.

guile. Before the game, general manager Steve Phillips, who'd fired two of Valentine's coaches in June, said he'd like the manager back next year. Fine, fine, but the fans want him back here to manage *next week*. Kevin Young, the only threat in the dilapidated Pittsburgh lineup, singles in Al Martin in the first inning. Benson stymies the Mets for the first three innings.

Mid-season pickup Darryl Hamilton hits a ball down the left-field line...fair! The game is tied. It stays that way through rallies that pan out to nothing. Benson finally leaves. Five Mets pitchers allow one hit after the first inning.

Journeyman Greg Hansell, who will never pitch in another major league game, begins the bottom of the ninth for the Pirates. Rookie sub Melvin Mora—where'd he come from?—singles, and Edgardo Alfonzo does the same to send Mora to third with one out. Up comes John Olerud, the club's most consistent player and murder against right-handers. They walk him—the 125th time he's drawn a base on balls, adding to a team record he shattered weeks ago—because the Bucs want to pitch to Mike Piazza. He's a super-star, but he hasn't had a day off in two weeks and he's bounced into 27 double plays. In jogs Brad Clontz, a submariner who threw two games for the '98 Mets but used to be a Brave. The Pirates look for two.

The tension. It's been 11 long years since the Mets made the postseason. The Yankees have done it five seasons in a row. Think that's crossing anyone's mind? Pittsburgh. Pittsburgh's not good, but you look at those uniforms and think of all those Pirates who've pillaged the Mets over the years: Stargell, Clemente, Parker, Drabek, Bonds, and that sidewinder they never hit: Tekulve. Clontz dips down, fires, and...and it's nothing like Kent Tekulve. Wild pitch! It's the greatest gift in Pirates–Mets relations since the Carom in '73. The relief. The Mets live for another day.

Catcher Joe Oliver doesn't even look back, and Mora touches down into the waiting arms of the jubilant Mets. Shea Stadium shakes as strangers hug and brave souls plan rendezvous for the Division Series. You say this place was like a morgue Thursday night?

Forget September, burn the past. October is a new month.

# 25 Benny's Blast

For a large-market team, the 2000 Mets had a low-budget outfield. The team's anger at Rickey Henderson's contract carping and his assumption that a long fly to left was a home run (it wasn't) made it obvious that year two of the Rickey experience would be difficult. Henderson was released and Joe McEwing took his place on the roster in May, but Benny Agbayani took his spot in left field.

Agbayani was already a Mets folk hero, homering 10 times in his first 27 games in 1999, and batting .400 in that span. Wearing No. 50—like fellow Hawaiian Sid Fernandez before him—Agbayani brought a football player's body and mentality to Shea Stadium. A 30th-round pick out of Hawaii Pacific University, he advanced against the odds in the minor leagues, and—despite solid 1999 numbers (14 homers, 42 RBIs, .286 average)—was on the outside looking in to make the 2000 team. Luckily, the Mets started the season in Japan several days before other teams; that roster flexibility enabled the Mets to take a couple of extra hitters on the long trip. Agbayani hit a game-winning grand slam as a pinch-hitter and he landed in the United States a Met.

Agbayani added punch to the lineup wherever he batted in the order. He was batting fifth when the Mets hosted the Giants for Game 3 of the National League Division Series (he'd batted first and sixth earlier in the series) and Agbayani was having an off day. But it was better than San Francisco's.

The Giants had failed to build on a 2–0 lead, and were just 2-for-14 with runners in scoring position in the game. The series was tied, but the Mets were happy to have salvaged a win at Pac Bell Park after a bullpen meltdown nearly cost them Game 2. The Mets evened up Game 3 after the Giants brought in closer Robb Nen to face Edgardo Alfonzo with two down in the eighth, a man on first, and the Giants ahead 2–1. Lenny Harris stole second, and Fonzie knocked him home.

Then stalemate. Both teams were on their sixth pitcher as the game reached into the thirteenth. Rick White, acquired in July for bullpen depth, gave the Mets just that as he pitched out of his second straight two-on, two-out jam. San Francisco's Aaron Fultz had dodged a bullet in his inning of work. One thing that seemed to no longer be a factor was the home run. The wind had been howling in over Barry Bonds's and Agbayani's shoulders in left the whole game and it had only gotten more blustery as day became night. The crowd sensed it and—a year removed from a 15-inning marathon playoff win at Shea—seemed spent from the tense game, trying to save up the energy for one last, big moment.

With one down, Agbayani watched the first pitch for a ball. He waited for the delivery, raised his left leg like a right-handed Mel Ott, made contact, and defied the wind. Gary Cohen made the call:

A high fly ball, deep left field, back goes Bonds, looking up at the wall, that ball is…outta here! Outta here! The Mets win the ballgame! Agbayani hit it up into the bleachers in left field. Benny Agbayani wins it with a home run for New York. And the Mets take the lead in the series, two games to one. And all the Mets are out of the dugout to greet Agbayani as he jumps on home plate.

The crowd chanted "Benny, Benny" over and over, the tension as long gone as his stirring home run. While Barry batted .176 for San Francisco, Benny continued defying the odds and wound up at .333. The Giants' left fielder would end the series the next afternoon in a way that made fans at Shea exult once more.

# 26 Jonesing

The Mets lost 103 times the year prospect Bobby Jones debuted in New York. In his seventh season they won 97, but he was injured and missed the postseason. In 2000 the Mets were having another outstanding year. And Bobby Jones was in the minor leagues.

On the recommendation of Bobby Valentine and his staff, Jones agreed to go to Class AAA to work on his fastball and curve. Although a soft thrower, Jones was often compared to Tom Seaver, a Mets broadcaster at the time, because they both hailed from Fresno. Jones swallowed his pride and went down, determined to earn his way back to Shea.

When Jones went to Norfolk in June, he was 1–3 with a 10.19 ERA. He came back stronger and went 10–3 with a 3.69 ERA. An All-Star in 1997 and a 74-game winner as a Met, Jones, in the last year of his contract, was the fourth starter on a talented club. Valentine toyed with starting lefty Glendon Rusch or bringing back southpaw Mike Hampton on three days' rest for Game 4 of the Division Series, but the Mets went with the right-hander. Jones took the mound in his first postseason game with a chance to clinch the series; he also needed to give the team innings because of a 13-inning classic the previous evening. He did both.

After Jones retired the Giants in order in the first, Robin Ventura gave the Mets the lead with a two-run homer in the bottom of the inning. Jones set down San Francisco in order in the second, third, and fourth. Just as fans were starting to murmur no-hitter—no Met has ever thrown one—Jeff Kent lashed a double to left in the fifth after just missing a home run earlier in the count. A short fly kept Kent on second, but a walk to J.T. Snow put the tying runs on base. Jones got the second out and walked Doug Mirabelli, bringing up the pitcher. Manager Dusty Baker let Mark Gardner bat. His pop-up ended the inning.

The decision came back to haunt the Giants because the Mets knocked out Gardner in the bottom of the fifth. Jones struck out but reached on a wild pitch and he scored along with Timo Perez on Edgardo Alfonzo's double.

Jones retired the last 13 Giants. He fanned Barry Bonds twice and got him to line out to center to end the game and the series. Jones's one-hitter was the first in Mets postseason history and was reminiscent of the better days of Shea's more well-known Fresno native. Jones allowed base runners in only one inning in one of the most dominant performances in club history. It turned out to be his last win in a Mets uniform—he got a no decision in the NLCS and lost in the World Series—but it couldn't have come at a better time.

# 27 Joan Payson

Joan Payson was both the patron and the matron of the Mets, giving them unquestionable support and reaping her reward with one of the most unlikely world championships of all time. With a Whitney family pedigree, numerous interests, and a fortune estimated at between $100 and $200 million in the 1950s, Payson did not need the Mets; the Mets needed her.

She had owned 10 percent of the New York Giants and had been the lone dissenting vote when the baseball team moved to San Francisco. She jumped on board Bill Shea's Continental League venture, owning equal shares with well-heeled Dwight Davis and Dorothy Killian, a rabid Dodgers fan. When the league dissolved without playing a game as the concession for major league expansion, Killian pulled back and Payson wound up with 60 percent of the team. And what a team.

Though she favored the name "Meadowlarks," she followed the public sentiment for "Mets," which edged out "Skyliners" in a fan poll. She watched with glee as the team readied the Polo Grounds for baseball after four seasons of decay. She was on a cruise for the start of her club's maiden season but left instructions to be wired the scores of every game. As the losses mounted—the Mets lost their first nine—Payson sent a wire back:

Please Tell Us Only When the Mets Win.

She later recalled, "That was about the last word I heard from America."

The 1962 Mets set the 20th century mark for losses with 120, not to mention other dubious marks like most home runs allowed (192), but the club also set a record for most fans to see a last-place club (922,530). The Mets drew at least one million every year after that until 1979.

Progress was slow. The Mets found every way to lose that's ever been imagined, plus a few more that hadn't. Yet Payson never skimped. She paid six figures (plus Bill Denehy) to bring Gil Hodges from Washington to manage the Mets after the 1967 season and then paid him more than he'd ever earned as a player. She took over the mantle of team president in 1968—George Weiss and Bing Devine had held it previously—and remained in the position until her death in 1975 at the age of 72.

# The Original Original Mets

In case further explanation is needed as to why the Mets were so bad in 1962 and for the six seasons after, take a look at how it started. The eight National League teams pocketed $1.8 million from the Mets by foisting 22 unwanted players on them in the expansion draft of October 10, 1961. Both the Mets and Houston Colt .45s (forerunners of the Astros) were on their own.

"I want to thank all these generous owners for giving us those great players they did not want," Mets manager Casey Stengel deadpanned. "Those lovely, generous owners."

Players on the list below are broken down—with broken down being the operative phrase—into several categories, including years spent in New York. Twelve of them lasted a year or less as Mets.

| Price | Position | Name (Previous Team) | Years as Mets |
|---|---|---|---|
| $125,000 | Pitchers | Jay Hook (Reds) | 1962–64 |
| | | Bob L. Miller (Cardinals) | 1962, 1973–74 |
| | Infielder | Don Zimmer (Cubs) | 1962 |
| | Outfielder | Lee Walls (Phillies) | None (Traded) |
| $75,000 | Pitchers | Craig Anderson (Cardinals) | 1962–64 |
| | | Roger Craig (Dodgers) | 1962–63 |
| | | Ray Daviault (Giants) | 1962 |
| | | Al Jackson (Pirates) | 1962–65, 1968–69 |
| | Catchers | Chris Cannizzaro (Cardinals) | 1962–65 |
| | | Choo Choo Coleman (Phillies) | 1962–63, 1966 |
| | | Hobie Landrith (Giants) | 1962 |
| | Infielders | Ed Bouchee (Cubs) | 1962 |
| | | Elio Chacon (Reds) | 1962 |
| | | Sammy Drake (Cubs) | 1962 |
| | | Gil Hodges (Dodgers) | 1962–63 |
| | | Felix Mantilla (Braves) | 1962 |
| | Outfielders | Gus Bell (Reds) | 1962 |
| | | Joe Christopher (Pirates) | 1962–65 |
| | | John DeMerit (Braves) | 1962 |
| | | Bobby Gene Smith (Phillies) | 1962 |
| $50,000 | Pitcher | Sherman Jones (Reds) | 1962 |
| | Outfielder | Jim Hickman (Cardinals) | 1962–66 |

She watched from her box to the right of the Mets' dugout through the bad times, and it was from there she saw her lovable losers become overnight champions. She also witnessed the twilight of the career of her favorite player, Willie Mays, whom she had always wanted to bring back to New York.

Payson's daughter, Linda de Roulet, inherited both the team presidency and spendthrift chairman of the board M. Donald Grant, who helped chisel away the goodwill and good team Payson's money had built. The family sold the Mets in 1980 for a then-record $21.3 million (the team had originally cost $2 million). The new regime began a Mets Hall of Fame the following year and, fittingly, Joan Payson and Casey Stengel comprised the inaugural class.

# 28 David Wright

Plenty of third basemen have come up through the Mets' system with the hopes of the organization, fans, and the city heaped on their shoulders. It finally all came together with David Wright.

Taken with a bonus pick in the 2001 draft—compensation for Mike Hampton signing with the Rockies—Wright had been a three-time All-State choice at Hickory High School in Virginia. He even grew up a Mets fan, having followed the club's Class AAA team in his Norfolk hometown. Showing he could handle pressure, he hit .298 with the Tides in front of family and friends every night while displaying power and speed. By the end of July he was in New York at the tender age of 21.

The Mets sputtered the last two months of the season, but it had nothing to do with Wright. He batted .293 with 14 home runs

*Third baseman David Wright is one of the cornerstones of the modern-day Mets.*

in 69 games and was successful in his six stolen base attempts. Manager Willie Randolph tried to bring him along slowly and bat him sixth and seventh in 2005, but as he moved toward 27 home runs, 102 RBIs, a .306 batting average, and 99 runs scored, Wright was fifth in the order behind Mike Piazza, who showed what a superstar in New York can be. Wright and Jose Reyes made the '05 Mets the first team in history to have a left side of the infield both appear in 150 games apiece at 22 years of age or under.

The obsequious third baseman was on the cover of every sports publication possible in 2006, but he remained the same quietly confident yet outwardly humble person. Wright got off to a terrific start, and the Mets jumped out to a huge first-half lead and never faltered. Wright was the starting All-Star third baseman and finished second in the home run derby. He homered in the All-Star Game and appeared on *Late Night with David Letterman* the next night. His next two months didn't match up with his first four, but the Mets rolled on to their first division title since 1988, and Wright put together a 12-game hitting streak to end the season. That carried over into '07 with hits in his first 14 games to give him a 26-game hitting streak, albeit over two seasons.

After four straight seasons with at least 26 home runs and 102 RBIs (plus successive Gold Glove and Silver Slugger trophies in 2007 and 2008), Wright was clearly affected by the cavernous dimensions at Citi Field. Though he hit .307 and collected the first Mets home run at the park, Wright fanned an alarming 140 times in 2009; his 10 homers were fewer than he had even in his abbreviated rookie season and his slugging percentage was 76 points below any other year. Still, Wright remains the team's best hope for baseball success in Queens.

# 29 The Big Shea

Shea Stadium was a lot like the 1960s: colorful, loud, versatile, and the best we thought we could be. Four decades later it was padded in a few more places, had lost some of its natural color, and was a little worse for wear…just like a lot of children of the '60s. And it was still pretty loud.

Ground was broken on Flushing Meadow Park on October 28, 1961, less than three weeks after the Mets selected their first 22 players in the expansion draft. Only seven of those players saw Shea Stadium as Mets. And what a sight. After extensive construction delays, the ballpark—now named after Bill Shea for landing the franchise—opened for business on April 17, 1964. The original plan was to enclose the stadium, but that—like the dome idea bandied about early on—never happened. There wasn't the money, but hundreds of pitchers would come to applaud the decision as the open-air stadium and winds off Flushing Bay helped turn countless home runs into easy outs.

The World's Fair was right next door, and the place was jammed with more people than any place in baseball other than Dodger Stadium. That remained the case for the first three seasons of Shea, even while the Mets produced a hideous record of 169–316. Joe Namath kept fans coming in the fall to see the Jets play the AFL's best. The dead of winter marked the only time Shea turned quiet. Even LaGuardia's airplanes took other routes.

When the Amazin' Mets became the best team in baseball in 1969, they drew more fans than any major league club. It continued for three more seasons, drawing more than 2 million fans each year. The Mets put together a stunning push to claim the 1973 pennant and nearly stole another world championship. In 1975 the Mets, Yankees, Jets, and Giants shared Shea for a total of 173 games. The Yankees returned to rejiggered Yankee Stadium and took control of the town with three straight pennants. Fifteen years into Shea's existence the Mets drew a franchise-low 788,905. The only thing amazin' about Shea then was that two teams—Atlanta and Oakland—actually drew fewer people in 1979.

With an ownership change, the removal of the signature aluminum siding shingles from the exterior, and the installation of a giant top hat complete with an apple to signal home runs, the Mets started the long road back in the 1980s. A massive color screen, known as Diamond Vision, arrived in 1982, and the picnic area for special groups and events appeared a little while later. The Jets left for New Jersey, but baseball fans returned to Shea in droves as the Mets became the hottest ticket in town. A year after their thrilling

## Mr. Met

A clever drawing on the 1963 yearbook marked the birth of Mr. Met, the dean of the major league mascots. A year later a man dressed as the mascot roamed the stands at new Shea Stadium, the first time a team had a character in the stands. Dan Reilly was the man inside the mask. The head was smaller than today's version, but kids have been in love with Mr. Met from the start.

Mr. Met spent close to 20 years in hiding—M. Donald Grant scared everybody—but he returned in 1994 as part of an amusement park at Shea that Nickelodeon was pushing. The amusement park died off during the strike, but Mr. Met stayed. In 2007 he was inducted into the Mascot Hall of Fame. At 6'10" he's the tallest Met in history and is certainly the most recognizable.

1986 world championship, the Mets became the second team in major league history—and the first in New York—to draw 3 million fans. They did it again the following year.

The team slipped and fans started dribbling away—and then running fast—as the team tumbled to 103 losses in 1993. Two strike-shortened seasons plus a Yankees resurgence made Shea look and feel prematurely old in its thirties. Yet it was refurbished Yankee Stadium that dropped chunks of concrete in 1998 and forced the Yankees to play their first home game at Shea since 1975. A winning team, interleague sellouts against the Yankees, plus the arrival of Mike Piazza and a couple other Florida refugees pushed the Mets back into the public eye. Shea Stadium literally shook once more during the first postseason game in more than a dozen seasons in 1999. The next year brought the most people to Flushing since 1989. Shea saw its third world championship celebration that fall, but it belonged to the Yankees. That marked the first time in 12 postseason series that the Mets were eliminated in New York.

Shea had more important work than baseball after the World Trade Center catastrophe in 2001. Shea served as a staging center for rescue workers—even housing many between shifts—and 10 days after the attacks the stadium hosted the first post-9/11 outdoor event in New York. It was as moving a night as Shea has ever seen…and Shea had the pope in 1979.

The Bobby Valentine era dissolved in 2002, and Art Howe failed to light up Shea with a last-place club. The National League's switch a decade earlier to count attendance as seats sold instead of bodies in the building made the annual 2 million attendance figures hollow. Changes in the front office and manager's chair, plus high-profile free agents from around the globe, brought pride, purpose, and people back to Shea Stadium in 2005. Home-field advantage in 2006 couldn't push the Mets beyond the NLCS. The Mets drew more than 4 million fans during Shea's farewell season in 2008. Hard as it was to look.

Shea remained relevant until the last day of its sporting life—perhaps too relevant. The Mets suffered a final Sunday letdown against Florida for the second year running with a postseason spot on the line. Disappointed to say the least, the fans didn't take it out on Shea, thrilling to the inspired postgame closing ceremony after one of the toughest losses in the building's existence. A gamer til the end.

# 30 The Team to Beat

What the hell happened?

Seven games up with 17 to play, the wheels came off the 2007 Mets and they careened over the cliff to immortality, becoming the first team to blow a lead that large with such few games remaining. The 1964 Phillies squandered a similar lead—6½ games over their last 12—but that was in a world where one team per league reached the postseason. The 2007 Mets could have blown the divisional lead they had held nearly all season and still have made it to the playoffs as a wild-card team, but they couldn't even manage *that*.

The Mets' demise began, ironically, after beating archenemy Atlanta for the fifth time in six games. September 13 was the Mets' final off day, and they lost a half-game off the lead when the Phillies beat the white-hot Rockies. Then the Mets started their run to infamy. They were swept at home by the Phillies and lost two of three in Washington. They actually won three of four in Florida, but then returned home to get swept by the Nationals, lost a makeup game to St. Louis, and then dropped two of three to the Marlins.

When the Mets' 5–12 slide finally ended, the scapegoat frenzy was on. But the Mets' collapse was a full team effort. Here are 12 reasons it happened, or one for every loss:

**XII. Age.** The creakiness of the team was apparent from the start. Six players were 40 or older, and 13 were at least 35. The Old York Mets ran out of gas.

**XI. The bullpen.** It was ridiculously overused all season. For the first time in Mets history, no pitcher went nine innings in a game (their two complete games were rain-shortened affairs). So with the abundant appearances by their top four relievers—Aaron Heilman (81), Pedro Feliciano (78), Scott Schoeneweis (70), and Billy Wagner (66)—it's no wonder the pen came up dry at the end. Pampering starters while simultaneously abusing relievers is an epidemic in the game. The disease proved fatal in this case.

**X. The starters.** The staff got by until the last two weeks. They even got two strong starts against the Phillies on September 14 and 15, but lost both. The Mets had just three starts of six or more innings the rest of the way: Oliver Perez's win in Florida, the night when Pedro Martinez and Cardinals journeyman Joel Pineiro seemingly switched bodies (or teams), and John Maine's flirtation with a no-hitter in the penultimate game of the year.

**IX. Tom Glavine.** The only Met to start four times during the 5–12 skid, he got progressively worse. The Mets lost all four of his starts, culminating with his ⅓ of an inning, season-killing performance on the final day of the season.

**VIII. The Nationals.** The Mets had won seven straight series at RFK before their last visit. Washington went 5–1 against the Mets over the final two weeks and 2–5 against the Phillies. History would chillingly repeat itself in many ways in 2008, not the least of which was dropping the first two games of a must-win series against the last-place Nats.

**VII. The Marlins.** For a team with the highest ERA and the most errors in the league, the Marlins sure did the job against the

*Shawn Green (left) and Carlos Delgado can barely stand to watch as the 2007 Mets collapsed down the stretch in historic fashion.*

Mets. New York was 8–1 in Florida and 3–6 against the same bunch at home, losing two of three to the Marlins each series at Shea.

**VI. Two games.** Two more wins over the final two weeks and the Mets would have survived. While many games slipped through their grasp in that stretch, two hurt the most. On September 20 in Miami, Glavine blew a 3–0 lead, but the Mets rallied to score four times in the ninth, three runs coming on a tremendous bases-clearing double by Marlon Anderson. Billy Wagner's back kept him from closing, which led to Jorge Sosa giving the lead back in the ninth and—still inexplicably in the game an inning later—allowing the game winner. And at Shea on September 26, Philip Humber had a 5–0 lead over Washington in his first major league start (injuries and circumstance left little choice but to give him a try), but the relievers spit this one out in the fifth. The Mets proved powerless to retaliate as their lead shrunk to one game. The dam was about to burst.

**V. An inability to win at Shea.** Their 47–34 road mark was the best in baseball, but they were just 41–40 at home. And this was as they drew 3.8 million, as many people as any team in the league (the Dodgers drew 3,000 more, but LA-LA Land doesn't have to contend with real-world weather issues). Who would be blamed for this unprecedented failure?

**IV. The players.** To fans living and dying with each game, it is sometimes difficult to relate to what the professionals say. Here are three quotes from a *New York Observer* article written just before the final homestand:

"We have so much talent that sometimes we relax a little bit and then we get ourselves in trouble."

—Pedro Martinez

"Sometimes when you're a team as talented as we are—I don't know if I'd use the word 'bored,' but I guess you can get complacent sometimes. You don't pay attention to details every now and then because you do have a ton of talent and think you can, on most days, do everything you wanna do."

—Tom Glavine

"I think at times we can get a little careless. We've got so much talent I think sometimes we get bored."
—Carlos Delgado (originally uttered on WFAN)

Mets fans found October especially boring with their team out of the playoffs, but in a way it beat the meaningful games of September.

**III. The general manager.** Omar Minaya was credited for trying to keep the talented young players in the organization and not breaking the bank for some overrated free agents (Barry Zito comes to mind). The failure of this team, though, falls on him.

**II. The manager.** Whenever a team falters, especially in New York, the first reaction is to fire the manager. Willie's unflappable demeanor and confidence was refreshing amid all the negativity, but when the failure became a reality, the manager looked aged and shaken. Minaya announced Randolph would return in 2008, but Willie only made it to mid-June before he was replaced by Jerry Manuel. The new skipper got the Mets back into the race, but ultimately let another September lead get away to the Phillies.

**I. The Phillies.** Simply put, the Phillies deserved it. They went 13–4 to end the 2007 season. They beat the Mets eight straight times in head-to-head competition. They swept the Mets three times (twice at Shea). They survived Chase Utley missing a month. They survived numerous injuries to their pitching staff and a porous pen. They truly became, as eventual NL MVP Jimmy Rollins said amidst a spring furor, "The team to beat."

# 31 To Cheer Again

September 11, 2001, dawned with the Mets in Pittsburgh. Winners of 17 of their last 22, the defending National League champs finally awoke after a long slumber. They were two games under .500 and creeping up in both the division and wild-card standings. And then it didn't matter at all.

The attacks that brought down the World Trade Center shattered daily life in America. After a week of pain, grief, and soul searching, those normally obsessed with work and career let their desks pile up, spent more time with loved ones, and remembered what was really important. The games that dominate America's leisure time were humbled, laid barren of meaning. That would change with time. The cycle would renew itself, but the missing element was time. It was too painful, too soon.

When September 17 dawned, the Mets were again in Pittsburgh. Even this was an alteration in the understood order. The Mets were supposed to be hosting the Pirates, but Shea Stadium—that maligned old building—was doing its duty as a staging area for rescue workers. People rested there, decompressed there, thought about things a lot more significant than baseball even as a huge banner of celebrating ballplayers hung in the corridor overhead.

With the sites flipped and the team in Pittsburgh instead of the Pirates coming to Shea, the Mets went about their jobs for their first game at the immaculate Pirates facility, PNC Park. The Mets were more concerned about wearing the hats that honored the emergency service personnel who'd put everything on the line for their city and country. As the Mets swept Pittsburgh to move above .500 for the first time since April 5 in Atlanta, their thoughts were never far from their country, their city, or the big concrete building that stood for home. On Friday, September 21, 2001, the Mets borrowed the building they'd known as home for 37 years. They kept it working as a place to send out supplies; Mets manager Bobby Valentine made sure of that. But the time had arrived to return Shea to its intended use as a place of diversion.

The first major event in New York following the attacks brought out emergency workers from every part of the city, plus counties and states far beyond. Fans waved flags and kept getting lost in thoughts that strayed far from baseball. A 21-gun salute and a moment of silence honored the fallen victims. Every member of the Mets donated a day's salary, totaling approximately $440,000, to Rusty Staub's New York Police & Fire Widows & Children's Benefit Fund. Many of the players spent time with the families of victims and continued to take time for them months and years later.

The rival Mets and Braves embraced before the game, and Chipper Jones, despised by Mets fans for the way he worked over the club with his bat, picked up a shell casing from the ceremony and put it in his pocket. Six years later he told SNY's Kevin Burkhardt he still had that casing to remind him "never to take anything for granted again."

Diana Ross performed "God Bless America," and Marc Anthony followed with the national anthem as 41,235 all sang along. Liza Minnelli would later sing a rousing version of "New York, New York" and hug Mets center fielder Jay Payton in the on-deck circle amid thunderous applause. With eyes moist and lumps still in plenty of throats, Bruce Chen threw the first pitch, and then it was time to try to concentrate on the game. It wasn't easy.

Atlanta took a lead in the third and the Mets tied it. The Braves went up 2–1 in the eighth inning. Flushing native Steve Karsay, trying to save it for first-place Atlanta, walked Edgardo Alfonzo on

*An emotional Bobby Valentine (left), Mike Piazza, and the rest of the Mets hosted the Braves on September 21, 2001—the first game played in New York City following the terrorist attacks of 9/11.*

a close pitch. Mike Piazza, the team's star looked up to in good times and bad, drilled a high fly to center that cleared the wall and cleared the throats of everyone who had watched the game but hadn't known what to think or do. They cheered. It was all right to cheer. Never forget, but remember how precious each moment is. That moment certainly was.

Curmudgeonly Braves manager Bobby Cox, whose club seemed to delight in tearing down Mets hopes year in and year out, thought about that night's game as more than just another one-run loss. "It didn't bother me, losing that game," he said. "A little, but not much. That was New York's night."

It didn't turn out to be New York's year, but that night remains one of the most heartfelt in the history of the Mets, the stadium, and fans of both the team and the city.

# 32 Mookie Wilson

"MOOOOOOOOK!" The sound still follows him whenever Mets fans see him, now almost a generation after his last game. Even those champagne-soaked images of Mookie in a Cardinals cap behind Preston Wilson during their 2006 celebration will never change all the hard times he endured as a Met…or that one ground ball.

Drafted in the second round in 1977 out of the University of South Carolina, William Hayward Wilson landed in New York in September 1980 sporting No. 1 and providing a glimpse of a future that had to be better than what fans had spent the last four seasons watching. Mookie, who picked up his name because he had trouble saying "milk" as a child, made things happen. His numbers that first month were intriguing. He stole seven bases yet was nailed seven times, and he drew 12 walks in a month. His stolen base success rate would increase, and he had the team record for steals his first season playing a full schedule in 1982. His ability to get on base, however, declined as he got older. Mookie would have to hit his way on.

He did, hacking away from the leadoff spot and coming through with big moments once he got on base. Twice in a week in August 1983 he scored from second base on infield outs in the final inning to win games. The Mets needed all the victories his legs could provide because the team finished fifth or sixth in each of his first four seasons as a Met. That changed in 1984 with a jump to second place. Wilson went on the disabled list the following year, and Lenny Dykstra arrived from the minor leagues. Dykstra had more power, reached base more often, and had a far better arm in center field. The two split time in center, and Wilson spent more

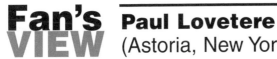

# Fan's VIEW
## Paul Lovetere
## (Astoria, New York)

### The '86 Conundrum

Given the choice of attending your first two World Series games with free tickets, which would you pick, Games 1 or 2 or Games 6 and 7? That thankfully was my greatest dilemma during the Mets' 1986 season. My allegiance to the Orange and Blue goes back to 1970 when I was five (don't quite remember too much from '69 besides my sister being born and wrecking my Camelot). Growing up not far from Shea on Long Island, I witnessed enough of the good, the bad, and the ugly of the 1970s and '80s to greatly appreciate the '86 season.

Naturally the World Series stands out as the highlight, with October as the most memorable month of that year. This is a very bold statement because 1986 was the end of my junior and beginning of my senior year in college. It is at Roanoke College—almost 500 miles from Shea Stadium—that my trip to the World Series began.

As the Mets and Astros were knee deep in their epic pennant battle, a good college buddy and fellow Mets fan offered me a chance to see the World Series if the team made it. The offer was simple and mind-blowing: if I could make it to New York (from Salem, Virginia) I would get a free seat to two games and a way back to school after it was over. Yee-ha, I'm in—minus the fact my car died right before senior year began and had no ride or funds to make it up to New York in a conventional matter (plane or bus). Bah, mere technicalities.

The logistical aspect would work itself out; we had more important decisions to make. Which games to attend? After great deliberation with others in the dorm room, we decided to take the safe bet to guarantee seeing the World Series. We chose Games 1 and 2.

Trust me, I know how close we came to seeing the greatest single World Series game ever (perhaps a biased opinion) and then a clinching Game 7 at Shea. I did see one close shutout loss in freezing temperatures and a blowout in Game 2. The finish looked just great on the little TV in my dorm room.

Twenty-odd years later, I would make the same decision again without the aid of hindsight. Now with hindsight, well, what would you do?

and more time in left field and less time leading off. In the destiny season of 1986 it all worked out.

A thrown ball in spring training shattered Mookie's sunglasses, and the resulting eye injury forced him to miss the first month of the season. A sort of platoon emerged, with Wilson, Dykstra, George Foster, and rookie Kevin Mitchell all spending time in the outfield with Darryl Strawberry a fixture in right. By the postseason Foster had been released and Mookie saw regular duty.

In a singular at-bat in Mets history, Mookie stepped up to the plate with the team down to its last out in the 1986 World Series, the tying run at third, and new pitcher Bob Stanley on the mound. Mookie fouled off six pitches and jackknifed out of the way as the ball bounced to the backstop and brought in Mitchell with the tying run. When he finally put the ball in play, it found Bill Buckner at first base. Buckner never touched it, and the Mets tied the Series, forever linking their names. Wilson led off and started in center field in Game 7, singling as part of the tying rally in the sixth inning. He was on the field when Jesse Orosco, a teammate through the lean times, got the final out.

The full-fledged folk hero missed his only .300 season by a point in 1987. Despite a solid season in 1988, Wilson saw action in only four of the seven games in the NLCS loss to the Dodgers. In 1989 he was traded to Toronto at the July deadline, just a few weeks after Dykstra had been dealt.

Wilson saw the postseason twice more as a Blue Jay. Former Mets teammate Rick Aguilera, who had gotten the win in Game 6 of the 1986 World Series thanks to Mookie's miraculous at-bat, retired Wilson his last time up in the major leagues in Game 5 of the 1991 ALCS. Mookie became a gospel singer and was later a minor league manager for the Mets. He served as a coach under Bobby Valentine from 1997 to 2002. Mookie was inducted into the Mets Hall of Fame in 1996.

# 33 Cleon Jones

Of the many things Cleon Jones did as a New York Met, he'll always be remembered for shoe polish and brushing the grass with his knee. On October 16, 1969, a bit of polish started a Mets rally. When the last out of the World Series came his way three innings later, he genuflected as he caught it in left field at Shea Stadium. Jones touched off a mad celebration on the field, in the locker room, and all over the city.

When Jones debuted under Casey Stengel, the Mets were so bad they could have been barred from watching the World Series, much less playing in it. He came up in 1963, the same year he signed out of Alabama A&M (he also scored 17 touchdowns in two years playing football). He made the Mets out of spring training in 1965. Hitting .156 in spot duty for a terrible team, the Mets sent him back to Buffalo. He was a regular the next two seasons at Shea, playing mostly center field. When Gil Hodges took over after the 1967 season, he pushed to acquire a Gold Glove center fielder who was Cleon's high school teammate in Mobile: Tommie Agee.

Jones shifted to left field and hit .297, sixth-best in the league in the "Year of the Pitcher." After the mound was lowered the next year, pitchers couldn't get Cleon out. He hit .400 the first month of the season and only once did his average drop as low as .333. The Mets were just as hot.

The Mets stayed well above .500 all summer and tried to stay near front-running Chicago. One of the low moments came in a doubleheader on July 30 when Jones did not hustle after a Johnny Edwards double during a 10-run Astros inning. Manager Gil Hodges walked out of the dugout, past the mound, and out to left field, calmly coming face to face with Jones. After talking briefly, both men headed back to the dugout. The Mets, citing a muscle pull, did not start him in any of the next three games. But Jones drove in crucial runs in consecutive one-run wins against Atlanta as a pinch-hitter and was thereafter back in left field. His .340 average for the year was third behind Pete Rose and Roberto Clemente for the batting crown. It remained the highest figure by a Met for 30 seasons; his .422 on-base percentage was likewise the highest in team history until 1998.

## TRIVIA
### Question

The 1969 Mets won more one-run games than any team in club history. How many times did the 1969 Mets win by one run? (Hint: the answer is a familiar number to Mets fans.)

Trivia answers on page 256

Jones pounded the ball at a .429 clip in the NLCS sweep of the Braves. He didn't hit much in the World Series, but it was a ball that hit him that caused much ado in Game 5. After a pitch at Cleon's feet skipped into the Mets dugout, Hodges emerged, brandishing a ball with shoe polish on it—proof that Jones had been hit by the pitch. Jones was sent to first and scored on Donn Clendenon's home run. The Mets rallied to take the lead, culminating with the fly to left that put Cleon on a knee.

He hit .319 in 1971, and the next year the Mets got Rusty Staub for left-handed lineup protection for the right-handed hitting—but lefty throwing—Jones. Injuries sapped his productivity, further damaging an already weak-hitting club. The night of September 20, 1973, a deep drive by Pittsburgh's Dave Augustine in the thirteenth inning hit on top of the wall and, instead of bouncing over for a home run, caromed right to Cleon. The relay nailed the go-ahead run at the plate, the Mets won the game in the bottom of the inning, and New York went on to win the division title after being in last place at the end of August. Jones hit .300 in the NLCS and .286 in the World Series, but the Mets lost to Oakland in seven games.

Two years later he was in Florida following knee surgery when local authorities caught the married Jones in a compromising situation with a young woman. He was forced to make a public apology to his teammates with his wife by his side and then rode the bench as his knee healed. He refused to take the field as a substitute in a July 18 game and argued with manager Yogi Berra. Jones declined a trade to the Angels and, despite his apology to Berra, was released. Berra was fired shortly thereafter. Jones spent 1976, his last season in the majors, with the White Sox.

Ed Kranepool and Jones were the last Mets to have played at the Polo Grounds. Cleon spent a dozen seasons as a Met and at the time of his release led the club in several categories, including hits (1,188), extra-base hits (308), runs (563), and RBIs (521). He is still among the team leaders in most offensive categories. He was inducted into the Mets Hall of Fame in 1991.

# 34 Fallen Stars: Doc and Straw

Two of the best players in Mets history were elected to the team's Hall of Fame in 2010. It was a long, strange trip for each of them.

Darryl Strawberry was National League Rookie of the Year in 1983; Dwight Gooden won the award the following year. In 1985 Gooden produced a season as remarkable as any in franchise history. Straw hit a home run in Game 7 of the 1986 World Series to give the Mets a championship cushion, and the next year Strawberry and Howard Johnson became the first teammates in history to hit 30 homers and steal 30 in the same season. Strawberry, who led the National League with 39 home runs in 1988, is still the club's all-time home-run leader, with 252, and hit

*The future was bright for the Mets' 1984 All-Stars: (from left) Darryl Strawberry, Dwight Gooden, Jesse Orosco, and Keith Hernandez. Sadly, Strawberry and Gooden would soon face struggles both on and off the field.*
Photo courtesy of AP/Wide World Photos.

more homers at Shea than any other player, with 127 (123 hit as a Met). He also leads the club in RBIs (733), extra-base hits (469), and runs (662). Doc and Straw made the All-Star team 11 times as Mets, with Strawberry making the team every year as a Met except for his rookie season.

Yet when you ask why the 1980s Mets failed to reach more than one World Series, one of the first questions is, "What if Doc and Darryl hadn't gotten mixed up with drugs?"

Cocaine was prevalent throughout society at that time, and the two young superstars were heavily involved in the booze and drug scene during their athletic peak. A powerhouse 1986 team that won 108 games covered Gooden's slip from his ridiculous '85 numbers and won a world championship, despite Doc losing three of his four postseason starts. Maybe Gooden pitched too many innings at too young an age and that contributed to his numbers after age 21 never approaching their previous heights. But if a manager took out a stud pitcher who averaged almost 10 strikeouts per nine innings in that era, people would have thought the manager was on drugs instead of the other way around.

Doc went into drug rehabilitation in 1987. His only season with an ERA under 3.19 after that was an injury-shortened 1989 season. Though he pitched until age 35, he never made the All-Star team after age 23. Gooden remained a Met until 1994, when he tested positive for cocaine a second time. He tested positive again and was suspended for the entire 1995 season. The next time he pitched at Shea Stadium was as a Yankee.

As for Strawberry, who also had a comeback with the Yankees, it always seemed that desire was at the heart of the issue while he was a Met. Davey Johnson, who managed Straw for most of his Mets career, said of his star slugger, "When he wanted to be, he was as good as it gets. But the thing is, I don't think he was hungry enough to do the 600-home run deal. Darryl is no dummy. He was comfortable hitting 34 home runs and stealing 30 bases. He knew what it would take to do more and he didn't want to do it." Strawberry averaged 32 home runs and 24 steals in his Mets career.

Troubled pasts and all, Doc and Straw have returned to the Mets fold: Strawberry is a host on SNY, and Gooden, a minor league executive in Newark, visits Citi Field with his family.

# 35 Bobby Valentine

Bobby Valentine became a Met on one of the worst days in Mets history. Some two decades later he became manager and helped guide the Mets out of one of their longest dry spells.

He came to the Mets on June 15, 1977, the same night Tom Seaver was traded. (Valentine was acquired in another one-sided deal, with slugger Dave Kingman going to San Diego.) A multiple-sport star at Rippowam High School in Stamford, Connecticut, Valentine's coming home was not what he would have imagined. Taken with the fifth overall pick by the Dodgers in 1968, a grotesque leg injury had stolen his speed and left him a utility player. Brimming with energy, Valentine became a restaurateur and took on coaching, joining George Bamberger's staff in 1983 and remaining with the Mets as third-base coach for Davey Johnson until the Texas Rangers tabbed him to replace Doug Rader in May 1985.

In his first full year he led the Rangers to the second-most wins in franchise history to that point (87), but he never surpassed that figure. Opponents who resented him referred to him as "Top-Step Bobby" because of his fiery temper and the position he adopted in the dugout. Yet Bobby V. knew the game and its rules better than quite a few umpires and opponents. He was never afraid to argue—at length—his point of view. After Rangers managing general partner and future U.S. President George W. Bush fired Valentine in 1992, Bobby V.'s next job was in Japan. He became the first American manager to be hired—and fired—in that country.

He returned to the United States and the Mets, managing in Class AAA Norfolk until he replaced Dallas Green late in the 1996 season. Valentine liked to juggle the lineup and try new things—having the first baseman hold a runner on from several steps away from the bag was a favorite—and he excelled at uncovering talent. Tarnished replacement players Rick Reed and Benny Agbayani thrived under Valentine, while the manager had conflicts with a few established players, notably Todd Hundley and Pete Harnisch.

Bobby V. proved loyal to his people, bristling when general manager Steve Phillips fired coaches Bob Apodaca and Tom Robson during an eight-game losing streak in June 1999. He considered quitting but instead declared that, if the next third of the

## We Three Kongs

Dave Kingman clubbed 36 home runs in 1975 and broke his own club record with 37 in 1976. The disgruntled slugger was traded to San Diego for Bobby Valentine and Paul Siebert on the infamous night of June 15, 1977 (the Padres and two more teams tired of Kingman during the season). The '77 Mets had three players tie for the team lead with 12, the lowest output for a club homer leader (tied by Daniel Murphy in 2009). Add up the totals of John Stearns, John Milner, and Steve Henderson, and it still falls one shot shy of Kingman's '76 total. Kong had nine for the Mets before the trade and 26 all told in '77.

season went poorly, he would step down. The Mets actually took control of the wild-card race...until the last two weeks of the season. A seven-game losing streak—reminding jumpy Mets fans of the five-game, season-destroying skid in late September 1998—plus an ill-timed and too-frank profile in *Sports Illustrated*, coming three months after his suspension for wearing a cheesy disguise in the dugout following an ejection, seemed to spell the end of the Bobby V. era. Yet the Mets won their last four, including a one-game playoff. They beat the Diamondbacks in thrilling fashion in the Division Series and nearly pulled off a miraculous comeback against the Braves in the NLCS.

His status rose even higher the next year when the Mets won the wild-card again and reached the World Series against the two-time defending world champion Yankees. His decision to let Al Leiter throw 142 pitches in Game 5 ended badly when the Mets lost a heartbreaker and the Series in the ninth inning.

The 2001 season was a dud for the first four months, but just when the Mets started to turn it around, everything changed on September 11. Amid Valentine's efforts to help in the aftermath and continuing long after the catastrophe, the Mets played the first outdoor sporting event in the city since the attacks. He'd refused to change out of his tribute "NYPD" cap during a game, and the team followed his lead. The Mets won that first game in New York but invariably came up short. Valentine, Mike Piazza, and a lot of often forgotten everyday public servants showed what an actual role model looked like.

The team around Valentine, however, fell apart. Phillips traded away the good fundamental ballplayers who'd helped the Mets achieve five consecutive winning seasons, the second-longest streak in club history. The new stars Phillips brought in wilted on the New York stage, and Valentine paid the price. He was fired the day after the 2002 season ended; Phillips stayed as the Mets sank even deeper.

Valentine proved a natural in the ESPN studios, but he jumped at the chance to return to Japan to manage. He took over the Chiba Lotte Marines, the same team that fired him in 1995, and guided them to their first championship. Back in America in 2009, he remains beloved in Japan if still misunderstood in his native land.

# 36 Ryan vs. Kazmir

It is almost unbearable to think what the Mets lost when they traded Nolan Ryan to the Angels on December 10, 1971. The man won 324 times and threw seven no-hitters. With his record 5,714 strikeouts and 2,795 walks (plus 158 hit batters, still in the top 10 all-time)—figured at his average of 836 batters faced over a 27-year career—Ryan spent more than 10 years with no one putting a ball in play! Ironically, his 61 shutouts are the same number as another great Met who also never should have been traded: Tom Seaver.

The Mets sent Ryan and three prospects who never panned out (Frank Estrada, Don Rose, and Leroy Stanton) to California for Jim

Fregosi, who spent all of 146 games as a Met, hit .233, played a lousy third base, and was hurt constantly. Twenty years after the Mets got rid of Fregosi, he had managed three clubs and taken two to division titles. Nolan Ryan? He was still pitching.

The 1977 Seaver trade aside—they did get three regulars who lasted several years as Mets—dealing Ryan was the worst trade in club history. Could it ever be topped?

The Mets have tried. Yet the one that produced the greatest outcry in recent decades was made at the July 2004 trading deadline. The deal was officially Scott Kazmir and Jose Diaz to Tampa Bay for Bartolome Fortunato and Victor Zambrano. In bad trade shorthand, that's Kazmir for Zambrano. It was poorly conceived

## Whitey Herzog: A Mets-Made Man?

An image from the mid-1980s is the hated Whitey Herzog scowling in his Cardinals cap as he watched his switch-hitters hop around the bases and Jack Clark hit balls 400 feet. But Herzog cut his management teeth with the Mets. He could have—no, probably should have—followed either Johnny Murphy as general manager or Gil Hodges as manager after their untimely deaths. Bob Scheffing got the former job and Yogi Berra the latter. Joe McDonald, who had once done Whitey's paperwork, got the GM job after Scheffing, but by then Herzog had gone where his prospects were better.

As director of player development, Herzog said that the Ryan-for-Fregosi trade was a mistake. (Whitey joined Ryan in Cooperstown in 2010.) He was responsible for putting together the talent that won two pennants in five seasons after the Mets had been the worst team in baseball for seven. He did wind up benefiting from one of those bad Mets deals. Amos Otis—part of a historically bad Mets trade after the 1969 season—was Herzog's center fielder in Kansas City, as that expansion team quickly became a dominant force. Herzog did help the Mets out 14 years later by angrily dropping Keith Hernandez in their lap.

Herzog's biggest problem during his Mets tenure was his outspokenness. He told board chairman M. Donald Grant not to meddle in baseball personnel affairs. Whitey was right about that, too.

from the start. Even if some in the organization weren't big on the little lefty, Kazmir could have been used in a trade after the season for the likes of Tim Hudson or any of the other top pitchers on the market who would've put up better Mets numbers than Victor Zambrano (10–14, 4.42 ERA in 39 games).

The reverberations and the outrage by fans shook the Mets to the core. Two months later, general manager Jim Duquette was demoted, manager Art Howe was fired, and the Wilpons had gone to Montreal to give Omar Minaya anything he desired to take over the franchise. Other GMs and pundits still use the term "Kazmir trade" as a cautionary tale of giving up future top-of-the-rotation pitchers. If Zambrano hadn't immediately gotten hurt, and if the Mets had actually contended for the wild-card instead of collapsing, maybe the team wouldn't have changed course and it might've taken longer for the Mets to realize the ship needed righting.

Kazmir has been good, but in his first seven years in the majors he hasn't been Nolan Ryan—though Ryan was only starting to become the Ryan of legend in his seventh season. There are similarities between Kazmir and Ryan's upbringing in the Houston area, to sharing late January birthdays, to frustrating their teams with their wildness and inconsistency, to getting traded to the Angels at the age of 25. Tampa Bay felt comfortable enough trading Kazmir in 2009, happy to shed the lefty's salary while bringing back three minor leaguers with potential.

The Ryan deal, however, started everything slowly spinning out of control for the Mets, even with them winning a pennant two years after the trade. The Kazmir deal actually resulted in changes for the better. But if you ever come across a time machine that lets you make two stops to right baseball wrongs, after you visit GM Bob Scheffing the week after Thanksgiving 1971, make sure to set the controls for Jim Duquette's office the morning of July 30, 2004, armed with medical reports and a stack full of tomorrow's headlines.

# 37 The New York Press

A look at the Mets franchise wouldn't be complete without a few words on the press. It can be a ballplayer's greatest friend when he or the team are going great, or it can be like a millstone around his neck during the tough times. The press never rests.

Winners of the J.G. Taylor Spink Award, given annually by the Baseball Hall of Fame to recognize journalistic excellence over a reporting career, have included several men who covered the Mets at some point in their careers, such as Red Smith, Dick Young, Jack Lang, Leonard Koppett, Joseph Durso, Murray Chass, and Bill Madden.

"[Bill] Shea, in his work to bring the team to New York, had forged a strong alliance with the newspapers, who also wanted a team to replace the Giants and Dodgers because baseball interest sold papers daily," Koppett wrote. "It happened that, through no particular plan, the older baseball writers in New York had been covering the Giants in the middle 1950s. When the teams left, most of them shifted to the Yankees, with attrition taking care of the surplus. The Dodger writers, on the other hand, were a younger and more aggressive group, and they included the single most influential (and, in the opinion of many, the most talented) baseball writer in America: Dick Young, columnist of the *Daily News*, the paper with the largest circulation in the country."

Young pushed for bringing a team to New York, and when it got here, he helped push it along. His status and sense of humor in the press box helped set the tone for, in Koppett's words, a "joyful irreverence" in covering the club. Casey Stengel's gravelly voice became an oracle of wisdom and laughter on the keyboards of Young and the other talented men on the beat. Stengel called the club "amazin'" so frequently that the tabloids started referring to the club as "Amazin's" in their headlines. The close relationship between this "new breed" on the field and the one at the typewriter lasted through the '69 "Miracle" and '73 "Ya Gotta Believe" seasons and into the mid-1970s. The stories mostly stuck to the game and matters concerning baseball. Private things were brought up if it was in an endearing light or was well known.

Dave Kingman was a favorite of fans who had long waited for a slugger at Shea, but he was mean and often rude to the press. While writers played up his mammoth home runs and dubbed him "Kong," they weren't about to paint him as something he wasn't off the field. Free agency reared its head, finally putting player and management on a more even keel, and the cracks in the relationship came through in the newspapers. Young, who sided with management in Tom Seaver's contract dispute (while Lang handled the pitcher's angle), formed a schism between media and Met. Young's words about Nancy Seaver's feelings put the best Met in history on the phone to demand a trade. He was dealt that night. Kingman, too.

Young was booed when he received his Spink Award in Cooperstown a year later. It didn't bother him. He jumped to the *New York Post* and, a decade after he helped get Seaver out of town, advocated that Mets fans "stand up and boo" Dwight Gooden upon his return from drug rehabilitation.

The press voraciously covered the mid-1980s Mets, who played the role of controversial winners that the Yankees had in the late 1970s. It often got ugly as back-biting teammates openly disdained Darryl Strawberry's nagging injuries that seemed to be exacerbated by partying all night. The era ended with a book about the 1992 club titled *The Worst Team Money Could Buy*, written by Bob Klapisch of the *Daily News* and John Harper of the *Post*. That book called out the team on its off-field troubles and labeled them as jerks; a characterization that Bobby Bonilla proved accurate when he threatened Klapisch in the locker room. By the time Bret Saberhagen sprayed the press with bleach that summer, the Mets were on their way to 103 losses and it would be years before any newspaperman besides the beat reporters felt compelled to spend time at Shea.

Bobby Valentine gave them a reason. Smart, successful, and combative, Valentine was the definition of "good copy," even if the way it came out in the press wasn't always good for him. Ten years after the '92 debacle, the Mets went down the drain and took the manager with them. The Mets beat became purgatory with the dull Art Howe and his equally lifeless club. There was still controversy, but it seemed like everyone was just going through the motions.

Manager Willie Randolph and general manager Omar Minaya helped restore credibility and a "back page" presence in the tabloids once more. An NL East title became a crushing NLCS loss in 2006, and a seeming repeat division title turned into the worst collapse in baseball history the next year. The story of the closing of Shea Stadium became secondary with a reprise September swoon in 2008. Jerry Manuel had replaced Randolph, who'd been fired after a month-long "Willie Watch" stemming from a disastrous newspaper interview followed by an even worse road trip. A year later, Minaya's press conference fumbling resulted in the outlandish accusation of a reporter's improper motives. That July 2009 brouhaha was the last blip of attention in a season of irrelevance in Citi Field's inaugural season. It would take more than a new ballpark to bring that back.

# 38 The FAN

It is hard to recall what life was like before WFAN, the radio home of the Mets and the country's first 24-hour sports talk station. The Mets have traveled the dial in their existence, but WFAN has been their home since 1987, including two years when WFAN was at 1050 AM before replacing WNBC at 660. The 50,000-watt "clear channel" station enables the Mets to be heard across several states at night and lets people in Virginia know what Short Al in Brooklyn thinks about the latest move—or lack thereof—in Flushing. No shortage of opinions here.

The long-running afternoon team of "Mike and the Mad Dog" dissolved into just Mike (Francesa) when Chris "Mad Dog" Russo moved to satellite radio in the fall of 2008. Francesa's alternating Mets bashing and baiting continued solo, simulcast on the YES Network, driving fans to distraction like a Tokyo Rose they just can't turn off. The current midday team of Joe Benigno and Evan Roberts are big Mets fans, and there are several other indispensable people (from a Mets point of view) at that station.

Ed Coleman has been the Mets' pregame host since Howie Rose moved up to TV play-by-play in 1996. Eddie C. is a veteran reporter who interacts beautifully with the players, yet he never forgets they are his beat. When permitted, he calls a good game, too. The station's weekly baseball program, *Ed Randall's Talking Baseball*, is often preempted for other sports, but the show provides a forum for all things baseball and extends beyond the local teams. Update vet Bob Heussler is a huge Mets fan and became a personal hero by indoctrinating his kid so deeply into Metdom that the boy sat around in a soaked shirt at a friend's house rather than put on a dry one offered with a Yankees insignia. We can all only hope the future is in such good hands.

Bob Murphy guided countless Mets fans through the best summers of their lives, and his voice acted like an arm around my shoulder on that long drive following the disturbing events at Shea on October 26, 2000. Murph will never be replaced. Rose is the keeper of the flame, taking a lifetime of study and passing the history and wonder along in his own way. Rose is a Mets fan in the booth, doing what we'd all kill to do…and doing it better than any of us ever could. His perfect partner was Gary Cohen, who moved—deservedly so—to SNY.

Steve Somers isn't new, but his tweaking of Yankees fans (and Icelanders fans) is what makes AM radio worth listening to, even with outer space crammed with satellites plus every song in the world at your fingertips. Somers has brought many a Mets fan home after a late-night game, adding some schmooze to the happy recap.

# 39 SNY: So Not YES

In 2006 SportsNet New York freed the Mets from SportsChannel, MSG, and Fox Sports New York, past providers of the Mets on cable dating to 1980. Although Cablevision paid the Mets hefty rights fees, the club wanted control of the product and the cash from advertisements and other programming. SNY is owned by the Mets (d.b.a. Sterling Entertainment Enterprises), Time Warner, and Comcast.

SNY has so far not been able to land another New York team's games in a major sport. The station talks about the Jets constantly, but the NFL still carries local games on network TV. To fill the hours, SNY broadcasts events like college football and basketball, Canadian football, boxing, pro lacrosse, extreme volleyball, street games, and poker (sigh), plus paid programming during odd hours. All that is nice, but what SNY is really there for is the Mets. That they do extremely well.

SNY not only has Mets games with in-studio shows before and after the games, there are several daily rebroadcasts, plus a shortened version that acts a little like a DVR for those of us without. For my money, the current announcing trio is the best since Murphy–Kiner–Nelson. There's Ivy League pitcher Ron Darling telling you everything Johan Santana is thinking, batting champ Keith Hernandez detailing what the hitter's doing wrong while tossing out lines from *Caddyshack* and unabashedly wearing a "man fur" in April, and Gary Cohen, the career professional, drawing good stuff out of the pair while deftly mixing recent observations with arcane Mets history. Even the cartoon commercials they had of the trio in odd circumstances were humorous (or at least funnier than the original ads with the talking TV head).

> **TRIVIA Question**
>
> **Which one-time Met allowed the record-breaking home run 756\* to Barry Bonds in 2007?**
>
> Trivia answers on page 256

*Mets Weekly* has a lot more information than its predecessor on Cablevision (and, full disclosure, invited me to talk on the program). *Mets Hot Stove* gets fans through the winter, and *Kids Clubhouse* does the Lord's propaganda by brainwashing kids blue and orange. The 1969 World Series rebroadcast was captivating TV, taking viewers back to a time when the game seemed purer, batters stayed in the box, umpires called letter-high pitches strikes, postseason games were played during the day, and the screen wasn't littered with ads and inconsequential graphics. In 2009 SNY unearthed the Mets highlights films of the club's first 25 years and aired the capsules as *Mets Yearbook*.

One thing SNY does not do is bathe all things in a wave of pompousness like the YES Network, broadcasters of the Yankees. There's no Joel Youngblood "Metography" or annoying fan-based reality shows (at least not now). The Yankees trade credibility for schtick with dozens of bad announcers, none of whom would dare bash the product. The Mets have traditionally been straight shooters—their sports news show, *Geico SportsNite*, has even led off many times covering the Yankees. Think that would ever happen on YES? No.

# 40 Trophies for the Living Room

While no Met has ever been named league Most Valuable Player, four Mets have taken home hardware as postseason series MVPs. Here's how they did it.

## Donn Clendenon, 1969 World Series MVP

A midseason pickup from Montreal, Clendenon platooned much of the time—he did not play in the World Series game that Baltimore righty Jim Palmer started—but he certainly hit lefties well. Clendenon batted .357 with four of his five hits going for extra bases, including three home runs. Jerry Koosman may have been a more inspired choice, but Clendenon put the runs on the board.

## Al Weis, 1969 Babe Ruth Award

You may not even know about this award. It has been around since 1949 (longer than the MVP) and is decided on and distributed by the New York chapter of baseball writers. It is often given to the same player as the World Series MVP, but in this case it wasn't. Weis led all hitters with a .455 average, and his rare home run in Game 5 tied the game in the seventh inning.

## Ray Knight, 1986 World Series MVP

Knight kept the rally going in Game 6 and danced home with the winning run on Bill Buckner's infamous error. Knight snapped the tie in Game 7 with a home run and made the cover of *Sports Illustrated*. While Gary Carter drove in nine runs, it's hard to go against Knight (.391), which was reinforced by the Ruth award a little while later.

# Back in Time

Not every postseason series has an MVP. The NLCS added one starting in 1977 and amazingly no sponsor has slapped a name on an MVP for the Division Series. We'll do it for them for every series the Mets have won that hasn't yet been covered. Call these guys the Rheingold Extra Dry "Heroes of Yore" presented by RC Cola.

## 1969 NLCS: Cleon Jones

The pitching wasn't up to snuff, and five regulars hit .333 or higher. Cleon's .429 was the highest of the lot in the three-game sweep of Atlanta, so crack open an ice cold Rheingold for him.

## 1973 NLCS: Tom Seaver

Rusty Staub hit all three Mets home runs in the five-game shocker against the Reds, but Seaver won twice with a 1.62 ERA after winning the NL East clincher on the last day. Not only was he superb after club doctors and officials wondered about his arm, Seaver also helped calm the angry Shea mob in left field after Pete Rose pounded Bud Harrelson.

## 1986 NLCS: Jesse Orosco

Yes, yes, they gave out an MVP, but it was a travesty to give it to Houston's Mike Scott. He may have beaten the Mets twice, but Orosco won three times, including twice in 26 hours while pitching on fumes. Oh, let Scuffy keep his trophy; spray some more of that dry beer on Jesse's head.

## 1999 NLDS: John Olerud

It is oh-so-tempting to give this fictional honor to Todd Pratt, ably filling in for injured Mike Piazza and hitting a homer for the ages to end the series. Yet it was Tank's only hit and Johnny O. laced liners all over the place against Arizona to the tune of a .438 average. Edgardo Alfonzo hit three homers, and Rickey Henderson batted .400 and stole six bases, but give Olerud anything if we can go back in time and make him stay at Shea.

### 2000 Division Series: Bobby Jones

It's tough to give it to a pitcher based on one start, but what a start! Jones tossed a one-hitter in the clincher, allowing base runners in only one inning. It would be nice to give it to Bobby Valentine, who managed the jock off Dusty Baker. The Mets got game-winning hits in extra innings from Jay Payton and Benny Agbayani and survived a Derek Bell injury (that's a bad thing?) plus an Armando Benitez breakdown to beat the Giants.

### 2006 Division Series: Paul Lo Duca

A crazy choice for a crazy guy, but when he tagged two runners out at home on one play in the second inning of the first game, it was all over right there. He hit .455 with vengeance in his eyes against his former team. Carlos Delgado (.429), Cliff Floyd (.444), David Wright (.333), and even Shawn Green (.333) helped the Mets momentarily forget their mounting pitching injuries.

## Mike Hampton, 2000 NLCS MVP

It's easy to hate Mike Hampton now, but Mets fans loved him after his complete-game shutout beat the Cardinals in the NLCS. While five Mets hit .300 or better in the five games, Hampton threw 16 shutout innings in his two wins. He took the hardware and ran…to the Colorado school system as a free agent.

# 41 Seaver's Unbreakable Pitching Records

It's been more than 25 years since Tom Seaver threw his last pitch as a New York Met, and most of his single-season and career team records still stand. Which ones will still be standing in another 25 years? Well, the crystal ball's warranty runs out before 2035, but if you happen to come across this book then—besides having a collector's item on your hands (the future's about hope)—you should find that Tom Terrific (1967–1977, 1983) is still tops on the Mets' charts in at least these five categories. Barring a return of Sidd Finch.

## Wins

Pitchers don't accrue wins like they once did because of the blind allegiance to pitch count and unjustified faith in middle relief. If Seaver's 25 wins from 1969 somehow gets broken, it either means that sanity has returned and starters are allowed to pitch longer,

### Sidd Finch, Figment

Mets had this kid back in spring training 1985. Finch. Knew Eastern philosophy and played a mean French horn. Wore one hiking boot and his hat backwards to pitch. Could throw 168 miles per hour. He could pitch more often than other pitchers. He rendered the flame-throwing Dwight Gooden obsolete. Or at least bumped him down to a very distant second spot in the rotation. The Mets not only had the pennant sewed up, they'd revolutionized the game. On paper.

The *Sports Illustrated* article, "The Curious Case of Sidd Finch," appeared around the end of spring training. The article's subhead was cryptic: "He's a pitcher, part yogi and part recluse. Impressively liberated from our opulent lifestyle. Sidd's deciding about yoga—and his future in baseball." Take the first letter of each word and it read: "H-A-P-P-Y A-P-R-I-L F-O-O-L-S D-A-Y." The rest of the code was "A-H F-I-B." But no matter what it said, there was no Sidd Finch. Wouldn't be. Couldn't be.

George Plimpton, he of *Paper Lion* and the *Paris Review* fame, made the whole thing up. *Sports Illustrated* had set up photo shoots and even tried to perpetuate the hoax. The cat was out of the bag. Gooden was still the Mets' star pitcher and he would have his best year ever. Still, one couldn't help thinking that first week of October 1985 as the Mets desperately tried to get past St. Louis, where they would be if Finch had been a little bit real. Why couldn't Plimpton have picked on the Yankees?

some Met has an unworldly year, or the season has been extended to 200 games. Likewise, his career mark of 198 wins should also still be standing 25 years hence. Dwight Gooden—24 wins in 1985 and 157 career victories—couldn't touch the marks while going nearly the same number of years as Seaver, although Doc was far less durable or reliable.

## Strikeouts

See above. Seaver's total of 2,541 was not approached by Dr. K, so do you think someone else will come close? Someone might, but it's doubtful, given the short leash starters have today. Gooden didn't even break Seaver's single-season mark of 289 in 1971 or 283 in 1970, but one extra start in his rookie year and his 276 (best since the 1800s by a first-year hurler) could have gotten him there.

## Complete Games

This is what they call a sure thing. Seaver's 21 complete games in 1971 would be impressive if the Mets team reached that in a season over the next 25 years. Not only will Seaver's complete games mark of 171 still be standing, but Jerry Koosman (108) will still be holding firm in second place (first among Mets southpaws). Gooden threw complete games at the third-highest rate for a Mets pitcher, and he's more than 100 behind Tom Terrific. Since shutouts are dependent upon complete games, we'll put down double that Seaver's 44 will also stand the test of time. Doc did throw eight in '85 to beat the seven by Koosman (1968) and Jon Matlack (1974).

## Innings

Seaver holds both the single-season mark of 291 in 1971 and the career record (3,045). His career total is exactly 500 better than Koosman's and 875⅓ ahead of Gooden. What made Seaver stand out is that he didn't consider the job done unless he finished a game...and when was the last time you heard that?

## Cy Young Awards

This is one wild-card that doesn't take an iron man to break. It's the easiest of these categories, yet it pretty much takes a Hall of Fame candidate to do it. Seaver was the first right-hander in history to gain three Cy Young Awards (1969, 1973, 1975) and he probably should have taken another in 1971. (This section doesn't really even address ERA—2.57 for his career—but '71 was Seaver's best year in several categories, including his 1.76 mark that only Gooden topped in 1985.) Winning the Cy Young isn't just about accruing statistics, although it helps. The Cy Young is voted on by writers, who have traditionally been influenced by number of wins, where a team finishes in the standings, and sometimes how good the pitcher has been in the past. Dwight Gooden (1985) is the only other Met to have won the award, but a Pedro Martinez–type pitcher in his prime could equal Seaver's mark. Break it? You might want to look back in 50 years on that one.

# 42 Rusty Staub

Rusty Staub had two different Mets careers. Le Grande Orange—a Colt .45s regular as a teenager and Montreal's first All-Star—was coerced from the Expos for three talented everyday players: Ken Singleton, Tim Foli, and Mike Jorgensen. The Mets desperately needed someone for the middle of the lineup, but the timing was awful. The 28-year-old, red-haired outfielder with the strong arm and solid bat became a Met on April 5: the day before Gil Hodges's funeral.

Three days earlier the Mets' manager had died of a heart attack in Florida. General manager Bob Scheffing, already criticized for

## Trusty Rusty

Rusty Staub is remembered today as a pinch-hitting star in his waning years as a Met. Big of frame and slow of foot, it's hard to imagine him as a young red-haired kid. Staub's walk-off—because he sure couldn't run—pinch-hit homer beat Philadelphia at Shea Stadium on September 25, 1984, but it couldn't change New York's doomed postseason chances. It did, however, put him in elite company because of something that had happened 21 years earlier. Coupled with the six home runs he hit at age 19 for the 1963 Houston Colt .45s (forerunners of the Astros), Staub became the first National League player to homer as both a teenager and as a fortysomething. Ty Cobb had done it in 1905 and 1928 in the AL. Staub hit one more homer in 1985 before calling it a career.

hiring Yogi Berra hours after the death, had been working on the Staub deal before the tragedy, but the announcement of the trade seemed callous to some. But the game moves on—Hodges had wanted Staub and his lefty bat in the cleanup spot and Rusty indeed transformed the lineup.

Staub was hitting .313 with 27 RBIs when George Stone—later a teammate but then with Atlanta—hit him on the right hand on June 3. The right fielder continued playing for the 31–12 Mets, whose five-game lead was the largest in baseball. Two weeks later, however, he dropped the bat in pain in Cincinnati. A broken bone in his wrist essentially ended his season…and his team's.

He started slowly in 1973, but a 5-for-9 performance with a tiebreaking double in the nineteenth inning at Dodger Stadium brought Staub's average out of the low end of the .200s. He saved his best for last, as the Mets tore from the bottom of the standings to the top in the final month. He had three hits and drove in three in the game that clinched a tie for the division and added four hits the next day as the Mets captured the division in their 161st and final game. Staub homered three times in the NLCS shocker against Cincinnati, but he injured his shoulder in a collision with the wall making a brilliant catch in Game 4. He somehow batted .423 in the World Series, despite discomfort that forced him to throw underhand. The Mets lost to Oakland in seven games.

Staub slumped along with the team in a downer year in '74, but he followed that with his finest season as a Met. Staub knocked in 105 runs to shatter the club mark of 97 set five years earlier by Donn Clendenon. Staub's mark was equaled in 1986, but 105 remained the club record until 1990. Rusty came and went as a Met twice in that time.

The December 1975 trade to Detroit for portly veteran southpaw Mickey Lolich was a shock. Staub prospered in Motown; Lolich retired after one poor year at Shea. Staub, getting a little chunkier himself thanks to his own top-notch restaurant in Manhattan, became accustomed to life as a designated hitter in the American League. He returned to the Mets as a free agent in 1981, batting .307 as a part-time first baseman but a wicked .375 as a pinch-hitter. The chef had a new gig.

After a year as player/coach—his pinch-hitting average plummeted to .211—Staub shifted back to full-time bench god. In 1983 he tied records with eight consecutive pinch-hits and 25 RBIs, while setting another mark with 81 at-bats off the bench (batting .296). He struck out just six times in a pinch and 10 times all year. The 1984 Mets surged back to contention for the first time since 1976, and Staub was a key contributor. He finished his long career a year later as an adored cog in a revitalized team that once again had New York's full attention.

His No. 10 was retired in Montreal—although the Expos' American descendants, the Washington Nationals, don't recognize his feats—and Staub and Bud Harrelson became the first Mets players inducted in the team's Hall of Fame in 1986. He spent seven years as a Mets television broadcaster and has worked tirelessly for the New York Police & Fire Widows & Children's Benefit Fund.

# 43 Gary Carter

In the context of the rough-and-tumble 1980s, Gary Carter was known as a goody-good. Religious, hard-working, and a star in a foreign market, some Expos intimated that he was too interested in his numbers. What Carter was interested in was winning, something that didn't happen as often in Montreal as it once had. And his numbers were good.

A seven-time All-Star—and two-time All-Star MVP—in Montreal, the mantle of best catcher in the National League passed from Johnny Bench to curly-haired Kid Carter. He'd foregone numerous baseball and football scholarships to sign with the Expos as a shortstop. He learned to catch and also played right field his first two years as an Expo, but by the time the team moved to Olympic Stadium in 1977, Carter caught every day and was at the heart of a formidable order. That's what the Mets wanted when they went shopping for an experienced catcher to work with their talented young pitching staff.

It took four players, including Shea favorite Hubie Brooks, to pry Carter from a division rival. He homered to win Opening Day 1985 and brought right-handed power to the middle of New York's order. Years of playing on artificial turf had taken a toll on his knees, but Carter received many cortisone shots, and trainers wrapped his legs before every game. "By the time they finish with him," general manager Frank Cashen said, "he looks like a gladiator." He played like one, too.

Carter caught the most innings of his career in 1985, despite requiring surgery as soon as the Mets were eliminated, which didn't happen until the penultimate day of the season thanks to Carter's 32 homers and 100 RBIs, by far the most ever by a Mets catcher to that point. He got more rest the next year and his numbers improved as the Mets cruised to their first division title since 1973.

Carter was mired in a 1-for-21 slump in the NLCS when he stepped to the plate in Game 5, score tied, series tied, twelfth inning. He singled up the middle to give the Mets the victory.

**TRIVIA**
**Question**

**What year did the Mets first have a pitcher not lose in double figures?**

Trivia answers on page 256

The next afternoon he caught all 16 innings in Houston, calling Jesse Orosco breaking balls for the final strikeout (following a recommendation/threat from first baseman Keith Hernandez). Carter homered twice in Game 4 of the World Series and knocked in nine runs against Boston, but his greatest contribution was his two-out single that started the legendary rally in the bottom of the tenth inning of Game 6.

Repeating proved much harder, especially with a hobbled pitching staff. Carter, who'd finished third in the MVP running the previous year, batted just .235, his lowest average since becoming an everyday catcher. The Mets picked up another division title in 1988 with Carter now cocaptain with Hernandez (an honor Kid lobbied for after Mex was named the first captain in team history a year earlier). The season was tough, however. Carter went an embarrassing 86 days and 225 at-bats between his 299th and 300th career home runs. He hit just 11 homers all season, his fewest in a decade. He batted .222 in the bitter seven-game NLCS loss to the Dodgers.

His 1989 season, shortened by injury, proved a long, slow good-bye for cocaptains Carter and Hernandez. The Kid, now nearing 35, headed to San Francisco as part of a platoon while earning 10 percent of the $2.1 million he'd made as a Met in '89. After a year as a Dodger near where he grew up, Carter returned to his first major league home in Montreal. The Expos retired his

No. 8, and "M" was the insignia on his cap when he went into the Hall of Fame in his sixth try in 2003. A one-time minor league manager for the organization, Carter had been inducted into the Mets Hall of Fame two years earlier. The Mets have not issued No. 8 since Carter reached Cooperstown.

# 44 Jerry Grote

Tough as a dollar steak, Jerry Grote came to New York for peanuts and was a crucial figure in nurturing the young but explosive Mets pitching staff of the late 1960s and early 1970s. Hard to steal on, harder to strike out, and a man not afraid to argue, Grote reigned in his pitchers if they ever tried to take it easy.

A San Antonio track standout, the Houston Colt .45s signed him out of his hometown Trinity College in June 1963, kept him in San Antonio with their Class AA club, and brought him to the majors that September. He spent 1964 with the club but hit just .181. Grote, 23, spent the entire next season in Class AAA and was then sent to the Mets for Tom Parsons, who had a 2–13 career record and never pitched in Houston.

Grote didn't hit much better in New York, but the Mets liked the way he took charge and called a game. A year after hitting .195 over a full season with 12 extra-base hits in 344 at-bats, Grote was the starting catcher in the 1968 All-Star Game. He had one passed ball all season.

With his cap turned around (never a helmet) and bill flipped up under the mask strap, Grote pounced on bunts and pitchers like a drill sergeant. When he didn't like a pitch or the way a pitcher was working, he fired the ball back as hard as he could. Tom Seaver set him straight in one of their first encounters. Grote also worked diligently with fellow Texan Nolan Ryan, who battled blister and control problems. Both pitchers mentioned Grote in their Hall of Fame induction speeches.

Grote started all 20 postseason games the Mets played during his tenure. He never had a chance for a Gold Glove with Johnny Bench in Cincinnati, but base runners feared him and no one looked forward to a home plate run-in with the grisly Grote. Nearing 35 and with John Stearns handling most of the catching—Grote even played 13 games at third base—the Mets peddled the veteran to the Dodgers at the postseason roster deadline on August 31, 1977. After the "Midnight Massacre" deals in June, this barely caused a ripple among the numb or apathetic fans remaining at Shea Stadium. Grote wound up in the World Series in New York that fall as a Dodger. He later managed in the minors and still reigns in inexperienced pitchers at Mets fantasy camp. He was inducted into the Mets Hall of Fame in 1992.

# 45 Tommie Agee

Tommie Agee was the first Met to steal 30 bases in a season, the first to hit 20 homers in consecutive years, the first to score 100 runs, the first to win a Gold Glove, and the only player in history to hit a home run into the upper deck at Shea Stadium. But when Agee's name is mentioned, the first thing that comes to mind is the two catches he made on a Tuesday afternoon in October 1969.

A Grambling alum and a high school teammate of Met Cleon Jones's in Alabama, Agee came to the Mets from the White Sox at the behest of Gil Hodges, who had himself just arrived from the

Washington Senators in a trade. Hodges knew Agee from the American League and figured the 1966 AL Rookie of the Year was available after a terrible sophomore year. Agee and second baseman Al Weis arrived for Tommy Davis, Jack Fisher, and two others. Agee tied Don Zimmer's dubious club record by going hitless in 34 straight at-bats, but Hodges kept playing him even as he hit just .217 with 17 RBIs in 132 games.

The next year was a thrill from start to finish. Agee hit his titanic upper deck blast in the third game of the year and finished with 26 homers and 76 RBIs—leading the club in both categories—from the leadoff spot. The Mets stunned the world by beating out the Cubs in September for the division title. Agee finished sixth in the MVP voting. He continued hitting in October as the Mets won the first NLCS, with Agee batting .357 with two homers and two steals. Agee went hitless in the first two World Series games in Baltimore, but the first World Series game at Shea Stadium would forever belong to him.

Agee homered leading off against Jim Palmer. As it turned out, that was the only run the Mets needed in a 5–0 win, but there was a little more to it than that.

With the Mets leading in the fourth, 3–0, Elrod Hendricks unloaded on a Gary Gentry pitch to left-center with two on and two out. Agee kept running and snagged it backhanded on the warning track, using his right hand as a cushion against the wall at the 396-foot sign. There was a lot of ball showing, but the inning was over.

Gentry walked three straight with two down in the seventh, and Nolan Ryan replaced him. Paul Blair lashed a two-strike fastball to right-center that Agee chased down to the right of that 396-mark, catching the ball in the webbing as he sprawled across the warning track.

"The wind brought the ball back to the infield a little bit [which was] the reason I had to dive for it, I think," Agee said after the game about catch number two. "When I got to the ball, I felt

# Fan's VIEW
## Lou Longobardi
## (Valley Stream, New York)

### An Amazin' Number

In early 1970, when I was a freshman at St. John's University, I went to Shea Stadium to purchase tickets for Opening Day. As I walked toward the ticket office, I noticed a lot of refuse strewn around the parking lot, including one large piece of green plywood sheeting lying face down on the ground. It was pretty dirty and stained and appeared to have been lying there for quite some time. Since the color had a familiar look, I decided to lift it up and look at the underside. As I suspected, it was a section of Shea Stadium's outfield wall. I knew this for certain because this wall fragment had a white numeral "3" on it, indicating that it had once been part of either the 396 or 371 distance markers from either left-center or right-center field.

Upon closer examination, I noticed graffiti written in both ballpoint pen and magic marker on the white background of the numeral

*Fans stormed the field and scooped up pieces of the Shea Stadium grass to celebrate the Mets' Game 5 victory over the Baltimore Orioles in the 1969 World Series.*

"3." One inscription said "Joan & Bill and the Mets are #1."
Another marking said "Steve B———" and included a date under his
signature… "10/16/69." That was the very date the Mets won their
first world championship! I broke the large sheet into a small
enough piece to fit into my friend's car, all the while keeping the
numeral "3" intact. I brought it home and stored it in my parents'
garage in Queens.

Recently, I decided that I would finally give that piece its right-
ful treatment by having it mounted and framed. When I found it in
the garage, I noticed it had inexplicably been cut into four pieces.
No one was around to explain. Fortunately, the pieces fit together
neatly, leaving the numeral "3" intact. I then decided to peruse my
library for a suitable photo to include with the memento.

I stumbled across a photograph taken an hour or so after the
last out of the 1969 World Series. The photo portrayed Tom Seaver
and Gary Gentry, walking around the pitching mound, surrounded
by huge divots of grassy turf liberally lying all over the field. At
first, I didn't think the photo would suit my needs. But when I
looked beyond the main subjects, in the background, I could clearly
see that where the right-field wall stood 371 feet from home plate,
only the numerals, "71" were visible. As I looked closer, the section
of the wall bearing the numeral "3" was clearly missing. After all
this time, I finally knew exactly from where and when that piece of
wall came. It actually was, and still is, a tangible link back to that
magical moment in Mets history.

like I was going to catch it, but when I started after the ball, I didn't
know whether I was going to catch it or not."

Agee, as luck would have it, led off the bottom of the seventh
to thunderous applause. The Orioles had challenged him enough
for one day. He walked. His five runs saved were the difference. The
Orioles scored just four runs in three games at Shea Stadium.

Agee repeated his productivity in 1970, but the team did not.
Although he hit .285 in 1971, his knees were problematic. The next
year the Mets traded for Willie Mays, and center field grew more

crowded even as the team's offense left room for improvement. Agee led the Mets with just 96 hits, the lowest such number in club history. He was peddled to Houston after the '72 season for what would be his last season.

Agee's name and No. 20 were painted near the spot he reached in the Shea upper deck. He also operated a lounge near the ballpark. After his death from a heart attack in 2001, the Mets displayed the numbers of Agee and minor leaguer Brian Cole, who died during a spring training car accident, on their sleeves on Opening Day. Tommie Agee was inducted into the Mets Hall of Fame in 2002.

# 46 Swoboda Happens

Ron Swoboda had been in Casey Stengel's camp—called "Saboda" by the Ol' Perfessor—and possessed power among many holes in his game. He was still around in 1969 and was a key part of Gil Hodges's platoon system in right field.

Swoboda, nicknamed Rocky and considered shaky with the glove, hit nine home runs in 1969. The lefty-swinging Art Shamsky had five more homers, despite 24 fewer at-bats. He also hit .300, while Rocky came in at .235. Yet things just seemed to happen when Swoboda was around, as they did on September 15, 1969.

That night Steve Carlton became the first pitcher in history to strike out 19 batters in a nine-inning game. Carlton, pitching because the Cardinals had moved up Bob Gibson to face the Cubs the day before, whiffed every Met in the starting lineup, including Swoboda in the first and sixth innings. But Swoboda homered his other two times up against 24-year-old Lefty. They were the only two homers he ever hit off Carlton in 52 career plate appearances (.130 average).

The Cardinals were ahead in the fourth, 1–0, when Swoboda followed a Donn Clendenon walk with a blast to left. With Carlton protecting a 3–2 lead and Tommie Agee on first in the eighth, Swoboda blasted another pitch to almost the same spot in the Busch Stadium mezzanine. This came on the heels of Swoboda's tiebreaking grand slam in the eighth inning two days earlier in Pittsburgh. The Mets now led the division by 4½ games.

"Swoboda," explained Mayo Smith, manager of the defending world champion Tigers, "is what happens when a team wins a pennant."

How about a World Series? Swoboda didn't play against Atlanta's right-handed pitching staff in the NLCS, but Baltimore had two tough left-handers in Dave McNally and Mike Cuellar. Swoboda batted .400 against the Orioles and knocked in the winning run in the clincher. His biggest moment, however, came with his glove.

With Orioles on the corners in the ninth and the Mets clinging to a 1–0 lead in Game 4, Brooks Robinson lashed a Tom Seaver fastball to the gap in right. Swoboda's one chance was a headlong backhanded dive. He caught the liner inches off the ground, hopped up, and threw the ball back in. Frank Robinson tagged up and scored to tie the game, but Swoboda's diving catch, coming the day after the two miraculous grabs by Agee in the Shea outfield, had prevented Baltimore from a big inning and evening the Series. The Mets won an inning later. And, behind Swoboda's only career postseason RBI, took the world championship the next day.

"We had no preconceptions," Swoboda told Stanley Cohen years later. "We had the innocence of someone who had never been there before. Hell, what did we have to lose? We had no thoughts of what happens if we don't get there. We were ingénues. We had that wonderful, clear-minded innocence of not having the responsibility of winning it, of not having to doubt ourselves if we stumbled, and that's a marvelous state to achieve."

# 47 The Friggin' A's and Damn Yankees

In their first 47 seasons of existence, the Mets made the World Series four times and won twice. The two failed trips followed a similar script: the rush to reach the postseason, the beating of veteran-laden opponents to claim the pennant, and that one moment where a world championship seemed there for the taking...and then it was gone.

## 1973

The Mets were in last place at the end of August and division champions by the end of September. How'd that happen? A mediocre division of historic proportions kept the Mets in it, even when they were at their worst. When the Mets got hot, the starting pitching, timely hitting, and daily doses of Tug McGraw's "Ya Gotta Believe" mantra and screwgie made it happen.

The schedule helped, too. A makeup doubleheader was held the Monday after the season ended, but after the Mets won the opener and clinched the division, the second game was called because of wet grounds—or champagne—in Chicago. A change that year in the ending date for the season gave the pooped Mets and Tom Seaver's weary right arm four days off before the NLCS in Cincinnati. At the time the divisions alternated who would host more games, so by rotation the Mets got the last three games of the best-of-five series at Shea Stadium. A decision to play the opening two games at Riverfront Stadium in the October twilight—thanks to the football schedule—gave the pitching-superior Mets an advantage over the squinting Big Red Machine. New York had just three hits in the first game and then allowed only two singles in the second game to even the series. Bud Harrelson's fight with Pete Rose made a Mets rout a sideshow in Game 3; Rose homered to tie the series the next day. The Mets rolled to the pennant behind Seaver in Game 5 as fans rioted at Shea after the final out.

Defending world champion Oakland was waiting. The Swingin' A's wouldn't be shaken by owner Charlie O. Finley pretending slumping second baseman Mike Andrews was hurt (it was quickly overturned) or Dick Williams telling the team he was quitting after the Series. Manager Yogi Berra rode the Mets' pitchers hard—McGraw threw eight innings of relief over the first two days in Oakland, Berra pitched his aces on short rest, and the team lost both of Seaver's starts—but New York was still one game from victory as the Series shifted to Oakland for Game 6.

Catfish Hunter and Ken Holtzman were up to the task, winning the last two games. Rollie Fingers pitched six times for the A's, and teammate Darold Knowles became the first pitcher in history to appear in all seven games in a World Series. Rusty Staub gamely batted .423 despite an injured shoulder, and Willie Mays collected his final hit in baseball during the winning rally in Game 2. It wasn't enough. The A's won—and would win their third straight title the following year (with Alvin Dark at the helm)—while the Mets would not see the World Series again until 1986. The wait would seem endless.

## 2000

The 1973 season had seen the introduction of the new rule known as the designated hitter, with a crucial double by Oakland pitcher Ken Holtzman against the Mets in his first at-bat all season (the first World Series DH didn't appear until 1976). By 2000 the wild-card was an accepted part of baseball. Bobby Valentine's club captured the NL wild-card for the second straight year after finishing second to Atlanta. The Mets even spotted San Francisco a game in the Division Series and nearly blew Game 2 when Armando Benitez allowed a game-tying home run in the ninth, but some unexpected heroes saved the day. Jay Payton drove in the tiebreaking run to win Game 2 in 10 innings, Benny Agbayani homered to win Game 3 in 13, and Bobby Jones (sent to the minors earlier in the year) tossed a one-hit shutout to clinch the series in four games.

Mike Hampton beat the Cardinals twice in the NLCS, and five regulars hit .300 or better as the Mets made surprisingly easy work of the Cardinals. The jubilation was heightened and then tempered by the task of facing the Yankees in the World Series, the first such "Subway Series" since 1956. The Yankees had a 10–3 mark against New York's previous NL teams in the World Series. Although the outside world didn't care a fig—as evidenced by the lowest World Series TV ratings to that point—the 2000 World Series meant everything in the Big Apple. At stake for Mets fans was a chance to change the pecking order of New York baseball. It looked very good for eight innings.

The Yankees tied Game 1 in the ninth on a Paul O' Neill walk and Chuck Knoblauch sacrifice fly. Former Met Jose Vizcaino ended nearly five hours of excruciating tension with a game-winning single in the twelfth. The focus of the second game was an anticipated confrontation that exceeded the hype. Mike Piazza broke his bat, Roger Clemens threw it back, and the Mets ran for cover until the ninth. The rally stalled just short of a tie.

Shea Stadium proved scant refuge for the Mets or their fans, but the Mets did end the Yankees' 14-game World Series winning streak on Agbayani's tiebreaking double in the eighth inning of Game 3. Momentum swung back immediately in Game 4 when

Derek Jeter led off with a home run, one of nine hits he had on his way to Series MVP. David Cone relieved wobbly Denny Neagle and got a crucial out in the fifth inning. The 3–2 loss put the Mets on the brink of their fans' worst nightmare. It became a reality in the ninth inning of Game 5. Al Leiter threw 142 pitches, but the last had little on it as Luis Sojo's single snapped a tie and the Yankees took the world championship. The celebration at Shea that followed was an eye-averting travesty to Mets fans. It was almost worse than no World Series at all. Big dreams can have bigger consequences.

# 48 Seventh Heaven and Hell

The Mets have gone to a Game 7 four times in 10 postseason series. The Mets won the 1986 World Series, but it hasn't gone so well otherwise. Here's a look at the ultimate games:

## 1973 World Series
A's 5, Mets 2

Jon Matlack pitched his third game of the World Series and had a horrible third inning. Bert Campaneris homered, and Series MVP Reggie Jackson introduced himself to New York's consciousness by graciously stomping on home plate after his homer made it 4–0. The Mets outscored mighty Oakland in the Series overall, but not in this game, managing just one run until the ninth inning.

Last out: Wayne Garrett popped up to Campaneris. Lefty Darold Knowles came in to face Garrett, making him the first— and still only—pitcher to appear in all seven games in a World Series.

## Endy's Catch

In the sixth inning of Game 7 of the 2006 NLCS, Endy Chavez made a catch for the ages. His leaping, snow-cone catch over the left-field wall not only robbed Cardinal Scott Rolen of a two-run homer, but it made fans think a Mets pennant was a matter of destiny. It wasn't. Yadier Molina's ninth-inning blast to the same spot, only about 10 feet higher, was confirmation that life can be cruel and the baseball gods fickle.

But Endy's catch lives on. As for its place among Mets postseason defensive gems, it rests right there with the three other great catches in Mets October lore, all made during the 1969 World Series: Tommie Agee's backhanded stab at the warning track in the fourth inning of Game 3; Agee's headlong catch on the warning track three innings later; and Ron Swoboda's backhanded dive in the ninth inning the next afternoon. All three plays, especially Swoboda's, came at crucial times with multiple men on base. The main difference is that those catches occurred as the underdog Mets won, and Endy's came as the favored Mets lost.

## 1986 World Series

Mets 8, Red Sox 5

This makes up for all the others. Of course, the Mets were facing a team that dropped Game 7 in the World Series four straight times over a four-decade span. The heartbreak on that end was exhilaration on this side. Keith Hernandez awoke the Mets from almost six innings of slumber with a two-run single off southpaw Bruce Hurst, and Gary Carter knocked in the tying run. Series MVP Ray Knight's line-drive homer gave the Mets the lead the next inning, they tacked on a couple more, and then held on for dear life as the Red Sox rallied in the eighth. Jesse Orosco snuffed that uprising and started another with his bat, pulling the old "butcher boy" play and singling in a run against the unsuspecting AL foe. Orosco then picked up his glove and flung it.

Last out: Marty Barrett, a .433 hitter in the Series, struck out swinging. Who can forget Bob Murphy's call?

"He struck him out! Struck him out! The Mets have won the World Series! And they're jamming and crowding all over Jesse Orosco. The dream has come true. The Mets have won the World Series, coming from behind to win the seventh ballgame."

## 1988 NLCS
Dodgers 6, Mets 0

Ron Darling is the only Met to start a Game 7 twice…and he didn't do well in either. Whereas Sid Fernandez and the Mets' bats rescued him against the Red Sox in 1986, Dwight Gooden came into a tough spot in relief in the second inning, and it was over quickly (except for watching series MVP Orel Hershiser complete his five-hitter). The Mets had this series seemingly under control until Mike Scioscia's home run against Gooden changed the series in Game 4.

Last out: Howard Johnson went down looking. That was child's play when compared to the backwards K in the next Game 7.

## 2006 NLCS
Cardinals 3, Mets 1

Great effort by unsung mid-season acquisition Oliver Perez, but St. Louis pitchers Jeff Suppan (NLCS MVP), Randy Flores, and Adam Wainwright stifled the Mets. Perez allowed one run through six innings, with a major assist by Endy Chavez for turning a home run into a double play in the sixth inning. A bases-loaded chance in the bottom of the inning went by the boards when Jose Valentin fanned and Chavez flied out. After Yadier Molina's home run off Aaron Heilman snapped the tie in the top of the ninth, the Mets loaded the bases again.

Last out: Carlos Beltran was frozen by a curve, and Shea seemed frozen in time. The cheers of the celebrating Cardinals on the field could be heard in the deathly-quiet stands.

# 49 No No-No

The Mets have seen some remarkable pitchers in their first 47 years of existence. Mets pitchers have won Cy Young Awards, victory crowns, ERA titles, strikeout championships, Sportsman of the Year nods, and postseason MVPs. One thing a Met has never done—as of this writing, or the writing of any previous Mets book—is throw a no-hitter.

Several have done it before they became Mets: Don Cardwell, Warren Spahn, Dean Chance, Dock Ellis, John Candelaria, Bret Saberhagen, Scott Erickson, Kenny Rogers, Al Leiter, and even Billy Wagner, who threw the last inning in a Houston no-hitter at Yankee Stadium in 2003 (1999 Met Octavio Dotel tossed an inning in that same game; one-time Met Alejandro Pena got the last three outs of a no-hitter for Atlanta in 1991). More famous are the Mets who threw no-hitters after leaving the club: Tom Seaver, Mike Scott, Dwight Gooden, David Cone, and, of course, Nolan Ryan, whose seven no-hitters are the most of all time. Hideo Nomo holds the distinction of pitching one both before and after being a Met.

So who's come the closest to a no-hitter while actually in a Mets uniform? Here's a list, including three of the franchise's 33 one-hitters. Interestingly, only the first of these five took place at night.

1. Tom Seaver, July 9, 1969, at Shea: The granddaddy of them all: a perfect game until one out in the ninth against the first-place Cubs before a packed house. Jimmy Qualls singled to left. Seaver had five one-hitters as a Met, but this one sure seemed like it would be the one.

   End game: Mets signaled they were contenders and inched closer to Chicago.

2. Tom Seaver, July 4, 1972, at Shea: First game of a Tuesday holiday twinbill. Seaver had tied the league mark in 1970 with 19 Ks of the Padres, plus the last 10 in a row. This time he fanned 11, but he kept the no-no going until Leron Lee, Derrek Lee's uncle, singled with one out in the ninth.

   End game: Seaver got Nate Colbert to ground into a double play to complete the 2–0 victory.

3. Tom Seaver, September 24, 1975, at Wrigley Field: This one was just cruel. Seaver had a no-hitter with two outs in the ninth. Scrub Joe Wallis became Jimmy Qualls for an afternoon, singling to break it up. What made this worse was that the game was scoreless, so if Seaver had gotten Wallis out, the game still would not be considered a no-hitter by MLB standards if he had allowed a hit in extra innings. Seaver and Rick Reuschel threw 10 scoreless innings each in front of 2,113.

   End game: Met Skip Lockwood walked in the winning run in the eleventh inning. Nice.

4. Tom Glavine, May 23, 2004, at Shea: This one had all the ingredients: Hall of Fame candidate, umpire calling the corners, facing a dead team with a Sunday lineup. Colorado's Kit Pellow hit a two-out double to right in the eighth.

   End game: One-hit shutout for Glavine and his first All-Star berth as a Met.

## Open Wide for Doc, Seaver

The Mets have the best record of any team on Opening Day (31–17) despite having lost the first eight openers in club history. The Mets tied the major league mark with nine straight lid-lifter wins from 1975 to 1983, and 18 of 20 from 1970 to 1989. Tom Seaver pitched every Opening Day he was a Met except for his rookie year (11 times). He won six times, as did Dwight Gooden. They are the only two Mets with multiple complete-game victories to open the season.

5. Pedro Martinez, August 14, 2005, at Dodger Stadium: Another Hall of Fame candidate cruising on a Sunday, this time one out in the eighth, Mets leading 1–0. Antonio Perez tripled just beyond Gerald Williams, playing in place of Carlos Beltran following a cataclysmic collision with Mike Cameron three days earlier. Then Jayson Werth homered. Marlon Anderson was thrown out at the plate in the ninth.

End game: Dodgers 2, Mets 1. Very long flight home.

# 50 Carlos Beltran

Center field for the Mets has been manned by Tommie Agee, Mookie Wilson, Lenny Dykstra, and even briefly by Hall of Famers Richie Ashburn and Willie Mays, yet none put up the numbers Carlos Beltran has as a Met. It has not always gone smoothly and it has not always ended ideally for Beltran, but no one promised that life in Flushing would be easy.

A second-round pick by the Royals out of Puerto Rico in 1995, Beltran was the American League Rookie of the Year four years later in Kansas City. He drove in 100 runs in four of his five K.C. seasons while displaying blazing speed and a stellar glove. The Royals, accustomed to not being able to afford these types of veteran players, sent him to Houston as part of a three-team trade in June 2004. He helped the Astros win the wild card and then batted .435 with eight home runs in 12 postseason games as Houston fell to St. Louis in the NLCS. Beltran was the hottest free agent on the market, but at that time big-ticket players only wound up in one borough of New York.

After three straight losing seasons, the disastrous trade of top prospect Scott Kazmir for a damaged Victor Zambrano, and the firing of both the manager and general manager, the Mets were no one's idea of a destination. Fred Wilpon told former employee and Montreal GM Omar Minaya, "We've become irrelevant in New York City. You've got to come home." Minaya came. Pedro Martinez came. And a month later, Beltran came. Carlos coined the phrase "the New Mets" (or at least agent Scott Boras did) during the press conference for his seven-year, $119 million contract.

Beltran had three hits on Opening Day, and after the 2005 Mets dropped their first five games, he homered to help give manager Willie Randolph—not to mention Martinez or the team—win No. 1. Beltran was at his best playing behind Martinez. Nine of his first 10 home runs as a Met came in Martinez starts. Mike Cameron, who'd moved from center field to right to accommodate Beltran's arrival, collided with Carlos in San Diego. Cameron, who took the brunt of the hit, missed the last eight weeks of the season. Beltran, who suffered a displaced facial fracture and a concussion, returned after less than a week. He wound up with 78 RBIs, about what the average player would accumulate in 650 at-bats, but for the money he was getting, fans demanded more.

Beltran was booed on Opening Day 2006. When he hit a key homer in the season's third game—Pedro's '06 debut, coincidentally—Beltran had to be pushed out of the dugout for the briefest of curtain calls. The quiet switch-hitter proceeded to change the tune at Shea. He tied the franchise record with 41 home runs, including a grand slam in late July that secured a sweep in Atlanta and all but assured the end of the Braves' 14-year postseason run. Beltran poured it on, finishing with 116 RBIs and earning his first career Gold Glove. The Mets won the division handily, and despite several injuries to the pitching staff won the Division Series with ease (Beltran had a .500 on-base percentage in the sweep of the Dodgers). He homered to bring in the only two runs of the NLCS opener, and after losses the next two nights to St. Louis, Beltran homered twice as the Mets evened the series. The teams swapped victories, forcing a Game 7. For the second time, Beltran's team lost to the Cardinals in a deciding NLCS game, but this loss ended with Carlos at the plate, forever frozen by an Adam Wainwright curve...with the bases eternally loaded.

That the Cardinals wound up winning the World Series stung, but Beltran stung the ball from the outset in 2007. His two homers helped the Mets complete a season-opening sweep in St. Louis. For the New Mets, the timing would always be just slightly off.

Beltran hit for one point higher (.276) and had nearly the same RBI total (112) as the previous year. The all-time leader in stealing successfully was at it again with a 23-of-25 theft rate in '07 that was his best season in that category since becoming a Met. But New York fizzled down the stretch as the Phillies exploited a tiny opening and dissolved a seven-game lead with 17 games to play. Beltran hit five homers with 17 RBIs in that stretch, but pitching was the team's ultimate downfall. It would be again in 2008, though relief pitching specifically helped do-in that year's Mets.

The 2008 club survived countless controversies, the heavy-handed firing of Randolph, and the elevation of Jerry Manuel to skipper, and went from 7½ games back in mid-June to 3½ up in mid-September...with 17 games remaining. Again the Mets folded down the stretch and again Beltran did everything in his power to stop it. After the Mets lost twice to the lowly Nationals, Beltran homered twice the next night and tracked down the balls being hit all over the yard against the helpless Mets bullpen. Beltran had hits in 13 of the last 17 games and knocked in 10, including the game-winner in a comeback win that kept the Mets tied for the wild card with three games left. With the Mets needing to win the last regularly-scheduled game ever at Shea Stadium, Beltran blasted a game-tying two-run home run that made Shea shake for a final time. His was the last run ever scored by a Met at Shea. Consecutive Florida homers doomed the Mets, their season, and their ballpark.

After three straight seasons of 112 or more RBIs, plus batting average and steal totals that rose each season, not to mention three consecutive Gold Gloves (he'd sewn up the '07 award in July with a sprawling catch with the winning run on third in extra innings on Tal's Hill in Houston), Beltran looked like a batting champ at spacious Citi Field in 2009. His average was .367 just after Memorial Day and still stood at .336 on Father's Day, but the latter was his last game until September because of a severe bone bruise in his knee that had doubled in size. He wound up hitting a career-high .325, but his 357 plate appearances were the fewest he'd had since his debut season in 1998. Lingering pain over the winter resulted in an operation—and a dispute with the Mets over the timing of the procedure.

While most of the great Mets center fielders have been leadoff hitters, Beltran has been at the heart of the batting order as well as the key to its up-the-middle defense. His knees require more rest and care than in years past, but his desire and skill have not been in question for a long time.

# 51 Jose Reyes

David Wright may get more magazine covers and quivery-knees among the fair sex at Citi Field, but Jose Reyes makes the Mets run. Literally.

When Reyes is not in the lineup, the Mets just aren't the same team. It's been proven throughout his tenure as a Met, which had been mostly injury-free from 2005 until May 2009, when a poorly diagnosed hamstring tendon strain went from day-to-day to month-to-month and Reyes missed the last four months of the season, only to have surgery in October. After Reyes's last '09 game in the leadoff spot, the Mets went 49–73. Granted, they were also missing several other key players in what became a lost season, and other Mets leadoff hitters actually did Jose proud with 13 triples— though his main replacement in the leadoff spot, Angel Pagan, is not a smart base runner. The seven shortstops who replaced Reyes, however, hit just .223, made 19 errors, and turned only 81 double plays. He was missed.

Reyes's antics and his unique handshakes for every player after they hit a home run rubs opponents the wrong way, though Jose is unfairly singled out in a league filled with showboaters. Without his energy in the dugout, in the field, or at the top of the lineup, the Mets aren't much fun to watch. Reyes holds the all-time Mets mark for steals in a season (78 in '07) and he was the franchise career base-stealing leader by age 25, the same year he set the club triples record; the old marks, 281 and 62, respectively, had belonged to Mookie Wilson for more than two decades. Like Mookie, Jose is not the game's most selective leadoff hitter, but there aren't many more explosive at the top of a lineup.

In 2007, *Baseball America* picked Reyes as the best base runner, fastest base runner, infielder with the best arm, and most exciting player for the second stright year. The National League managers whose opinions make up the *BA* rankings bestowed yet another accolade on Reyes: best defensive shortstop.

This is the same player who, after debuting in the major leagues at 19, was switched to second base his second year in favor of Kaz Matsui. That ridiculous idea didn't even last a whole season, much of which Reyes spent nursing leg injuries. In 2005 he played all but one game, became the second player in Mets history to steal 60 bases, and set the franchise record for at-bats. Reyes became a superstar in '06, doubling the previous season's walk output, knocking in 81, stealing 64 bases, and scoring 122 times as catalyst of the team that finally ended Atlanta's 14-year stranglehold on first place.

Yet Reyes was not at his peak during consecutive collapsing Septembers by the Mets. He batted .205 the final month in '07 and hit a slightly more respectable .243 in '08, after four straight months of .305 or higher. When he's hot, he can carry a team. Reyes hit for the cycle in 2006, reached base safely a club-record 33 straight games in 2008, is the only Met to lead off consecutive games with triples, has the most homers by a Met leading off a game (plus one in the '06 NLCS), stole bases in six straight games twice in his career, and even had a three-homer game in '06. In 2008, he was the first player in history to surpass 20 doubles, 10 triples, 10 homers, and 30 steals by the All-Star break…though he was not chosen to represent the National League. (He went 3-for-4 in his lone All-Star appearance in 2007; he was voted to start in '06 but missed it with a hand injury.) In 2008, Reyes joined Lance Johnson (1996) as the only Met to surpass 200 hits. He also owns the club record for four-hit games and highest career average by a Mets switch-hitter (.286 through seven seasons). Reyes bats 20 points higher from the right side (.301), yet has almost three times as many home runs batting lefty.

Obviously there's plenty Jose Reyes can do, and New York fans always want more. To get to the status of a truly elite Met, Jose will have to bounce back from the bad times and come through when the club needs it in September and—dare we dream—October.

# 52 Ed Kranepool

Ed Kranepool persevered. He played under eight managers, five general managers, and four team presidents. A local prodigy signed out of James Monroe High School in the Bronx, he was 17 when he first swung a bat for the original Mets. Neil Allen, the top reliever for Kranepool's last Mets club in 1979, was four years old when Krane debuted.

He certainly lived up to his name as "Steady Eddie." While Kranepool never had more than four hits or two home runs in a game, he also whiffed four times just twice in his career: both at age 18. Manager Casey Stengel kept the kid Kranepool around to start 1963, often batting him third or fifth. He did manage two home runs—still the youngest Met to homer—but he was finally shipped out to Class AAA Buffalo in July with a .190 average. The left-handed hitter pushed past New York's negativity, notably the headline asking if he was "over the hill" at 19. He showed he belonged, earning his only career All-Star berth at 20. Even more remarkable that year was that Kranepool, incredibly slow even at a young age, led the Mets in triples.

Over a 10-season span, Kranepool played 100 or more games every year except one: 1970. The Mets sent him to the minor leagues that year with his average at .118 in mid-June. He returned to New York in August and finished at .170, but it was the only time other than his very brief 1962 appearance that he went a year without homering. Even at his best, most of his managers sat him against left-handers. Six of his 118 career home runs came against lefties, and he hit only .220 against southpaws, compared to .268 versus righties. Still, his bat was potent enough for Gil Hodges to keep right-handed power stick Donn Clendenon on the bench for the entire 1969 NLCS—Kranepool hit .250—and for Game 3 of the World Series (Kranepool homered off Dave Leonhard). The pitcher he faced most in his career was Cardinals dominator Bob Gibson (126 plate appearances) and Kranepool batted .313.

He was especially popular with owner Joan Payson, who, according to longtime beat writer Jack Lang, gave orders that he should never be traded. He never was, even after she died in 1975 and her daughter took over. By then Kranepool was specializing more and more in pinch-hitting. He hit .300 or better off the bench each year from 1974 to 1978, including a league-best .486 in 1974. The last original Met retired holding nearly every team career record, and he still owns many marks, including pinch-hits (90), total bases (2,047), games (1,853), at-bats (5,436), hits (1,418), and doubles (225). A stockbroker, Kranepool was even part of a group that wanted to buy the team just after his retirement in 1979. The bid wasn't accepted, but Kranepool made it to the Mets Hall of Fame a decade later.

# 53 Scioscia vs. Molina

It's the ninth inning, National League Championship Series, man on first, and a catcher better known for his glove than his bat stands in at the plate. If the Mets get him out—or get him to tap into a double play—the pennant isn't clinched, but it will put the team in a much better position to win it. Same scenario, same stadium, same result: 18 years apart.

In 1988 Mike Scioscia homered to right field in the ninth inning against Dwight Gooden to tie Game 4 of the NLCS. The Dodgers won the game in 12 and the series in seven. If Gooden had gotten Scioscia, or if manager Davey Johnson had brought in lefty Randy Myers after Doc walked the leadoff batter, things might have turned out differently. Lefties hit just .180 off the hard-throwing southpaw Myers all year with no home runs. Instead of being up three games to one with a chance to finish the series the next day at Shea, the NLCS was tied and a trip back to the West Coast assured.

In 2006 Yadier Molina homered to left field in the ninth inning against Aaron Heilman. In a tie game Heilman was probably the best available reliever. He just threw a bad pitch at the worst possible time. Of course, if Duaner Sanchez hadn't gotten in a taxi accident in July, he might have been on the mound against Molina and the Cardinals. But then the Mets wouldn't have wound up trading for Oliver Perez, who started Game 7. Choose whichever "if" scenario suits you best.

Scioscia had three homers during the '88 season in 408 at-bats. Molina hit six in 417 at-bats in 2006. Both catchers wound up on World Series winners. It's the kind of thing that keeps going through your head as you watch the snow fall that winter, realizing how close your team was, and how it has to start all over again in the spring.

# 54 Howard Johnson

When you share the same name as a popular orange-roofed restaurant and hotel chain, people remember you. Howard Johnson outlasted his critics and the numbers still speak loudly. He remains among the leaders in virtually every Mets hitting category, including home runs (192), RBIs (629), steals (202), runs (627), doubles (214), and games (1,154).

The Mets were dealing from a position of strength when they sent pitcher Walt Terrell to the world champion Tigers for Howard Johnson in December 1984. The Mets had better prospects than Terrell and even though they had two third basemen at the time—Ray Knight and (the soon-to-be-dealt) Hubie Brooks—the Mets liked Johnson's power potential. The switch-hitting HoJo collected 11 home runs in 1985 while playing 126 games. His .242 batting average wasn't much, but it

## The '86 Effect

The 1986 season may be two decades in the past, but Davey Johnson's world champion Mets continue to have an impact on the game today. Of the 36 men who appeared on that year's team, 21 are known to have gone into managing, coaching, or broadcasting at the college or professional level, plus one executive.

The following list classifies the players by highest level managed or coached through 2009 (+ signifies that a major league coach was also a minor league manager; * signifies they worked for the Mets in the position listed). Brooklyn Cyclones manager Wally Backman's top level is listed as minor league manager although he served as manager of the Arizona Diamondbacks for less than a week after the 2004 season. Not reflected below are Rick Aguilera, Sid Fernandez, or George Foster, who coached baseball at the high school level, and Lenny Dykstra, who was hired as a Reds minor league manager in 2001 and quit during spring training. (Guest instructors are also not included in this list.) Ray Knight, Gary Carter, and others have served other major league teams as announcers. Barry Lyons served as announcer for Class AAA Nashville. Ron Gardenhire, successful manager of the Minnesota Twins and a Johnson protégé, spent the '86 season in the Mets' minor league system.

**Major League GM**
Ed Lynch

**Major League Manager**
John Gibbons
Ray Knight
Lee Mazzilli

**Major League Coach**
Rick Anderson
Howard Johnson+*
Dave Magadan
Roger McDowell
Randy Niemann*
Rafael Santana
Mookie Wilson+*

**Major League Announcer**
Ron Darling*
Keith Hernandez*

**Minor League Manager**
Wally Backman*
Gary Carter*
Kevin Mitchell
Tim Teufel*

**Minor League Coach**
Dwight Gooden
Bob Ojeda*
Darryl Strawberry

**College Head Coach**
Danny Heep

looked better than Knight's .218. HoJo repeated his numbers in 1986 even though his playing time decreased as Knight had a bounce-back year. HoJo was employed as a shortstop 34 times in Davey Johnson's "power lineup," including during the late innings of Game 6 of the World Series. He was on deck during Mookie Wilson's fabled at-bat in the tenth inning. If the wild pitch had hit Mookie, it would've been up to HoJo.

The Mets liked Johnson enough to offer World Series MVP Knight only a one-year contract. Knight went elsewhere, and HoJo became a star. Johnson and Darryl Strawberry both surpassed 30 home runs and 30 steals in 1987, the first teammates to ever do so. HoJo was a feared hitter, knocking in 99 runs, scoring 93, and getting his bat confiscated because a few skeptical opposing managers thought it might be corked. Results were always negative, and HoJo did his best to remain positive despite these slights.

His numbers were off in 1988—part of a frustrating odd–even cycle in which his best years alternated with disappointing ones—and Johnson was displaced late in the year by minor league phenom Gregg Jefferies. The brash third baseman had just turned 21 yet had already graced the cover of *Sports Illustrated*. Jefferies was never accepted in the Mets' locker room, and many were annoyed that he displaced the loyal and productive Johnson. HoJo started four games at shortstop in the NLCS, but sat out Game 7; a crucial Jefferies error at third base handed the Dodgers the pennant. HoJo fanned to end the series as a pinch-hitter, and many were convinced that would be his last at-bat as a Met.

But it was Jefferies who moved—to second base—while Johnson thrived at third. He led the league in runs scored with 104, knocked in 101, hit 36 homers, stole a career-high 41 bases, achieved his highest average as a Met (.287), and made the All-Star team for the first time. A modest 1990 was followed by a monster '91. Johnson became the first Met to lead the league in homers and RBIs in the same year (he's still the only Met to lead in the latter category) and he managed to do this while switching to right field during the season.

He spent all of 1992 in the outfield and switched back to third base the following year, but injuries and a poor team around him made them unproductive and unhappy years. He finished his career as a pinch-hitter for the Rockies and Cubs, retiring as the league's all-time home-run leader for switch hitters (that's no longer the case). A comeback try with the Mets didn't get past spring training. HoJo remained a Met, however, serving as a scout and then a coach and manager in the minor leagues. He was named a coach in New York in 2007.

# 55 Edgardo Alfonzo

Edgardo Alfonzo said that during his first five years as a Met, he was never once recognized on the street or asked for an autograph away from Shea Stadium. And he lived in Flushing! No matter how many key hits he got, how many rallies he snuffed with his glove, or how many times he coaxed a walk out of a pitcher who'd been sailing along, the next day it was guaranteed that a media outlet somewhere would spell his name "Alfonso."

People are bad spellers, so that's understandable, but it is hard to comprehend how Alfonzo could be so overlooked by the baseball cognoscenti. He has the most RBIs in a season by a Mets second baseman (108 in 1999) and more in his career than beloved Mets Cleon Jones, Keith Hernandez, and Rusty Staub. Alfonzo had more home runs and walks than Ed Kranepool, who had 1,539 more at-bats. Alfonzo was just 13 doubles off Kranepool's club record of 225, and his .367 on-base percentage, sixth on the list, is the highest of any Met who appeared in 1,000 games. His .292 average is tied for fifth in club history, but again, it's the highest of any Met who played that many games. Oh, and he did this while moving around the lineup and the infield to please his managers and teammates.

Dallas Green showed faith in the 21-year-old Venezuelan by playing him regularly at third base in 1995, even though he had as much trouble pulling a pitch as a 49-year-old Julio Franco. When Rey Ordonez came up in 1996, Alfonzo found himself on the bench while Jose Vizcaino played second base and Jeff Kent moved to third (that didn't work out). After Kent and Vizcaino were traded and Bobby Valentine replaced Green, Alfonzo was back at second. Carlos Baerga was the regular second baseman in 1997, with Alfonzo at third. Compared to some of the other stone-handed third basemen utilized at the time—Butch Huskey and Matt Franco among them—Alfonzo looked like Brooks Robinson. He also came into his own as a hitter, batting .315 and stealing a career-best 11 bases, batting mostly out of the two-hole.

Yet when the Mets signed Robin Ventura as a free agent in 1999, Alfonzo shifted back over to second base and responded with a career-best 27 homers and 108 RBIs. His defense was impeccable. He didn't boot a grounder all season—his five errors all came on throws—and was featured on the *Sports Illustrated* cover with John Olerud, Ordonez, and Ventura under the headline, "The Best Infield Ever?" To Mets fans, there was no question.

His most remarkable day came in the last Mets series ever at the Astrodome, when he set club records on August 30 by going 6-for-6 with 16 total bases and six runs; he also tied the club record with three home runs. More important was the homer he hit with Rickey Henderson on base, just two batters into the one-game playoff in Cincinnati. In the ninth inning the next night in the Division Series opener in Arizona, Alfonzo's grand slam snapped a 4–4 tie.

The 1999 season provided as much recognition as Alfonzo would ever receive: an eighth-place finish in the NL MVP balloting and a Silver Slugger. But he was snubbed for the Gold Glove. Alfonzo made the All-Star team in 2000 for the only time, but how could he not after batting .324 with an on-base percentage 101 points higher (slightly higher than the numbers he'd had at the All-Star break)? In typical understated Alfonzo fashion, in the midst of an eighth-inning uprising to overcome an 8–1 deficit on Fireworks Night against Atlanta, Fonzie singled in the tying run with two outs. Mike Piazza then followed with a three-run homer to cap the 10-run inning, relegating Alfonzo's clutch hit to the afterthought bin.

Alfonzo batted .444 in the Championship Series against the Cardinals, reaching base at a .565 clip in the five-game set. Of course, someone else was there to soak up the glory: Mike Hampton was named MVP. Alfonzo, Hampton, and the Mets laid an egg in the World Series against the Yankees.

Back problems eventually sapped Alfonzo of his power and sweet stroke. He batted just .243 in '01 and even the .308 season that followed wasn't enough to convince GM Steve Phillips to re-sign Alfonzo. Phillips was right that time. While Alfonzo had a good first year in San Francisco, he wasn't the dynamic player Mets fans remembered. Ditched by two American League teams in 2006, he wound up a Norfolk Tide. His progress at Triple-A wasn't enough for the Mets to call him up in September. Forgotten again.

# 56 Subway Mugging: A Brief History of Mets vs. Yankees

In the beginning there was no rivalry. The Yankees were world champions and the Mets—peopled by castoffs from other local clubs—could only hope to annoy the Bronx Bombers by winning exhibition games and outdrawing them at the gate. The Mets did just that. The teams generally came out about even in the spring training games, but the Mets got far more mileage out of the wins than the Yankees. In the first Mayor's Trophy Game in 1963, Mets fans poured into Yankee Stadium and put up banners faster than security could take them down. Casey Stengel, fired by the Yankees after a mere 10 pennants in 12 seasons, started his best pitcher—as he often did when the Yankees came up on the exhibition schedule—and won. Stern, straight-laced Mets president George Weiss, who'd been fired in the Bronx shortly after Stengel, smiled to himself.

The Mayor's Trophy Game continued and so did the exhibitions, but they lost their oomph and purpose. (The Mets went 8–10–1 in the Mayor's Trophy and 3–4 in later reincarnations held in New York just before the season started.) The Mets and Yankees, both in new sites in Florida, stopped appearing on each others' spring training schedules. In the first 35 years of their coexistence, the unimaginable—a World Series between the clubs—stayed just that. The teams never made the postseason the same year, although they came moderately close a few times. They did share the same field, however, when Yankee Stadium was renovated and Shea became home for both New York teams in 1974 and 1975. While the Yankees acted like it was beneath them to play there, they had a better record than the Mets during their two years there and saw fit to convene their Old-Timers' Day at Shea. (The Yankees would play a regular-season game at Shea on April 15, 1998, when falling concrete in the Bronx postponed a series; the Yankees hosted an afternoon game against the Angels at Shea in front of a crowd almost three times the size of what the Mets drew that night.)

Interleague play became a reality in 1997. For the first time, the Mets and Yankees met in games that counted. The first game was on a Monday at Yankee Stadium. It was a bizarre night, with catcher Todd Hundley stealing home and run-of-the-mill Dave Mlicki stealing the show with his first career shutout. Three-syllable "Let's go

*Yankees pitcher Roger Clemens and the Mets' Mike Piazza squared off in more ways than one during the World Series in 2000.*

Mets" chants rolled right into the extra-syllabled Yankees mantra; that first series seemed good-spirited (mostly), and the city reveled in it, even if the players protested for the first time—and certainly not the last—that it was just another series.

Shea Stadium was sold out the next year as the series was moved to the weekend permanently. It was also the last time the teams played just one series against each other per season. While it boosted attendance—every game has been a sellout at both stadiums—the fan bases became genuinely hostile when in proximity of each other. Whether it was anger about so many Yankees fans invading Shea,

George Steinbrenner and his minions constantly belittling the Mets, or the fact that the Yankees looked like they already had another world championship in the bag (they did); this was no longer an "I like both New York teams" town. If your friends didn't call such feelings Pollyanna, the sports talk show hosts certainly would.

In 1999 the teams split six games. The Mets beat Mariano Rivera for the first time when Matt Franco singled in the tying and winning runs in the bottom of the ninth at Shea. Mike Piazza, as big a star as anyone the Yankees could march out onto the field, seemed to rise to the occasion whenever the teams met.

And for the first time in history, both the Mets and Yankees made the postseason and each advanced to their respective League Championship Series. The Yankees' foes were the Red Sox, fanning the flame between two old rivals, eclipsing anything the Mets did in terms of market excitement. If you went to the Mets team shop now open in midtown Manhattan, you could get a checkers set featuring the Mets and the Yankees. If you went to the nearby Yankees' shop, you could get the Yankees and the Red Sox. It was bad enough being second banana, but now market research had bumped the Mets to third. The Mets lost in the NLCS, while the Yankees beat the Red Sox and took the world championship against the Braves. There was all winter to play checkers.

The 2000 season saw many firsts in the crosstown rivalry. A rainout at Yankee Stadium precipitated the first interleague, inter-city doubleheader in history, with an afternoon game in Queens and the nightcap in the Bronx. After prodigal son Dwight Gooden won his first start ever against the Mets, Roger Clemens beaned Mike Piazza and forced him to sit out the rest of the weekend and the All-Star Game. The Clemens incident ratcheted the series to an even higher level as the beaning dominated all discussion about the series for years to come.

Not only did both teams make the 2000 postseason, they each won the pennant to set up the first Subway Series in New York since the Yankees and Brooklyn Dodgers went at it in 1956. The Mets fared about as well as the Dodgers of yore in this do-or-die regional matchup. The Mets blew a lead in the ninth inning of the World Series opener at Yankee Stadium, and the latest installment of Clemens–Piazza the next night took a bizarre turn when the pitcher rocketed a bat shard at Piazza. The Mets played scared, Shea felt like the Bronx, and the Mets dropped four out of the five close games. The club's first pennant in 15 seasons didn't seem worth a plugged nickel.

Clemens finally pitched at Shea in 2002, but the retaliation the world anticipated missed the mark when Shawn Estes threw behind Clemens instead of at him. That Estes—and Piazza—homered that day in a rocking of the Rocket is a forgotten footnote.

Though the Mets have had their moments, the Yankees command the field even after taking the rivalry to two new venues. The Yankees held a narrow 17–16 edge against the Mets at Shea Stadium—plus 2–1 in World Series play—and a 20–13 mark at Yankee Stadium (2–0 in World Series). The first game at the newest stadium incarnation in the Bronx in 2009 ended with the catastrophic dropped pop-up by Luis Castillo. The Yankees later swept at Citi Field. Good grief.

# 57 Yogi Berra

When you think of Yogi Berra, the Mets aren't usually the first thing that comes to mind, but he was an important figure in Mets history. Wildly popular—he made Yoo-hoo sound good and inspired the frisky cartoon character Yogi Bear—Berra became available after 20 years in the Yankees organization. The Yankees fired him when he lost the 1964 World Series in seven games as a rookie manager.

The Mets signed him as a player/coach. He caught two games, pinch-hit in two more, and called it quits as a player. He spent seven seasons as a Mets coach, serving under Casey Stengel, Wes Westrum, interim Salty Parker, and Gil Hodges, and celebrated with the team in 1969. The newly minted Hall of Famer did not play golf with the manager and other coaches on April 2, 1972. Hodges died of a heart attack in the parking lot. The Mets front office acted quickly—some said a little too quickly—in tabbing Berra to take over.

The Mets had their best start in history under Berra (31–12), but the club slid to a distant third. The bad luck followed into 1973 as players kept getting injured, but Berra always had a positive outlook and good things seemed to happen around him, whether it was surviving the D-Day landing on Omaha Beach, winning three MVPs and setting 10 World Series records, or playing in 14 different Series and winning 10. Even as the Mets sputtered in a weak field in July, Berra uttered one of his most famous lines, "It ain't over 'til it's over." He was right.

The Mets finished the season at 24–9, going from last to first in the process. When they beat the Reds in the NLCS, the 82–79 Mets became the worst team in history to win a pennant. Yogi didn't care about style points. They could have used a couple more timely hits and, according to the critics, the manager could have used George Stone instead of Tom Seaver and Jon Matlack on short rest in Oakland. The A's won in seven games. Yogi, the second manager to win pennants in each league, had become the first to take both the Mets and Yankees to the World Series...and the first to lose with both.

After the Mets stumbled in 1974, new general manager Joe McDonald set to work on revamping the team. Joe Torre, Dave

Kingman, Del Unser, and Skip Lockwood arrived, but gone was Tug McGraw, and the rotation was barren behind Seaver, Matlack, and Jerry Koosman. They still had Cleon Jones, who had been involved in an adulterous scandal in Florida, forced to apologize, and benched. When Jones refused to enter a game as a substitute, management initially refused to back up the manager. Jones was eventually released, but the Mets fired Berra a week later.

Berra returned to the Yankees and was later fired as manager there as well, creating a long rift with owner George Steinbrenner. It was eventually patched up on the radio at the Yogi Berra Museum in New Jersey.

# 58 Bud Harrelson

Bud Harrelson was the glue on the Mets' infield when the other parts changed frequently. He was the first Mets infielder to win a Gold Glove and twice appeared in the All-Star Game. Harrelson's most memorable moment was fighting—and losing—against Pete Rose in their fabled dustup in the 1973 NLCS.

Derrel McKinley Harrelson was born the day of the Normandy Invasion in 1944 and hit the ground running. Although deemed too small to play for his hometown San Francisco Giants, the Mets weren't so picky. They signed the skinny shortstop out of San Francisco State the day after his 19th birthday. After hitting .108 as a 150-pound right-handed swinging call-up in 1965, he gained a little weight and learned to switch-hit the following spring. Pesky was the best way to describe his offense, fighting his way on base while hitting just .234 as a Met.

Despite numerous injuries, Harrelson still amassed the second-most at-bats in club history (4,390) and was once the club's career stolen base leader with 115. Harrelson collected 1,029 hits, 45 triples, and scored 490 times as a Met. He hit just six home runs in 1,322 games for New York...and if you saw him play, that homer total may sound high. Yet the slick-fielding Harrelson proved invaluable in both the 1969 and 1973 pushes for the pennant.

## TRIVIA
## Question

**What Mets pitcher allowed the 3,000th and final hit of Roberto Clemente's career?**

Trivia answers on page 256

If you count games wearing a Mets uniform, Harrelson stands apart. He spent five-plus seasons as coach—plus two years as minor league manager—and was the only Met in uniform for both world championships. The third-base coach hooped and hollered behind Ray Knight after Bill Buckner's error brought in the winning run in Game 6 of the 1986 World Series.

One job that did not work out was in the manager's office at Shea. It started off favorably after he replaced Davey Johnson in May 1990. Despite numerous injuries and a few questionable moves—such as starting Julio Valera in his second major league game against front-running Pittsburgh in September—the Mets weren't eliminated from the 1990 race until four games remained in the season. The next year was a disaster in every way.

The team fell apart during a 5–23 stretch that essentially ended their season. During the team's collapse, Vince Coleman got into a shouting match with coach Mike Cubbage; Harrelson dismissed the incident as "a moment of insanity." The insanity ended with a week to go when Cubbage replaced Harrelson as manager.

Harrelson stayed close to Shea Stadium as manager and later co-owner of the independent Long Island Ducks.

# 59 Jon Matlack

Jon Matlack was part of perhaps the greatest triumvirate in Mets history: Seaver–Koosman–Matlack. From April 1972 to June 1977 this trio made opponents wince. It was only New York's lack of offense that kept the club from dizzying heights of success.

Elders Tom Seaver and Jerry Koosman wound up accruing enough wins to be inducted in the Mets Hall of Fame (338 combined victories). Matlack went 82–81 despite the second-best ERA of any Mets starter in history (3.03), 26 shutouts (tied for second with Koosman), 65 complete games (fourth), and doing it all in just 199 starts (Seaver and Koosman totaled 741 starts for the club).

"That was a staff that knew how to compete and was willing to do whatever it took to be successful and put zeroes on the board," Matlack said. "We all fed off each other, and it snowballed into not wanting to be the one who was the weak link."

Jonathon Trumpbour Matlack was taken with the fourth overall pick in 1967, the only Mets top-10 overall selection in the first 15 drafts to become an All-Star with the club. The Mets being what they were at the time, the buzz was that the lanky lefty, who tossed eight high school no-hitters in West Chester, Pennsylvania, was ticketed for the majors sooner rather than later. Intimidated in his first spring camp, he tried to catch up with the hard-throwing big leaguers and soon lost his dominating curve. He did not find it until Puerto Rican winter ball in 1972, after San Juan manager Bill Virdon demoted him to the bullpen to work out his problems. When Matlack reported to spring training in St. Petersburg, he dominated and began the season in New York. His 2.32 ERA was the lowest on an impressive staff and fourth-best in the National League. Matlack took Rookie of the Year honors.

# Fan's VIEW

## Jim Starr
## (Boulder, Colorado)

### An Officer and a Ticket Seller

It was the 1973 World Series against Oakland, and I had assured my wife I could buy tickets at Shea for Game 3. She waited on a bench while I stood by the subway exit asking everyone if they had tickets to sell. A policeman approached me.

"Buddy, are you trying to sell tickets?"

"No, I'm trying to buy them."

"How many do you want?"

I told him I needed two, and the police officer surreptitiously showed me two $10 face value tickets. When I asked him how much he wanted for each of them, he told me $10 in a tone suggesting he had been affronted by the question.

"I'll take them."

"OK, I'll leave the tickets in that empty phone booth. You get them and leave the 20 bucks in there—we're not supposed to do this!"

I made the pickup and the drop, and triumphantly returned to my wife feeling like James Bond.

Then came the fractured skull. On May 8, 1973, a line drive by Atlanta's Marty Perez hit Matlack's forearm and struck him in the head. The ball ricocheted into the dugout for a ground-rule double, Perez eventually scored the go-ahead run, and Matlack was saddled with the loss while lying in the intensive care ward at Roosevelt Hospital. Matlack returned 11 days later, but his luck wasn't any better as he stood at 2–8 for a last-place team. Things turned around for Matlack and the Mets. He won 12 of his final 20 decisions, tossed the franchise's first complete-game postseason shutout in Cincinnati, and became the first Met to start three games in a World Series. He won Game 4 but lost the first and the last games in Oakland.

Matlack tied the then-club record with a league-leading seven shutouts for the fifth-place Mets in 1974 (he was 6–15 when he didn't blank the opposition as general manager Bob Scheffing pointed out). A 16-game winner in 1975, Matlack secured the win and co-MVP in the All-Star Game with Bill Madlock (think any of the voters got the names confused?). In 1976 he tied for the league lead with six shutouts and won a career-best 17 games. Then the bottom fell out. He went just 7–15 with career worsts across the board in '77. Complaints about the penurious front office and threats to become a free agent led to Matlack—and fellow '72 rookie hero John Milner—leaving New York in a four-team, 10-player trade. Matlack wound up in Texas, where his win totals were even less glamorous and there was no "big three" pitching staff. He became a pitching coach and eventual pitching coordinator for the Detroit Tigers system. The man knows pitching.

# 60 Groundbreakers: Bill Shea and George Weiss

One got the team in New York, the other got the team off the ground. Bill Shea's name has stood the test of time thanks to the former stadium's nameplate and a place among the retired numbers at Citi Field.

First came Shea. Mayor Robert Wagner assigned Shea, a prominent attorney, the task of bringing National League baseball back to New York after the Dodgers and Giants left for California in 1957. He first set his sights on luring an existing franchise to New York. When that didn't work—and the NL scoffed at the idea of expansion—Shea put together a third major league. He hired Branch Rickey as president of the Continental League. Though nearing 80, Rickey still knew how to get the attention of the press and major league owners. After much finagling and political wrangling, baseball

## First to the Plate and First Out the Gate

Richie Ashburn was the first batter in Mets history in 1962. He was also the team's first All-Star and received a $5,000 boat for being selected as the top player on the 40–120 club. Ashburn, who helped push Marv Throneberry into the spotlight as the poster child for the abysmal club, later lamented about his Mets award: "Most Valuable Player on the worst team ever? Just how did they mean that?" The future Hall of Famer retired after the '62 season and became a Phillies broadcaster.

agreed to its first NL expansion in 70 years. The Continental League never played a game yet helped get four new teams—the Mets, Astros, Angels, and Rangers—into the major leagues.

The new stadium was an important step in that process and a movement began to name it after the man who'd been so instrumental in getting the franchise. He christened Shea Stadium in 1964 using two champagne bottles: one with water from the Harlem River, which flowed beside the Polo Grounds, and the other from the Gowanus Canal in Brooklyn. Shea later helped get the NHL to award the New York Islanders franchise. He died in 1991.

George Weiss was a Yankee. After hiring manager Casey Stengel and putting together a 1950s dynasty, he was forced to retire after the Yankees lost the 1960 World Series. Stengel had been shoved out the door first.

Though Branch Rickey was considered to run the expansion Mets, ownership (namely M. Donald Grant) demurred at giving Rickey the power (or checkbook) he demanded to take on this challenge so late in life. Weiss emerged as president of the brand-new Mets and tabbed the popular Stengel to lead the team.

There were many poor decisions. Among them was to fill the team with names from New York's past. They had name recognition but could no longer play. The young players that came from other organizations—the dregs of the league that the Mets and Houston were forced to pay dearly for—couldn't play in the big leagues. The staid Weiss didn't like that the Mets were portrayed in the press as a sort of comedy troupe, but that was about the best way to spin a 40–120 team at the ancient Polo Grounds. They stunk up brand-new Shea as well. Weiss retired, this time of his own volition, in 1966. He was inducted in the National Baseball Hall of Fame in 1971, the third GM so honored (Rickey beat him to it). Weiss died a year later.

Weiss was inducted into the Mets Hall of Fame in 1982. Shea joined him in 1983.

# 61 Roger McDowell

Roger McDowell was known as the club clown on the top-notch Mets teams of the mid-1980s. He gave out hot foots on a time-release basis. He wore his uniform upside-down on national TV one time and often wore no clothes at all while shagging naked—fly balls, not the Austin Powers definition of "shag"—in the hours before the public entered the park. He gained lasting fame beyond the diamond as the "second spitter" in a famous *Seinfeld* episode, a role foreshadowed by his sprinkler spitting technique in the forgettable "Lets Go Mets!" (Go) video. He still makes appearances in New York as pitching coach of the hated Braves. What shouldn't be forgotten between his transformation from clown to coach, however, is how good a reliever McDowell was for the Mets.

New York selected McDowell in the third round in 1982 out of Bowling Green State University in his native Ohio, the third pitcher taken by the Mets after Dwight Gooden and Floyd Youmans. The postman's son idolized Tom Seaver…in Cincinnati. He wound up taking the number (42) one higher than Seaver's.

McDowell was a starter with just three relief appearances in three levels of the Mets' minor league system and missed almost an entire season after having bone chips removed from his right elbow. Manager Davey Johnson saw him in the Instructional League after the season and was impressed by the action on his sinker. Johnson liked the pitch enough the following April to keep McDowell on the team. He had two ineffective starts among his first seven appearances and then never started again in his next 716 games.

McDowell had a crucial role in 1985. Jesse Orosco stumbled after back-to-back brilliant seasons, and Doug Sisk's sinker reached

*What appears to be a Met walking on his hands is actually clubhouse clown Roger McDowell wearing his uniform upside-down.* Photo courtesy of AP/Wide World Photos.

the strike zone with far less bite or frequency than his. McDowell went 6–5 with 17 saves, and his 62 appearances fell just short of the rookie record set by Sisk two seasons earlier. McDowell was the only reliever to receive a vote for National League Rookie of the Year. Future Mets headache Vince Coleman won the award for the Cardinals, who edged out the Mets in a tight divisional race.

With New York's sights set on the divisional title after two straight near misses, McDowell was even better in 1986. He set a still-standing club record with 14 wins in relief and became the first Met to surpass 70 appearances. He played the outfield and alter-nated pitching with Orosco in a wild 14-inning game in Cincinnati in July (McDowell got the win). He threw five scoreless innings— the ninth through the thirteenth—in fabled Game 6 of the NLCS in Houston and got the win in Game 7 of the World Series.

McDowell underwent a hernia operation during spring train-ing in 1987. He experienced a different type of pain in September when Terry Pendleton's traumatic home run in the ninth inning changed the momentum in the divisional race. McDowell still managed a career-high 25 saves despite missing six weeks.

After Orosco was traded, McDowell worked with Randy Myers and helped the Mets win another division title in 1988. McDowell took the loss in crushing Game 4 of the NLCS against the Dodgers, surrendering a home run to gimpy Kirk Gibson in the twelfth after allowing only one home run all season.

His inclusion in a trade to Philadelphia the following June made the difference between a brutal deal and one of the all-time franchise blunders: McDowell and Lenny Dykstra to a division rival for Juan Samuel. He had a 1.11 ERA in 44 appearances for the Phils that year—Dykstra had even more success as a Phillie—while Samuel spent just 86 games as a Met and hit .228. McDowell pitched in the majors through 1996, when a series of shoulder operations ended his pitching career. He had a couple of stints as a minor league pitching coach before being elevated to the big leagues to succeed Leo Mazzone in Atlanta in 2006. The hot foots long past, now McDowell sits in the enemy dugout with the best Braves arms a phone call away.

# 62 Sid Fernandez

On a starting staff with Doc, Darling, and Bobby O., Sid Fernandez sat in the bullpen during the 1986 World Series. He made one start in the NLCS and lost to Mike Scott 3–1. Through the first six World Series games, Fernandez, one of five Mets All-Stars that year, had pitched twice in relief, both losses by Dwight Gooden. When Ron Darling couldn't make it out of the fourth inning of Game 7, in came El Sid.

Fernandez walked the first batter he faced, Wade Boggs, but he retired the next seven—four by strikeout—in what became the most important long relief outing in Mets history. Lee Mazzilli batted for him in the sixth inning and started a game-tying rally. El Sid was in the middle of the pile on the mound three innings later with a smile as wide as his frame.

Management tried several times to get him to slim down from 230 pounds to improve his stamina, but El Sid was pretty durable anyway. His 250 starts as a Met are fourth all-time. And he was hard to hit. With his deceptive motion and slingshot delivery, he led the league in fewest hits allowed three times and still stands as the fourth-best in major league history with 6.85 hits per nine innings. Fernandez was among the top five in the league in strikeouts six times, and his 1,449 Ks as a Met are fourth in club annals.

Even at a time when pitch counts were not a major concern, Fernandez often came out early because he got himself into trouble with walks. Ironically, in his 16-strikeout game against the Braves in 1989—the most by a Mets southpaw—Fernandez walked none and lost on a Lonnie Smith home run in the ninth. Despite his early exits, El Sid still won 98 times as a Met.

He arrived in a heist in December 1983: Bob Bailor and Carlos Diaz to the Dodgers for Ross Jones and El Sid. The Mets brought up the 21-year-old lefty in July 1984, and he remained in New York for a decade. He was the first Met to wear No. 50—in honor of his native Hawaii—and the theme from *Hawaii 5-0* played before his starts. He pitched for three clubs after leaving the Mets in 1993, retiring to his home state and becoming involved in sports development and amateur coaching.

# 63 Well Staffed

Which Mets club had the best pitching staff ever? The Mets have long been known for having strong pitching—playing in a tough stadium for hitting has had its benefits—and the numbers can be broken down several different ways.

The 1986 staff won 108 times, the most in franchise history, and had six pitchers with 10 or more wins, although no one won 20. The 1969 club was the first to win 100 games, with Tom Seaver capturing a quarter of that lofty total. The '69 Mets also won a club-record nine games by a score of 1–0, including two in one day. The 1988 club was the third Mets club to crack three-digits in wins, led by David Cone's 20. The '88 club was also the only Mets staff since the 1960s to have 20 or more shutouts in a season. Bob Ojeda collected five of their 22 shutouts, but he missed the postseason after a hedge-clipping accident.

## Incomplete

The 1997 season was a revelation after six straight losing campaigns, but it also marked the first 162-game schedule where the Mets did not have 10 or more complete games as a staff. (The 1981, 1994, and 1995 teams didn't reach that number either, but those schedules were truncated by strikes.) Seven times the '97 staff went the distance, with Bobby Jones and Rick Reed the only pitchers to do it more than once. Mark Clark had a complete game and was traded the next day. In the decade since '97, no Mets club has topped 10.

The lowest ERA in club history was recorded in 1968, a year the Mets finished ninth out of 10 teams in the NL standings. It was also the first year the Mets did not allow at least 124 home runs (they cut it down to 87). Granted, the '68 club had a second-year Tom Seaver, a brilliant rookie season by Jerry Koosman, and contributions from Nolan Ryan, Don Cardwell, Jim McAndrew, and others to top 1,000 strikeouts for the first time, but the club's 2.72 ERA was also a product of the "Year of the Pitcher." The entire league had a 2.99 ERA and three teams were ahead of the Mets. Still, the 449 earned runs allowed remains the fewest allowed by the club over a full season.

Strike-shortened 1981 saw the Mets allow 365 runs in 105 games, with a 3.55 ERA that was the lowest recorded by any Mets team between 1976 and 1985. (The 1994 team allowed 470 earned runs in an abbreviated 113-game schedule, but that came out to a not-so-special 4.13 ERA, the highest by a Mets club since 1966.)

The Mets had sub-3.00 ERAs in 1969, 1971, 1976, and 1988. The '86 club's ERA of 3.11, it should be noted, was the lowest in baseball (league ERA of 3.72). As for strikeouts, the 1990 staff, led by David Cone, Dwight Gooden, Frank Viola, and Sid Fernandez, set the club standard with 1,217.

What about the bullpen? The 1984 team was the first to crack 50 saves, shattering the previous best of 41 set in 1972. The '84 crew was led by All-Star Jesse Orosco with 31 saves; Doug Sisk had 15, Ed Lynch recorded two, while Brent Gaff and Wes Gardner had one apiece. That mark was snapped by the 1987 pen's 51: Roger McDowell had 25, Orosco 16, rookie Randy Myers six, Doug Sisk three, and David Cone added one.

With all these numbers meaning something different, the best Mets pitching staff can't really be pinned to one year. But since this began with a question inquiring as much, an answer should be given: 1988 gets the nod. The '86 team won more games, but the '88 club was the last in Mets history to be under 3.00 or log 30 complete games and the first to fan 1,100 or walk as few as 404 over a full season. (Though almost the same as the '86 club, this model did have the first full year of David Cone in his prime.) And then there's all those shutouts. The fact that there was more offense in baseball gives '88 the edge over the '69 team, even though both clubs won 100. If you're talking personnel, Seaver, Koosman, Ryan, and McGraw in '69 can't be topped. Twenty years makes a big difference in eras, but the pedigree's the same.

# 64 Closing Arguments

If you're ranking Mets relievers over the last 40 years, Tug McGraw stands at the top of the list in terms of quality and energy. After Gil Hodges put him in the bullpen to split time with reliable Ron Taylor in 1969, McGraw appeared in 305 games, threw 615 innings, won 43, and saved 85 for two pennant-winning Mets clubs. (He made only 11 starts in those six seasons.) Tug had one save more than Roger McDowell, who should go down as the best setup reliever in Mets history. In four full seasons with the Mets in the 1980s, he averaged 64 appearances, 117 innings, eight wins, and 20 saves. Both McGraw's and McDowell's numbers are hard to compare with anyone doing those jobs today.

Closing is a tough job. Frankly, today's closers should be held to a high standard because most closers are paid simply to accrue as many saves as possible. That's a far different role than in McGraw's day—or even McDowell's—when a team's top reliever was responsible to throw as long as needed to get the team a win. The modern closer generally works one inning. The save rule states that a reliever has to protect a lead of three runs or less, have the tying run on deck, or pitch at least the last three innings with a lead of any size. It sounds easy on paper.

According to *The Book*—an actual book about the proverbial "book" in baseball—teams score less than three runs in an inning 93.6 percent of the time; a team does not score 70 percent of the time. The odds are in favor of the pitcher, but baseball is all about defying the odds. The ninth is sweaty palms time with most relievers. That brings us to the top three men ahead of McGraw and McDowell (Billy Wagner is fourth) on the club's all-time saves list. They are three dissimilar pitchers who mean very different things to Mets fans.

**Jesse Orosco:** He clinched the unclinchable—or so it seemed to any fan of the team when he debuted as a Met in 1979—and Messy Jesse had quite a run. His first full season was 1982, when he set up for Neil Allen. An intangible in Jesse's corner: after losing his job to Orosco and trying to start for the Mets, Allen was sent to St. Louis for All-Star first baseman Keith Hernandez. Orosco then went on to have as good a year as any Mets reliever: 13–7, 62 appearances, 110 innings, 84 strikeouts, and a 1.47 ERA in 1983. The southpaw placed third in the Cy Young race and became the club's first reliever since McGraw in 1972 to make the All-Star team. His 17 saves sound puny today, but the '83 Mets were a last-place team that used Orosco for a lot more than just protecting what few leads the offense created. In '84 the Mets vastly improved, and he saved 31 while allowing a run more per nine innings. Orosco and McDowell accrued saves at almost the same rate after that—it's hard to imagine any self-respecting agent today allowing a manager like Davey Johnson to have two closers sharing the load and the glory for more than one year—but Orosco was still the man Johnson went to for the final outs in the 1986 postseason. He got three wins against Houston and saved two in four scoreless appearances against Boston in the World Series, pitching multiple innings in the deciding game in each series. He moved on after the 1987 season, but given that he pitched another 16 seasons for eight more teams, appearing in 872 games (a major league record 1,252 all told), he somehow kept busy.

**John Franco:** The little lefty had big shoes to fill. Not Orosco's either. He was traded straight up for Randy Myers, who, in his first year after the trade got the last out in Cincinnati's world championship clincher. Myers was one of the top closers of his time, but Franco outlasted Myers and far exceeded his major league saves total (424–347). Franco collected a club-record 276 saves for the Mets in a decade as their closer, becoming the first lefty to reach 400 saves and ending his career second on the all-time list to Lee Smith. (Less than two months later, Trevor Hoffman passed Franco for second on his way to eclipsing Smith.) Franco, a Brooklyn native and lifelong Mets fan, was a team captain—the only one in history other than Hernandez and Gary Carter—and became a solid setup reliever after the Mets went with a much harder thrower as the closer.

**Armando Benitez:** While Orosco has legend factor (his rejoicing face was plastered on the side of Shea Stadium) and Franco has the durability quotient (his 695 games as a Met are almost 300 more than runner-up Tom Seaver), Benitez was one of the most reviled stars in Mets history. Benitez averaged almost 40 saves per season as Mets closer (July 1999 to July 2003), recording 160 saves while blowing only 25. Franco (64) and Orosco (36) had exactly

100 failures for the Mets. But fans will contend that it was *when* Benitez blew saves that made him so easy to hate. To that I can only say…they're right. His blown save—after Franco's blown save—in Game 6 of the 1999 NLCS set the stage for Kenny Rogers to walk in the winning run an inning later. Benitez's inability to hold the lead in Game 1 of the 2000 World Series at Yankee Stadium will forever haunt Mets fans. His two meltdowns against Atlanta in as many weeks in 2001…let's just say, Benitez was not what you'd call a "big-game closer," and Armando is proof indeed of how fickle the position can be and how much is demanded of a closer. Get the save or get the blame.

The best of the three? It was Orosco all along. Besides his '86 mojo, he was acquired from Minnesota for the southpaw who got the last out in the 1969 World Series, Jerry Koosman. Francisco Rodriguez has a way to go to crack this list, but put K-Rod on that mound with his glove in the air after clinching a World Series for the Mets and we'll talk.

# 65 Lenny Dykstra

Lenny Dykstra was considered too small, but the Mets took the scrawny southern Californian in the 13th round of the 1981 draft and never regretted it. Known for carrying his glove everywhere in high school and for his willingness to take batting practice any time, anywhere, Dykstra was unstoppable in the minor leagues. Playing A-ball in Lynchburg (18-year-old teammate Dwight Gooden struck out 300), the left-handed Dykstra made the Carolina League tremble with 132 runs, 107 walks, and 105 steals.

*Center fielder Lenny Dykstra was the catalyst for the Mets' 1986 championship team.*

Dykstra arrived in New York in 1985 showing patience (30 walks) and speed (15 steals) in just 83 games. Manager Davey Johnson regularly juggled his outfield to get Dykstra into games in 1986. His defense and arm benefited the strong pitching staff—his perfect throw in San Diego on August 27 turned a potential game-tying hit into a game-ending double play—and he had pop at the plate. Right-handers dreaded facing the Mets with Dykstra and the equally feisty second baseman Wally Backman at the top of the order, a phenomenon known as "Backstra." (His partial platoon with Mookie Wilson, another speedster and crowd favorite, was referred to as "Mookstra.") Known as "Nails" because of his toughness, Dykstra stood his ground against left-handers. His pinch-hit triple against craftly southpaw Bob

Knepper started the celebrated ninth-inning rally against the Astros in Game 6 of the 1986 NLCS.

He became a mini-Bambino in October, homering 10 times in 32 career postseason games (as opposed to 81 in 1,278 games otherwise). His two-run home run in the bottom of the ninth in Game 3 of the 1986 NLCS won the first postseason game at Shea Stadium since 1973. (Dykstra said the last time he'd come through with a home run in such a situation was as a kid playing Strat-O-Matic against his brother.) He launched six homers over two career World Series, none more important than his shot in the first inning of Game 3 at Fenway Park in 1986, spurring the Mets to victory after they had dropped the first two at home. Dykstra homered again the next night.

He hit .429 against the Dodgers in the 1988 NLCS, but the Mets lost in seven games. The following year he was dealt to the Phillies with Roger McDowell for Juan Samuel, Dykstra's inadequate and short-term replacement in center field. It is still regarded as one of the worst trades in Mets history.

Dykstra put up some remarkable numbers with the Phillies—leading the league in hits, walks, and runs for the 1993 NL champions—but gambling, reckless behavior, and injuries marred his subsequent years in Philadelphia. He averaged just 60 games his last three seasons. He quit before he got started as a minor league manager, but he should have quit while he was ahead in business. Dykstra declared bankruptcy in 2009.

# 66 Al Jackson

Al Jackson started his pitching career as a Pirate and ended it as a Red, but in between—and almost every year since—he has been a

## Marvelous Marv: M.E.T. to Be

Marvin Eugene Throneberry had timing. He'd once been traded for Roger Maris (along with a few others), and the Mets, intrigued and needing a first baseman with Gil Hodges hobbled, got Throneberry from Baltimore.

Within a week of his arrival, the team embarked on a 17-game losing streak that saw the Mets get swept six times. The Mets won three times in Wrigley Field to end the skid, but the next weekend the Cubs came to the Polo Grounds. After a Throneberry error—one of 17 he made in 97 games at first base—allowed Chicago's Lou Brock to bat and connect for the first home run to the distant center-field bleachers since 1953, Marvelous Marv came up in the bottom of the inning and tripled in two runs. Unfortunately, he was called out for missing first base. Charley Neal immediately followed with a homer, and Casey Stengel scrambled out of the dugout and pointed at each base for him to step on. The Mets lost by a run, and the Cubs swept the four games.

Two weeks later, after Al Jackson had thrown the first one-hitter in team history in a crisp, errorless 2–0 win (with Hodges playing the last two innings at first base), Throneberry made three errors in the nightcap in a 16–3 Houston romp. When Marvelous Marv heard his teammates being booed, he cracked, "Hey, you're stealing my fans."

Met. He earned it. In the first four seasons of the club's existence, Jackson averaged 18 losses a year and had two 20-loss seasons. Yet Jackson deserved a better fate. Anybody did.

Signed out of Wiley College in 1955 and drafted from the Pirates in the 1961 expansion draft, the tough little Texan gave the Mets his best every time. The bumbling Mets didn't reciprocate in kind. Still, Jackson had some truly noteworthy performances for the young franchise. He threw the team's first shutout in April, and twice in nine days in August he threw 15 and 10 innings...and lost both. Jackson had the best ERA of any original Mets starter at 4.40, which was lower than only two teams in the major leagues. He was the first Met to win at Shea Stadium, pitching a shutout. With a pennant on the line—for St. Louis—Jackson beat Bob Gibson, 1–0, the last weekend of the 1964 season (the Cards took the pennant anyway). He led or tied the club for most wins, strikeouts, and shutouts three times in his first four years as a Met. It being the Mets and Jackson pitching 200 innings a year, he led the team in a few not so noteworthy categories as well.

Jackson left the Mets in 1965 with the most wins—and losses—in team history. Traded to St. Louis for Ken Boyer— Jackson was the only Cardinal not to play in the 1967 World Series win over Boston—he was shipped back to the Mets the day after the Series ended still owning his franchise marks. Tom Seaver broke Jackson's record for victories (43) less than a month after the southpaw was sold to the Reds in June 1969. (It took Seaver until 1974 to accrue 80 losses to break Jackson's hold on that category.)

Jackson finished out the year with the Reds and was released the following spring. What would he do now? While the Mets did not have a place for him on the roster, they did have a spot for him in the organization. He became a roving minor league instructor starting in 1970 and returned to that role three more times over the years. He managed in the Mets' minor league system and teamed up with original Met Don Zimmer as pitching coach in Boston from 1977 to 1979. He filled the same role for Orioles manager Frank Robinson from 1988 to 1991. Jackson served in New York as bullpen coach and assistant pitching coach under Bobby Valentine in 1999 and 2000. His son, Reggie, played in the Mets organization.

Still a pitching consultant, 41 of his 48 years in baseball since the expansion draft have been with the Mets. Jackson is even an ambassador to new lands for baseball: he and his wife Nadine were part of the contingent that traveled to West Africa to promote the game in the winter of 2007.

# 67 Welcome Home

Cities like St. Louis are renowned for making new stars feel at home. New York has a reputation for being too hard on its players, for making them prove themselves here before they'll be accepted, and for kicking a guy when he's down. All true. But New York fans know the game as well as anyone in any city and they've got heart. They also know a good deal when they see one. Following are just a few of the new guys whose New York arrival has been met with roaring approval. After that, they had to prove it. This is New York.

**Donn Clendenon (June 22, 1969):** Gil Hodges was strict, with his players and with his platooning. After an unheard of 8–4 road trip during which Clendenon was acquired from Montreal, the new first baseman sat in favor of Ed Kranepool for the first two home games against defending NL champ St. Louis because the Cards started right-handers. Clendenon finally played Sunday against Steve Carlton in the first of two before 55,862, the largest regular-season Shea crowd ever to see the Cardinals. Clendenon drew a walk amid cheers his first time up, and the appreciation grew as he singled in a run his next time up. The Mets won the game, the doubleheader, and eventually the world championship, defying logic and the odds with a lot of help from World Series MVP Clendenon.

**Willie Mays (May 14, 1972):** The Mets had tried to get the "Say Hey Kid" for years before the Giants finally agreed to deal the 41-year-old superstar. A week shy of the 21st anniversary of his debut as a New York Giant, Willie took his first bows as a Met before a Mother's Day crowd that included his biggest fan, Mets owner Joan Payson. Fittingly, the Giants were in town and the score was tied in the fifth when Mays, batting leadoff and playing first base, homered to left. The score stood, and the cheers rained down. Everyone knew this was his swan song—he'd retire after '73—but this was love.

**Steve Henderson (June 16, 1977):** Steve Henderson? Like Tom Seaver, who wouldn't have reached 300 wins if he'd stayed a Met, Hendu had no chance of breaking into Cincy's stacked lineup. He scored the go-ahead run as a pinch-runner and later received a standing ovation in his first major league at-bat. He struck out. Hendu knew how to hit—he became an established hitting coach—and he was a decent player who wound up getting traded for both Seaver and Dave Kingman (to the Cubs in 1981). Kudos to the crowd of 9,000 at Shea that night for trying. Henderson tried, too.

**Keith Hernandez (June 20, 1983):** Whereas the Tom Seaver trade in 1977 signified the demise of the franchise, the Keith Hernandez deal six years later created a seismic shift in the club's fortunes. Hernandez debuted with two hits and an error in Montreal on June 17—with the reunited Seaver taking the loss for the Mets—but Hernandez drove in a run with a groundout in his Shea debut before a handful of people in the opener of a twi-night double-header. With the crowd close to 17,000 for the nightcap, he got a bigger response when he hit his first homer as a Met with a man on against his former team. Neil Allen, the bargain price for Hernandez, blanked the last-place Mets the next night, but even then complaints were few.

**Gary Carter (April 9, 1985):** The Mets emerged as contenders in 1984 before coming up short at the end. They needed an established catcher and got the best one in the National League. Carter arrived in a ballyhooed four-for-one deal with the Expos and was greeted warmly by a packed house on Opening Day 1985. Joaquin Andujar drilled him in his first at-bat (he was hit by Bill Campbell in the eighth). Batting in the tenth inning against Neil Allen—remember the Keith Hernandez deal?—Carter lined a home run to left to beat the Cardinals and win over the crowd. Kid had them at "hello."

**Mike Piazza (May 23, 1998):** The night before had been giddy with John Franco getting the save after swapping numbers from 31 to 45 to make room for Mike. Saturday afternoon a police escort took Piazza from LaGuardia to Shea. The crowd roared long and loud when he first stepped up and again when his double knocked in a run in the fifth. His maligned defensive skills looked fine as he caught Al Leiter's shutout of Milwaukee. His defense wouldn't shine so brightly that first summer, and the crowd would often boo with little provocation, but he overlooked the rough patches and signed a seven-year deal. Mets fans fell hard for the slugger's power, class, and quiet leadership. They'd still be cheering his final game at Shea in 2005 if he hadn't broken away.

**Pedro Martinez (April 16, 2005):** The legend of Pedro landed in Flushing on a sunny Saturday afternoon. He'd already pitched two superb games on the road and now Shea got to see him in the flesh. A crowd of 55,351, larger than Opening Day, jammed the place to see Pedro fire away at Florida. Fans cheered every move Pedro made and rudely booed former ace Al Leiter in his return. Another much-watched new guy, Carlos Beltran, singled to tie it, and old pal Mike Piazza knocked in the go-ahead run in the eighth. Even a Braden Looper meltdown couldn't dampen the spirit as Ramon Castro knocked in the winner. Pedro's starts would be a happening and, after a brilliant 2005, a rare event indeed.

# 68 The Polo Grounds

The first place the Mets called home was a Giant leftover. The New York Giants played baseball in northern Manhattan at Coogan's Bluff, next to the Harlem River, from 1911 to 1957. Their various homes around the city had all been dubbed Polo Grounds since the franchise came into existence in 1883. The Yankees spent a decade at the Polo Grounds as well, with Babe Ruth swatting enough home runs to make the tenants a better draw than the landlord Giants. You could certainly call the old place venerable. Comfortable was a different matter.

Spruced up but still dank at 51 years of age, the Polo Grounds reopened for business on Friday the 13th. It was the stadium's first National League game since Pittsburgh's Bob Friend, who would later win the first game at Shea Stadium, threw the final pitch against the Giants on September 29, 1957.

When the Giants and Dodgers moved west, there was no guarantee baseball would ever again grace the Polo Grounds. Football returned first. The National Football League Giants had jumped ship to Yankee Stadium in 1956, but a new team and a new league arrived in 1960 with the New York Titans and the American Football League. The future Jets weren't nearly as bad as the original Mets would be, but they weren't very good and didn't draw well at all.

The 922,000 who came to see the 1962 Mets perform their singular magic at the Polo Grounds represented the highest attendance at Coogan's Bluff since the Giants won their final New York and last franchise world championship in 1954. (Take that, California!) The Mets surpassed 1 million fans in 1963, when the team was supposed to already be in Flushing. Construction at Shea took far longer than anticipated, and fans were able to ponder the Polo Grounds for a few months more.

It was very short down the lines—306 to left and 281 to right while the Mets were there—but a second-deck overhang was actually about 250 feet away for a ball hit just right. Center field, on the other hand, was several subway stops away at 475 feet. Two of the four balls ever hit to the center-field bleachers came on successive days by future Hall of Famers on June 17 and 18, 1962. They certainly weren't Mets (Lou Brock and Hank Aaron). The Mets' two-year record at the Polo Grounds was 56–105, which looked like a pennant-winner compared to the road mark of 35–126 their first two years.

Still, there was a group that loathed the idea of baseball vacating Manhattan for good. Among them was Robert Lipsyte of *The New York Times*. He lamented what was being left behind for Queens, "that smug borough of bourgeois achievement with its *nouveau riche* stadium." While it is quaint to look back at not-yet-completed Shea and snicker about how its "manicured greensward will be clearly seen from every cantilevered tier" or Lipsyte's extrapolation on the new parks of the day that have long since been replaced, the feeling was genuine.

Although the Mets tarried just two years at the Polo Grounds, they extended life of a grand old building that had seen the brilliance of Mugsy, Matty, and Mays while wincing at Marvelous Marv. "It will be a sad day," Lipsyte wrote of the closing of the old park. "They will leave their soul in the Polo Grounds."

Demolition began a few days before the Mets moved into Shea Stadium. There'd be no looking back now.

# 69 More than One Murph

Murphy is the only name that's in the Mets Hall of Fame twice. Of course, there's broadcaster Bob Murphy, who spent 42 seasons as the beloved voice of the team. The other is Johnny Murphy, no relation but also known as Murph (and "Fordham Fireman" from his days as relief ace for six world champion Yankees clubs in the 1930s and 1940s). He was chief scout for the Mets at their inception and later vice president.

**TRIVIA Question**

The Mets traded five pitchers—Rick Aguilera, Kevin Tapani, David West, Tim Drummond, and Jack Savage—to get one pitcher back. Who was he?

Trivia answers on page 256

You can't give him all the blame for the terrible teams of the early 1960s, nor should he get all the credit for the Miracle Mets as general manager in 1968 and 1969. Bing Devine put a lot of the bodies in place, and Whitey Herzog helped find and nurture the young talent from the farm. Murphy did acquire Donn Clendenon from Montreal in the middle of the season to bring life to New York's lineup. His last trade was his worst: Amos Otis for Joe Foy. Murphy died of a heart attack a few weeks later at 61 without even getting to see the championship banner raised at Shea. He was inducted into the Mets Hall of Fame in 1983. The top Mets rookie each year in training camp receives the Johnny Murphy Award. John Milner was the first recipient.

Murphy was the first Mets GM voted Executive of the Year by *The Sporting News* (Frank Cashen won it in 1986). Here's a look at the other Mets GMs who have made it to the postseason as well as their most notable transactions.

| GM | Years | Postseason(s) | Best/Worst Trades |
|---|---|---|---|
| Bob Scheffing | 1970–1974 | 1973 | R. Staub, F. Millan, G. Stone/ N. Ryan |
| Frank Cashen | 1980–1991 | 1986, 1988 | K. Hernandez, R. Darling, S. Fernandez, G. Carter/ J. Reardon, L. Dykstra, R. Aguilera |
| Steve Phillips | 1997–2003 | 1999–2000 | A. Leiter, M. Piazza, A. Benitez, M. Hampton/J. Isringhausen, M. Mora, M. Vaughn, J. Bay |
| Omar Minaya | 2004–Present | 2006 | C. Delgado, J. Maine, J. Santana/ H. Bell, B. Bannister |

# 70 Lost in Translation

## Imports

In 1995 the Dodgers' Hideo Nomo became the first Japanese pitcher in the United States in 30 years, winning National League Rookie of the Year honors and capturing the hearts of fans around the globe. Two years later, despite the Yankees' much-publicized transaction for Hideki Irabu, the Mets had the first Japanese import to actually play in New York: Takashi Kashiwada. He shriveled like a blossom in snowfall. The Mets' luck with players from Japan hasn't improved much since.

The 26-year-old Kashiwada fit in with Bobby Valentine's 1997 club as a player with minimal skill contributing to the team's winning ways. Despite control problems, the southpaw's 3–1 record remains the highest winning percentage (season or career) for any Mets pitcher from Japan. Masato Yoshii, the only Japanese pitcher to last more than one year with the Mets, won 18 times over two seasons for the club, including a 12–8 mark in 1999. As a Met in 1998, Nomo had the worst year of his otherwise successful career. Three others—Satoru Komiyama, Kaz Ishii, and Shingo Takatsu—combined to win four games. The Mets rolled the dice again with reliever Ryota Igarashi, signed to a two-year deal in 2010.

Position players from Japan have not excelled either. While flamboyant Tsuyoshi Shinjo had a solid 2001 season as a fourth outfielder, he was traded to San Francisco. When he returned in 2003, he couldn't hit a lick. Kaz Matsui's travails in New York are well documented—just typing his name makes one's ears ring with boos.

The Mets have tried to make diplomatic inroads in Japan even if they can't find someone from there who can play at Shea. Japan's

Prime Minister Shinzo Abe received a Mets pinstriped jersey with his name and the No. 1 from David Wright and Co. during a November 2006 visit.

| Player | Years with Mets (Years in Japan) |
| --- | --- |
| Ryota Igarashi | 2010 (1999–2009) |
| Kaz Ishii | 2005 (1992–2001, 2006–2007) |
| Takashi Kashiwada | 1997 (1994–1995, 1998–2004) |
| Satoru Komiyama | 2002 (1990–2001, 2004–2007) |
| Kaz Matsui | 2004–2006 (1995–2003) |
| Hideo Nomo | 1998 (1990–1994) |
| Tsuyoshi Shinjo | 2001, 2003 (1991–2000, 2004–2006) |
| Ken Takahaski | 2009 (1995–2008) |
| Shingo Takatsu | 2005 (1991–2003, 2006) |
| Masato Yoshii | 1998–1999 (1985–1997, 2003–2005) |

*The smiles would be few and far between for Matsui in New York. He homered in his first at-bat in each of his three seasons as a Met, but he didn't do encores in New York.*

## Are You with Me, Mr. Koo?

Dae-Sung Koo was a South Korean who came to Flushing via Japan in 2005. The Mets were in desperate need of relievers, especially left-handers. When asked in spring training what he liked to be called, he replied through an interpreter, "Mr. Koo."

Mr. Koo was actually mildly effective, with a 3.91 ERA in 33 appearances. He made the erroneous assumption that Carlos Delgado (the Marlin) would not swing at a 3–0 pitch, and the subsequent crushed meatball cost the Mets a sweep in Miami. Mr. Koo's lasting moment of fame, however, came at the plate. He walloped a double off Randy Johnson in a national telecast against the Yankees. When Jose Reyes sacrificed him to third, Mr. Koo kept running and splayed his jacketed self across the plate with a dramatic dive. He might have saved himself the trouble because Miguel Cairo followed with a home run, but Mr. Koo was all about style points.

## Exports

Mets who've gone from the United States to Japan have generally fared better than their Japanese counterparts. Early Met George Altman hit .309 in eight seasons in Japan and credited martial arts with the 50-point improvement over his American numbers. Roberto Petagine got on base constantly in the minors, but he never caught a break in America. Petagine became Keith Hernandez with 40-homer power in Japan.

Two of the most successful managers in Mets history have ties to Japan. Davey Johnson spent two years playing for the Yomiuri Giants in the mid-1970s before returning to the United States as a pinch-hitter and potential manager. Bobby Valentine never played in Japan, but he managed there both before and after his tenure as leader of the Mets. His candor, humor, eagerness to learn, knowledge, and devotion to the game have made Bobby V. a beloved figure in his adopted country. He also brought Benny Agbayani and Matt Franco with him; the trio helped the Chiba Lotte Marines win a championship in 2005.

Following are players not born in Japan who have played for both the Mets and in Japan. Years under contract in Japan are in parentheses.

| Player | Years with Mets (Years in Japan) |
| --- | --- |
| Benny Agbayani | 1998–2001 (2004–2007) |
| Edgardo Alfonzo | 1995–2002 (2009) |
| George Altman | 1964 (1968–1975) |
| Rigo Beltran | 1998–1999 (2002) |
| Mike Birkbeck | 1992, 1995 (1996) |
| Craig Brazell | 2004 (2008–2009) |
| Terry Bross | 1991 (1996–1999) |
| Brian Buchanan | 2004 (2006–2007) |
| Mark Carreon | 1987–1991 (1997–1998) |
| Joe Crawford | 1997 (1998–1999) |
| Elmer Dessens | 2009 (1999) |
| Chris Donnels | 1991–1992 (1996–1998) |
| Pedro Feliciano | 2003–2004, 2006–2009 (2005) |
| Tony Fernandez | 1993 (2000) |
| Julio Franco | 2006–2007 (1995, 1998) |
| Matt Franco | 1997–2000 (2004–2006) |
| Mike Fyhrie | 1996 (1997) |
| Karim Garcia | 2004 (2005–2006) |
| Shawn Gilbert | 1997–1998 (2001) |
| Dicky Gonzalez | 2001 (2004–2006) |
| Geremi Gonzalez | 2006 (2007) |
| Eric Hillman | 1992–1994 (1996–1998) |
| Jonathan Hurst | 1994 (2001) |
| Darrin Jackson | 1993 (1996) |
| Jason Jacome | 1994–1995 (1999–2000) |
| Mark Johnson | 2000–2002 (1999) |
| Mike Kinkade | 1998–2000 (2004) |
| Dae-Sung Koo | 2005 (2001–2004) |
| Brandon Knight | 2008 (2003–2005) |
| Pat Mahomes | 1999–2000 (1998) |
| Barry Manuel | 1997 (1999) |

| | |
|---|---|
| Jim Marshall | 1962 (1963–1967) |
| Felix Millan | 1973–1977 (1978–1980) |
| Kevin Mitchell | 1984, 1986 (1995) |
| C.J. Nitkowski | 2001 (2007) |
| Tom O'Malley | 1989–1990 (1991–1996) |
| Alex Ochoa | 1995–1997 (2003–2007) |
| Jose Parra | 2004 (1999, 2005) |
| Timo Perez | 2000–2003 (1996–1999) |
| Roberto Petagine | 1995–1996 (1999–2004) |
| Andy Phillips | 2008 (2009) |
| Jerrod Riggan | 2000–2001 (2003–2004) |
| Shane Spencer | 2004 (2005–2006) |
| Tony Tarasco | 2002 (2000) |
| Jim Tatum | 1998 (1997) |
| Ryan Thompson | 1992–1995 (1998) |
| Wilson Valdez | 2009 (2008) |
| Eric Valent | 2004–2005 (2006) |
| Pete Walker | 1995, 2001–2002 (2004) |
| Matt Watson | 2003 (2007) |
| David West | 1988–1989 (1997) |
| Don Zimmer | 1962 (1966) |

# 71 Ron Taylor

It was like he answered an ad in the paper: "Young team needs exp. leader, ability to deal w/pressure a plus." Ron Taylor was just what the doctor ordered…but more on that later.

Taylor spent six years in Cleveland's farm system partly by his own doing. He reported mid-season for five straight years to earn an engineering degree at his hometown University of Toronto. He threw 11 innings of shutout ball in his major league debut in

1962, allowing a grand slam to Boston's Carroll Hardy to end the game. Taylor pitched 54 times for the '63 Cardinals, followed by a career-high and league-best 63 outings for the world champions the next year, including two scoreless appearances in the World Series.

In 1967 he was sold by Houston to the Mets, just about the only team worse than the Astros. But something strange happened to Taylor when he arrived at Shea. He got better—a lot better.

Taylor's ERA of 2.34 was half that of the previous year, allowing just one home run in 73 innings. The Mets used him to finish games, even if they were losing (which was often). He put together nearly identical numbers in 1968 and '69 except for one department: a 1–5 record for a ninth-place club followed by a 9–4 mark for the "Miracle Mets." He led the team with 13 saves (Tug McGraw had nine wins and 12 saves) as the Mets overtook the Cubs for the first National League East title. Taylor earned the win that put the Mets in first place on September 10, and he later won the club's 100th game of the year. This from a team that lost 100 times in Taylor's first year there for their fifth such season in six years of life. Life was changing.

Taylor saved the first NLCS game in history and got the victory the next day in Atlanta when Jerry Koosman couldn't get through five innings. He pitched in the first World Series game in franchise history, but his biggest moment came the next day. Although Koosman was brilliant in Baltimore, he walked two batters in a 2–1 game with two down in the ninth. Gil Hodges brought in Taylor to try to even the Series. He induced Brooks Robinson to ground out, and the Miracle was on. The Mets won the next three.

In six career postseason appearances, Taylor did not allow a run and saved three games. He pitched two more years with the Mets before finishing in San Diego at age 34. That's when the real work began. He went back to the University of Toronto for his medical degree and joined yet another expansion club: the Toronto Blue

Jays. Dr. Taylor became team physician in 1979, often working in his practice all day, coming to the ballpark, and occasionally pitching batting practice while ballboys monitored his pager for emergencies. Now past 70, the Canadian Sports Hall of Famer doesn't pitch much anymore, but his son, Drew, a southpaw, pitched in the minor leagues for the Blue Jays.

# 72 Ron Hunt

Ron Hunt is remembered for being hit by pitches. A lot. The Mets liked him because he could hit. Some. Hunt was the first player to be a star for the Mets—not a huge star, but the 1960s Mets were willing to take any star they could find.

Hunt was one of several players mined from the Milwaukee Braves. A well-run organization, even if their fans' interest waned and the club moved to Atlanta in 1966, the Braves discarded a lot of players in New York's direction. Mets coach Solly Hemus had seen Hunt play for a low-lying Braves farm club and suggested the Mets buy the infielder. Hunt wasn't big and he wasn't fast, but he put the ball in play and had a knack for reaching base that was rare for the 1963 Mets.

He led the club in at-bats (533), hits (145), runs (64), doubles (28), and, not surprisingly, hit by pitches (13). Hunt placed second to a tough second baseman from Cincinnati named Pete Rose for Rookie of the Year, so Casey Stengel decided to move Hunt to third base. Hunt was hurt by the move. He had led second basemen with 26 errors, but he felt he had won the job. Stengel thought Hunt had the reflexes to play third, where his inability to cover ground wouldn't be as detrimental or as obvious. Four games into the '64 season Hunt was back at second base and the revolving door at third continued unabated. Then he got 73-year-old Casey beat up.

Hunt tried to jar the ball loose from Braves catcher Ed Bailey and started a brawl in Milwaukee. Stengel came racing into the mêlée and had his arms pinned back by Denis Menke. The manager survived, the team lost, and even as the defeats piled up, the Mets at least had a new home with its very own All-Star Game and very own All-Star. Hunt's scrappy play led his contemporaries to choose him as the starting second baseman for the Midsummer Classic. All these years later, he's still the only second baseman in club history to start an All-Star Game. He had a single in the National League's dramatic victory.

Hunt hit .303 that year, dropped 63 points the next, and went up 48 points in 1966 while earning another All-Star berth. The Mets decided to sell high and sent the popular Hunt and Jim Hickman to the Dodgers for Tommy Davis, who had one stellar season with the Mets before being moved in the Tommie Agee–Al Weis deal.

But Hunt left his mark, or more appropriately, his bruise. His 41 HBPs are still the club standard, and his 50 ouches as an Expo in 1971 remains untouched, even if his career major league record of 243 has been broken, no pun intended.

# 73 1964 All-Star Game

World Series home-field advantage or no, the All-Star Game has lost its luster. It's also lost New York. Even with the Yankees hosting the game in 2008, that was still a 31-year absence in this two-city market. Chicago, San Francisco/Oakland, Baltimore/D.C., and Los

Angeles have seen at least one site host the game in the past 15 years. Some said the New York teams haven't wanted it. Others mumbled that new stadiums had to be on the table before MLB would even consider the city. Whatever. The Mets are on the short list to get a Citi Field Midsummer Classic (though the home run derby might be a problem). Shea? Oh, it had an All-Star Game. Back when the paint was freshly dried and the game was still played in the afternoon.

It was an outstanding game. Ron Hunt became the first Met to start—and the only one until Jerry Grote in 1968—and he got a hit against American League starter Dean Chance. Hunt took the field on July 7, 1964, with five players who would one day be Mets (Willie Mays, Ken Boyer, Joe Torre, Chance, and Jim Fregosi, the AL's shortstop and leadoff hitter).

Don Drysdale allowed an unearned run in the first, but the National League took the lead in the fourth on home runs by Billy Williams and Boyer. Roberto Clemente dashed home from first on a double by Dick Groat to make it 3–1 in the fifth. Mays dove and just missed Brooks Robinson's drive as both Mickey Mantle and Harmon Killebrew scored to tie the game an inning later. Fregosi's sacrifice fly made it 4–3 in the seventh.

Once the AL had the lead, intimidating Red Sox reliever Dick Radatz was in for the duration. "The Monster" retired the side in order in the seventh and eighth, but he began the ninth by walking Mays. Willie stole second and came around to score on Orlando Cepeda's bloop single that was thrown away by Yankee Joe Pepitone. Radatz retired Boyer, but he intentionally walked Reds catcher Johnny Edwards to set up the double play. NL manager Walter Alston used Hank Aaron to bat for Shea's own Ron Hunt. Aaron struck out, leaving it up to Philadelphia's Johnny Callison with two down.

Callison, who played the last five innings because Aaron was ill, had flied out his first time up against Radatz. Using a lighter

## All-Star Mets

The Mets have only hosted one All-Star Game, but they've had no shortage of stars. Since Ron Hunt got the starting nod in 1964, a Met has started an All-Star game 27 times, plus three Mets who couldn't because of injury.

Darryl Strawberry was an All-Star in each of his seven full seasons as a Met. Though he didn't play in the 1989 game because of injury, he hit .333 as a Mets All-Star, was picked to start five games, and scored twice in the 1985 contest. Mike Piazza, likewise, was picked for seven All-Star games as a Met. He started six— batting .154—and missed a seventh assignment because of Roger Clemens's beaning at Yankee Stadium three days before the game.

Tom Seaver was named to nine All-Star teams as a Met. He pitched in six, but he had no decisions in nine innings over six appearances for an ERA of 3.60. Dwight Gooden pitched in three All-Star Games. He struck out the side in 1984—combining with Fernando Valenzuela to fan six straight AL hitters—but he lost both his starts in 1986 and 1988. Tug McGraw won the 1972 game, while Al Leiter lost the game in 2000. David Wright has appeared in four games through 2009, batting .364.

Gary Carter and Keith Hernandez played in three games apiece as Mets. John Stearns also played in three games—and was named to a fourth and did not play—but as the late-inning replacement catcher, his only at-bat was in the 1980 game.

Carlos Beltran has been an All-Star in four of his five years as a Met while batting .400 against the AL. He went 2-for-4 with a daring steal of third in 2006 and was in the running for the game's MVP until Trevor Hoffman blew the save for the NL. Jon Matlack, winner of the 1975 game, is the only Met to earn the game's MVP (he shared the award with Cub Bill Madlock).

Lee Mazzilli played in just one All-Star Game and had just one official at-bat, but he hit a home run that tied the 1979 game and then walked with the bases loaded against Ron Guidry to force in the go-ahead run. Maz lost out on the game's MVP trophy because Pittsburgh's Dave Parker won it with a superb throw. David Wright is the only other Met to homer in an All-Star Game.

Cleon Jones went 2-for-4 and scored twice in his only All-Star Game in 1969. Bud Harrelson was 2-for-3 in the 1970 game. Lance

> Johnson went 3-for-4, stole a base, and scored a run in 1996. Jose Reyes did the same thing in his All-Star debut in 2007.
> Billy Wagner allowed key runs in NL losses in both '07 and '08, a harbinger of how both Mets seasons would end. Francisco Rodriguez pitched a perfect inning in a losing effort. Fitting, once again.

bat borrowed from Cub Billy Williams, Callison had his mind made up before he stepped in the batter's box. "I said, 'I'm going to hit the first pitch I can and not let him work me,'" Callison said years later (he died at age 67 in 2006). "He threw me a high fastball, and I hit it. It was a big deal. It happened in New York, so that makes it bigger."

It was such a big deal it would have to do for All-Star excitement in these parts for four decades and counting.

# 74 40–120

Records are, by nature, made to be broken, but one club mark no Mets fan ever wants to see surpassed is the club's first-year record of 40–120. The 1962 Mets, a well-intentioned but poorly put together group, helped rethink the entire expansion draft. (It was set up in 1969 and subsequent drafts allowed new teams to pick from a larger pool of players.) But it was too late for the Mets.

The Mets dropped their first nine, won one, and then lost another three straight. The Mets rallied early on and, following two double-header sweeps of the Milwaukee Braves just over a week apart, the Mets stood at 12–19 on May 20. They then embarked on a 17-game losing streak that not only remains the franchise record, but it also set a New York baseball worst (breaking Brooklyn's 1944 mark of 16). The race to 120 losses was on.

The Mets were a source of comedy in New York and around the country. When everything was in, the Mets led the league in all sorts of categories. Offensively, they were last in hits (1,318), batting average (.240), and doubles (166). And for you OBP freaks out there, the original Mets actually drew more walks than any NL team (616). Fat lot of good it did them.

It was on the mound and in the field, however, where the original Mets really stood out. They led the NL in most hits allowed (1,577), most hit batters (52), worst ERA (5.04), most earned runs (801), and most total runs allowed (948), which brings us to the hallmark stat of the team: most errors committed (210).

Yet contrary to popular belief, others have actually lost more often than the 1962 Mets. The 1899 Cleveland Spiders were on the other end of the spectrum: a team leaving the league rather than entering it. Cleveland was contracted out of the National League—along with three other teams after the 1899 season—but the Spiders really deserved it. Part of a baseball syndicate that also owned the St. Louis club, any Spider even remotely talented was sent to St. Louis, including a pitcher named Cy Young. The Perfectos, forerunners to the Cardinals, had experienced a .221 winning percentage at 29–102 just two years earlier, and the restocked 1899 franchise finished fifth but were still 65½ games ahead of the Spiders. Cleveland wound up 84 games behind first-place Brooklyn. The Spiders' 20–134 record resulted in a winning percentage—and the term is used loosely—of .130.

Other 19th-century teams as bad or worse than the original Mets include the 1890 Pirates (23–113, .169), Louisville of the American Association in 1889 (27–111, .196), Washington's NL club in 1886 (28–92, .233), Detroit NL in 1884 (28–84, .250), Washington AA in 1884 (12–51, .190), 1883 Phillies (17–81, .173), Worchester NL in 1882 (18–66, .214), Milwaukee NL in

*Casey Stengel, shown here with Pirates skipper Danny Murtaugh, presided over the 120-loss Mets in their 1962 inaugural season.*

1878 (15–45, .250), and all the way back in the inaugural year of the National League in 1876 there were two such clubs: Philadelphia (14–45, .237) and Cincinnati (9–56, .138). Ties and the Union Association aren't included.

The 20th century and 154-game schedule had the 1916 Philadelphia Athletics in the American League with a percentage of .235 and a mark of 36–117. How about those Braves? The 1935 Boston club had Babe Ruth—he didn't stay long—and went just 38–115 for a .248 percentage.

A close one was the 2003 Detroit Tigers. That club endured 24-hour-a-day mockery via the Internet concerning their mythical "chase" of the Mets. A "walk-off" wild pitch by Jesse Orosco in his last career appearance helped the Tigers avoid their dreaded 120th loss. The '62 Mets had a tie and a rainout that weren't made up. The Tigers played straight through and finished with a 43–119 mark and .265 winning percentage. Three seasons later they were in the World Series.

That's not something the Mets could say. It took them seven losing seasons before they not only reached the World Series but won it.

# 75 Ron Darling

Ron Darling was Honolulu-born, Ivy-educated, and cover-of-*GQ* handsome, but with the game on the line he was all about pitching. Just four other Mets made more starts than Darling (241), and only Tom Seaver, Jerry Koosman, and Dwight Gooden exceeded his 1,620 innings. Likewise, those same three pitchers are the only ones to surpass his totals for walks and hits. Darling

*Current broadcaster and 99-Met game winner Ron Darling (third from left), along with Bob Ojeda, Sid Fernandez, and Dwight Gooden, pitched the Mets to the '86 world championship.*

just missed joining that trio in the 100-win circle, forever stuck on 99 as a Met.

Yet Darling is the only Met in history to start a Game 7 twice. He didn't pitch well either time, though the Mets rallied to win his final start in the 1986 World Series (they lost to the Dodgers in the NLCS two years later). Only Tom Seaver and Al Leiter, who pitched in an extra round of playoffs, started more postseason games than Darling. He and Jon Matlack are the only Mets to start three times in one World Series.

Darling also had that cock-of-the-walk manner like most of his '80s teammates. The longest-tenured Met on the 1986 starting staff, Darling was barely 26 when the team clinched the division crown.

The Mets acquired Darling and Walt Terrell from the Rangers for Lee Mazzilli on April 1, 1982. The April fool was on Texas. A first-round pick the previous year out of Yale, Darling got the instruction

## 300-W and 3,000-K Clubs

While 2007 will be remembered for its bitter ending, two Mets pitchers reached significant milestones less than a month apart during that summer. Tom Glavine became the first Met to reach 300 career wins—Warren Spahn, Tom Seaver, and Nolan Ryan all did it with other teams—and joined just 22 others in that exclusive club. Although coverage of Glavine's milestone at Wrigley Field was dwarfed by Barry Bonds setting the home run record that same week in August, and despite Glavine failing the Mets miserably at the end of the season before his retreat to Atlanta (where he won his first 242), 300 victories is still a special number. Glavine was the ninth pitcher since 1982 to reach the milestone, the biggest crop of 300-game winners of any quarter century. Randy Johnson reached 300 wins in 2009, but it doesn't seem like anyone else will be joining the club anytime soon.

While Glavine had to wait two starts to earn number 300, Pedro Martinez had to wait almost a year to notch his 3,000th strikeout. He fanned Reds pitcher Aaron Harang for the landmark strikeout in his first start after rotator cuff surgery on September 3. He was the 14th pitcher to reach the mark. No pitcher had ever come as close as Pedro to 3,000 without reaching it. Jim Bunning, he of the perfect game for the Phillies at Shea Stadium in 1964, came the closest, and he was still probably a year shy of the mark at 2,855. Martinez should join Bunning and the two former Mets who preceded him in the 3,000-K club— Ryan (who reached the mark with the Astros in 1980) and Seaver (with the Reds in 1981)—in the Hall of Fame in Cooperstown.

he needed in the minors and pitching-friendly Shea helped his confidence during his rapid ascent to the majors. One of Jesse Orosco's rare poor outings in 1983 cost Darling his first major league win, but he took care of it himself with a complete-game victory over Pittsburgh in his final start. Darling's name was written in ink for the 1984 rotation and he had a solid if completely overlooked rookie season because of Doc Gooden's explosive debut. Darling went 16–6 and 15–6 the next two seasons. He had an ERA under 3.00 both years but made the All-Star team only in 1985 because of the plethora of Mets worthy of the honor. He remained a Met until 1991; traded to Montreal, he lasted three games there before being sent to Oakland. He started for Tony La Russa until 1995.

Darling was the last Met to clinch a division title with a complete game (1988), the only Mets pitcher to win a Gold Glove (1989), and the lone relief appearance in his first 208 games was the last inning of the epic 19-inning game in Atlanta on July 4, 1985. As announcer for the Mets since 2006, brilliantly teamed with Keith Hernandez and Gary Cohen, Darling has become the last word on the franchise's execution, mindset, and motivation. When the usually collected Darling wore a microphone on the field for the 20th reunion of the world championship team and reported the memories and the crowd made him "a little verklempt," he made everyone at home feel it, too.

# 76 One Dog, One Season

Lance Johnson played just 232 games as a Met, yet he holds two significant team batting records. In 1996 Johnson, signed as a free agent from the White Sox, set still-standing club records for hits (227) and triples (21). Jose Reyes topped Johnson's record 682 at-bats in 2005, and others have passed his 117 runs. His 50 stolen bases fell short of Mookie Wilson's single-season steals record of 58 (1982) and his .333 average was seven points below the .340 mark set by Cleon Jones in 1969. (Both marks have since been surpassed.)

One Dog was no one-trick puppy, but he was a one-season Mets wonder. Originally signed by the Cardinals, he had 59 National League at-bats in 1987 before going to the White Sox and becoming a solid leadoff hitter with a propensity for triples. He led

# Generation Kaput

The 1996 season was supposed to mark the beginning of Generation K. Three young stud pitchers were set to emerge from the Mets minor leagues and unleash their fastball fury on big leaguers. It was going to be big. Even the two guys who fans at Shea had seen—Jason Isringhausen, who won 20 games over three different levels in 1995 (including a 9–2 record with a 2.81 ERA for the Mets), and Bill Pulsipher, with that wicked southpaw action (5–7, 3.98 ERA for New York)—would pale in comparison with Paul Wilson. The 1994 first draft pick in the nation, Wilson had led the Eastern League with a 2.17 ERA for Binghamton before moving up to Norfolk and putting together a 2.85 ERA. Fifty wins among them in '96 could put the Mets back over the hump. They won 11 and lost 26.

To their credit, two combined for 53 starts in 1996, which was 39 more than they would make the rest of their Mets careers. Pulsipher blew out his arm in spring training. Wilson showed flashes of brilliance before hurting his arm in September. He finished at 5–12 with a 5.38 ERA. His only complete game for the club ended with Sammy Sosa's "hop-off" homer across Waveland Avenue in the bottom of the ninth inning.

Pulsipher and Wilson never won again after their rookie seasons for the Mets. Isringhausen slowly progressed through injuries and ridiculous behavior (playing softball for a team from Hooters while on a rehab assignment comes to mind). In 1999, with the Mets needing relief pitching and Isringhausen showing no signs of filling that void, general manager Steve Phillips traded Izzy and sidearmer Greg McMichael to Oakland for completely shot Billy Taylor. Izzy was an All-Star closer the following year. A much better trade was worked out the next summer with Wilson (along with Jason Tyner, who couldn't hit a home run in a Wiffle ball game) going to Tampa Bay for useful reliever Rick White and bench bopper Bubba Trammell. Pulsipher? Phillips traded him away twice and acquired him once in a three-year span without any results. It was hard for Mets fans—or the Mets GM—to have much faith in the club's farm system after Generation K's early TKO.

the American League in three-baggers for four straight years, but he never put up numbers like he displayed as a Met.

The 33-year-old Johnson was chased around the bases by the best-hitting Mets team to that point (.270), fueled by monster seasons from Todd Hundley, who set the club and NL catcher's mark with 41 home runs, and Bernard Gilkey, who established the Mets' record for doubles (44) and tied the club RBIs mark (117). Johnson had his tongue hanging during the dog days of summer, going 24 games without a triple. Yet One Dog had already broken the club record a month earlier. His 31 doubles weren't near the club mark, but it was 13 more than he ever collected in a season. His 69 RBIs represented a dozen more than his previous best. Alas, his 33 walks angered those who demand on-base percentage, especially from a leadoff hitter. Johnson didn't have time for OBP. He was too busy hitting everything in sight.

His average crept steadily all year: .285 in mid-May; .306 on June 9; .322 at the All-Star break; it reached .333 when he broke Felix Millan's 21-year-old hits record of 191 in early September; it reached as high as .336 the last week of the season before a 2-for-13 finish left it at .333. Johnson had 35 infield hits and 75 multihit games, both tops in the game.

He even hit in games that didn't count. The All-Star Game—still just a little old exhibition—belonged to Lance with a 3-for-4 night with a stolen base and a run as he played the entire game because of an injury to Tony Gwynn. The MVP went to some guy named Piazza (still a Dodger then). Through 2009 the NL hadn't won an All-Star Game since Lance's big night.

Too bad the Mets couldn't pitch. The club's 4.22 ERA was the highest since the year Shea Stadium opened (4.25 in 1964). Manager Dallas Green was fired in August 1996 and the team lost 91 times. Johnson had leg problems and Bobby Valentine issues in 1997 and wound up a Cub in a six-player deal, replaced in center field by Brian McRae. B-Mac was no '96 Lance Johnson. No one's been.

# 77 Hendu Can Do

Any purported fan who rips the Mets when they're in first place—or within hailing distance of same—should try to recall what life was like in days gone by. One might suggest a daylong loop of the 1979 Mets highlight film (entitled *Fireworks*), and if the subject is reluctant, perhaps strap him or her into one of those old wooden seats from Shea with eyes forced open like Alex in *A Clockwork Orange*. Real horror show.

The last three years of the 1970s tested a Mets fan's will to continue following the team or even the game. The 1980 season started with little reason for optimism. A 15–4 loss to Cincinnati in mid-May left the Mets at 9–18, the worst record in baseball. Over the next month the Mets—the same team that had been forced to win their last six games a year earlier just to avoid 100 losses—went 17–9.

A 12-game homestand in June began with two losses, but the Mets rebounded with four straight wins, including three in a row against the defending world champion Pirates. The Mets then swept the Dodgers—punctuated by Mike Jorgensen's game-ending grand slam—to give the club seven wins in eight games. This was heady stuff. Warner Wolf and other local sportscasters admonished Mets fans for not supporting their team. Only 16,580 a night had come to Shea for the first 10 games of this eye-opening homestand. The team's hokey advertising campaign under the new Doubleday/Wilpon ownership—"The Magic Is Back"—couldn't be true, could it? The Mets were still only in fourth place, six games out. But these were Joe Torre's Mets, featuring the likes of Joel Youngblood, Elliott Maddox, and Frank Taveras. Fourth place meant they were ahead of two teams!

The bravest among the 22,918 who filed into Shea for the first Saturday night game of the season on June 14 had visions of 1973, when this underdog club with a beleaguered manager dared to paw through a mediocre division to win the pennant. Back in the present, Pete Falcone was knocked out in the second inning by last-place San Francisco. Sigh.

But the game moved on. The presentation of the fan of the night, chosen by whirling a camera several times before stopping on a lucky individual to the cue of Jay & the Americans' version of "This Magic Moment," brought a few smiles, but the Giants increased their lead to 6–0.

The Mets showed their first stirrings of life when a single, an error, a patented Taveras bunt single, and a sacrifice fly by new guy

## Joe Torre, Player/Manager

Joe Torre was the only player/manager in Mets history. He was also the only person ever elevated from the club's active roster to make out the lineup card. The overall results between 1977 and 1981 weren't good (286–420), but his first few weeks on the job were.

With the Mets in last place at 15–30, manager Joe Frazier was fired on May 31, 1977. Torre, 36, had been secretly called back to New York at the end of a road trip a week earlier to discuss taking over the team. Nearly traded to the Mets in 1969 before the Braves sent him to St. Louis, where he earned the 1971 NL MVP and batting championship, Torre was a career .297 hitter. The Mets, in desperate need of hitters, kept him on the active roster after his 1977 promotion.

Torre sent himself up to bat twice. The first time he batted with men on second and third in the tenth inning of a tie game against the Phillies on June 5. He was intentionally walked, and the Mets won on a subsequent wild pitch. The second time he flied out in the ninth inning of a blowout loss against Houston on June 17, two days after the devastating trades of Tom Seaver and Dave Kingman. This was obviously a youth movement now, and Torre took a seat for good. His Mets tenure started off at 10–4, but it would be a long time before Torre or the Mets saw that kind of record again.

Claudell Washington made it 6–1 against John Montefusco. The rally was snuffed, however, when Steve Henderson struck out. Hendu singled in a run in the eighth to knock out Montefusco, but John Stearns ended that rally by whiffing against Greg Minton.

Some fans had long since tuned out the game when the bottom of the ninth began. It seemed like the smart move when the Mets sandwiched a Doug Flynn bunt single between two ground-outs. Lee Mazzilli kept the game alive with a single to make it 6–3. Then Frank Taveras walked. He never walked. A year earlier he'd drawn just 33 in 164 games—both bizarrely true numbers—and now the game continued due to his sudden patience. Fans who'd left their seats peeked their heads back in. Now Washington singled in the fourth run. Allen Ripley, a starting pitcher, came in from the bullpen to face Henderson, the cleanup hitter with no home runs.

The Mets didn't do home runs—the club's meager season output, the *Daily News* constantly reminded, couldn't even keep pace with Roger Maris's total from one season—and opposite-field home runs were so rare as to not even be thought to exist. So Henderson's drive to right field seemed like the end the moment it left the bat. It was. Just not in a way Mets fans had any reason to expect. It was gone. The Mets won!

To anyone who was there, watched it on Channel 9, heard it on WMCA, or just read about it in the Sunday paper, Hendu's home run was a touchstone moment. Yes, the team lost the next seven and would drop 95 games despite a dalliance with first place in July, they would only match Maris's 61 in '61 output, and the team would not have a winning season until 1984. But June 14, 1980, to loyal Mets fans of the day, was like finding a $10 bill in the street. It came out of nowhere, would be spent quickly with little to show for it, and did nothing to keep the wallet full. Yet every once in a while, you thought about the moment you looked down and it appeared out of nowhere. This Magic Moment.

# 78 Cast of Characters

Lastings Milledge was probably the most notorious Mets character of recent vintage. He raised eyebrows when he high-fived fans after his first major league home run—a game-tying shot in extra innings—in June 2006. A year and a poorly received rap single later, Milledge ruffled some feathers when he showily celebrated pitcher John Maine's first career home run and then his own shot later in the game. Some insist his showboating even fired up the last-place Marlins to beat the Mets in the 2007 do-or-die finale.

"I like to call it colorful. I don't like to use the word flamboyant," Milledge said. "It's kind of like if you have two TVs. And if you've got a black-and-white and a color one, which one do you choose, you know? They both show the same thing, but one is more appealing to the eye."

The Mets, tired of Milledge's act, traded him late in '07 to Washington. Characters usually don't last long in Flushing unless their play is as memorable as their antics.

**Jimmy Piersall:** This certified baseball nut ran the bases backwards after his 100th career home run in 1963, against future Mets manager Dallas Green. It was his only homer as a Met because upstaged Casey Stengel and company released him a few weeks later.

**George Theodore:** Flaky to a fault, he personified the skinny kid in us all with more heart than talent. The bespectacled Stork is known in Shea annals for dislocating his hip in a scary collision with Don Hahn in 1973, but he showed chutzpah as a minor leaguer writing farm director Joe McDonald with a list of demands, including a raise and promotion from Class A to AAA (plus athletic glasses, stickers, bats, and an introduction to Yogi Berra). He got everything he wanted, plus a 105-game Mets career.

# Fan's VIEW

## Robert Pizzella
## (Wellesley, Massachusetts)

### The Dog Days of the '70s

On November 16, 1975, I was turning 10 years old and my mother walked into our house in New Rochelle, New York, with my birthday present: a new puppy. This little lab/cocker spaniel pup looked like a winner to me, so I named him Seaver to honor the best pitcher in baseball. Even on his tough days, the thrill never faded watching Tom Terrific.

I had 41's pitching motion down cold, and I always rooted for Tom Seaver to win the coveted "Gillette Foamy Face of the Game Award," even if he didn't get the W. I now live in Massachusetts (haven't converted, don't worry) and just around the corner from me is Seaver Street. Interestingly enough, there is no number 41.

I can still hear Bob Murphy saying, "And then it all (singing the word) broke loose in the bottom of the ninth when Ed Kranepool hit a pinch-hit Baltimore chopper over the head of the first baseman to score the winning run. Robert Apodaca gets the win" (not Bob Apodaca, as everyone called him and as it read on his baseball card). Then there was Lindsey Nelson. The handoff would go something like this:

Ralph Kiner: "And now for the play by play, Lindsey Nelson…"

Lindsey Nelson: "Thank you very much Ralph Kiner and HELLO (very loud) again everybody. Let me remind you now that the Mets are winning 4–1 in the top of the fifth inning with Tom Seaver on the mound."

Who could forget that famous Kiner refrain: "It's going, going, it is gone, good-bye. That's Dave Kingman's 28th home run of the year."

I was such a Mets fan that my brother Don and I would pray for coach Joe Pignatano's tomato plants in the right-field bullpen! I think Rick Baldwin and Skip Lockwood were good gardeners.

I would practice being Wayne Garrett with the barehand play on the grass near third after a bunt. I never was able to find those flip-up sunglasses.

Still, I wouldn't trade those years as an early Mets fan for anything. It showed me that I can take a punch and hang in.

**Willie Montanez:** Snatch catches and stutter-strutting around the bases after home runs brought a slight pulse to the corpse in 1978. It wasn't nearly enough.

**Wally Backman:** The Mets' version of Paul O'Neill, only shorter. The scrappy second baseman was always dirty and mad about something. His drag bunt and dive in Game 3 of the 1986 NLCS was out of the baseline, but it was so typically Backman to get Houston all riled up minutes before serving up Lenny Dykstra's home run. Backman was fired days after Arizona hired him in '04 because of personal issues. The Mets hired him to manage Class A Brooklyn in 2009.

**Turk Wendell:** He slammed the rosin bag to excited cheers at Shea and groans on the road. A good-natured guy whose stated goal was to play one year for free (didn't happen), he wore a necklace of animal teeth around his neck and was one of the most durable pitchers in Mets history.

**Rickey Henderson:** A teammate of Wendell's and a coach of Milledge's, he talked to fans while in left field, played cards with Bobby Bonilla while the Mets lost in the 1999 NLCS, and ended his tenure as a Mets player after admiring a long fly that would end up being a long single for the stolen-base king. "People used to think I was showing them up," Henderson said. "I just kept on doing it until they got the message, 'This is who I am.' That's what makes the game fun."

**Paul Lo Duca:** Like having Wally Backman behind the plate. Lo Duca kept the players loose and wasn't afraid to tear into anybody, as his "Captain Red Ass" moniker clearly signified. A horse owner who loves the track and the young ladies, he can be hot with the bat and under the collar. The Mets let him go after the 2007 season, even before he was implicated in the Mitchell Report.

# 79 What's with All the Different Uniforms?

It's all about marketing. The Mets sell a lot of uniforms and having a variety seems to increase sales and produces a coveted revenue stream for the club. This supposedly trickles back to you—the fan—in that the extra money may be used to acquire better organizational playing talent or to pay off the debt on Citi Field, though ticket sales will also cover that.

That's the short answer. You really thought that would be the end of it?

In the beginning there was blue and white with a little orange. Starting from scratch, the Mets had almost 200 seasons of cumulative New York baseball history to keep them grounded. It was the early 1960s, and fashion hadn't yet gone loopy. The Angels had halos and the Colt .45s were working on a gun motif, but the other ostensibly new clubs—the new Washington Senators and the old Washington Senators, now called the Minnesota Twins—hadn't exactly set the fashion world on fire. The Mets used old ideas: orange from the departed New York Giants, blue from the Brooklyn Dodgers, and pinstripes from the Yankees. They had a patch with a "skyline" logo on the sleeve of their gray "New York" road uniforms; after four seasons they added it to the home duds.

That's pretty much how the uniform stayed until 1978, when the Mets went to a pullover with piping on the sleeves and neck. An alternate blue jersey and the racing stripes followed in 1982. The racing stripes weren't great fashion, but they did look cool flying through the air onto a pile of wriggling bodies in 1986.

The racing stripes lasted a decade, replaced by a flashy line underneath "Mets," just in time for their first 100-loss season in more than a quarter century. After the 1994 strike they came back

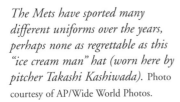
*The Mets have sported many different uniforms over the years, perhaps none as regrettable as this "ice cream man" hat (worn here by pitcher Takashi Kashiwada).* Photo courtesy of AP/Wide World Photos.

with no underscore on the team or city name. The Mets went to an all-white alternate uniform in 1997 and made the first change to the hat since 1962. The white alternate hat was called the "ice cream man hat" and was rarely worn after the first few weeks of the season. The next year the Mets added black to the hats—black was all the rage in sports colors just then—and in 1999 they added black home and road jerseys plus all-black hats. The team got matching batting helmets as well.

The Mets didn't discard any uniforms—and even added batting practice duds—creating myriad potential outfits each night for equipment manager Charlie Samuels to choose from. (The Mets have also occasionally worn special one-time jerseys, such as Negro League uniforms to honor the past, the hideously futuristic "Mercury Mets," and the "Los Mets" look on their annual Latin night.)

So what will the Mets wear tonight? Anything goes. Will you remember which outfit it was the next day? Magic 8-Ball says, "Doubtful."

## Meet the New Duds

A month and a half after the end of the 2009 season, the Mets announced a new alternate uniform that combines "new and old elements of Mets uniforms," according to the press release. The cream-colored uniform includes pinstripes, the number on both front and back, as well as the player's name…and the black "drop" shadow that has irked Mets traditionalists for more than a decade. It's close, though not a direct copy of the 1969 retro jersey worn by the Miracle Mets for the night in their honor in August 2009 (the '09 Mets, however, did not wear retro uniforms for a throwback night).

The 2010 uniform change was part of a series of alterations to both the uniform and Citi Field in an effort to honor the team's past, which many critics felt had been overlooked in the new stadium. Initial reaction to the new duds was mixed. Others didn't seem to care what the team wore, as long as there were players of talent wearing the uniform. Fair enough.

The Mets announced that the white uniform, which had become the home uni of choice for the Mets, would be worn more than any other. The new jersey would slide in front of the black alternate jersey. How the laundry shakes out, only time will tell.

# 80 What Are Those Numbers on the Wall for?

Perhaps 90 percent of first-time visitors to Citi Field, plus some stadium employees, ask the question in some form or another. Few get all four on the first try, unless they've been following along at home: Casey Stengel, Gil Hodges, Tom Seaver, and Jackie Robinson. How did they achieve their raised station above the left-field wall? One broke his hip, another died suddenly, the Franchise was forever destined for the honor, and the fourth of this group retired before the Mets even existed. But here's a little more—oh, what the heck—a lot more background on the names and numbers.

## 37: Casey Stengel (Retired September 2, 1965)

Hall of Fame manager of the Yankees and humorous narrator of the spectacularly bad New York Mets of the 1960s, Casey Stengel dubbed the club many things, the most lfamous being "Amazin'." Just as some people grumbled the team should be making more progress in its fourth season of existence, Stengel broke his hip. Doctors told the 75-year-old manager, who'd debuted as a big leaguer in Brooklyn 53 years earlier, that it was finally time to take off the uniform. Stengel made the awful Mets a joy to be around.

## 14: Gil Hodges (Retired June 9, 1973)

Gil Hodges was a Brooklyn folk hero and the first Met to set a positive record. He hit the first home run in Mets history in 1962 and broke Ralph Kiner's mark for most career home runs by a right-handed batter in the National League at 370, a number nearly doubled later by Hank Aaron. But Hodges's slugging prowess had nothing to do with his elevation to the wall. He managed the 100–1 shot Mets to the 1969 world championship less than a year after suffering a heart attack. He got everything he could out of his players and even willed a baseball to bleed shoe polish. He died of a heart attack while still manager in April 1972. In September 2007 the Mets had a night for Hodges (though hundreds of people lined the field during the ceremony for some unrelated event) to honor his induction into the Marine Corps Sports Hall of Fame. Former Marine Tom Seaver, a 2003 inductee, spoke passionately about his manager. Brooklyn's own Joan Hodges was, as always, beautiful, humble, and appreciative.

## 41: Tom Seaver (Retired July 24, 1988)

The Mets Hall of Fame had no five-year waiting period to bring in Tom Seaver, and the club retired Tom Seaver's number to boot, four years before he was eligible to glide into Cooperstown. A three-time Cy Young winner and the team leader in his first decade as a Met (plus a too-brief comeback in 1983), Seaver *was* the Mets to a

# Who Else Wore Those Numbers?

Well, someone asked.

No one else has ever worn 37. Casey Stengel had it before he ever came to the Mets and he brought it along when he was hired as the first manager. When he was forced to retire in 1965, his 37 went with him.

Gil Hodges likewise brought his number with him, but then he was traded to Washington to manage. While he was making the expansion Senators semi-respectable, a couple of others slipped on 14 in New York. Ron Swoboda tried it first and then Ken Boyer suited up. Boyer, two years removed from NL MVP for the 1964 world champion Cardinals, had the first solid season by a Mets third baseman: .266 average and 14 home runs while leading the club with 61 RBIs and 28 doubles for the first Mets club not to lose 100 games. Although Boyer slipped in '67, the Mets were still able to send him to the White Sox in a deal that returned J.C. Martin, whose wrist would prove supple enough to deflect a throw to win Game 4 of the '69 World Series.

Before Tom Seaver, there were four other pitchers in 41. Clem Labine was done, while Grover Powell and Jim Bethke didn't have much to give. Gordon Richardson fit the same category. Gordie had been a rookie on the '64 Cardinals and pitched twice—badly—in the World Series to qualify for a ring. The gravy train ended there. A few weeks before Christmas the lefty learned he was going to the Mets. He combined on a spring training no-hitter with Gary Kroll, but when Richardson couldn't get people out during the actual season…well, 41 was sitting vacant when Tom Seaver arrived in camp in 1967.

Number 42 was a different story. From the time Larry Elliott first wore it in 1964, the number had somewhat consistent wearers. It had key roles in two world championships with Ron Taylor and then Roger McDowell and was owned in between by other relievers—Chuck Taylor, Hank Webb, and Tom Hall—plus a "country gentleman," as Bob Murphy used to call perennial backup catcher Ron Hodges. Butch Huskey switched to 42 in 1995 to honor Jackie Robinson, little knowing that he would be in the starting lineup the night it was retired forever. Or until Mo Vaughn.

> Vaughn, like Huskey, was grandfathered in for 42. On a team with a long tradition of slothful first basemen, the one-time AL MVP's gimpy knees may well have made him the slowest of them all...plus a glove seemingly made of stone. On May 2, 2003, after grounding out to drop his average to .190, Vaughn came off the field for what turned out to be the last time. No. 42 would only exist on the wall.

generation of fans and the voice to another as a broadcaster (though his skills in the former far exceeded those in the latter).

### 42: Jackie Robinson (Retired April 15, 1997)

President Bill Clinton, Rachel Robinson, and numerous baseball greats were upstaged at Shea Stadium by commissioner Bud Selig, who announced that Robinson's 42 would be retired by every team "in perpetuity." Since that night at Shea to celebrate the 50th anniversary of Robinson's breaking of the color barrier, every professional ballpark has followed by hanging 42 in a spot of honor.

### Shea: William A. Shea (Retired April 8, 2008)

No numbers but letters spelling the name of the man most responsible for the Mets coming into being. The final Opening Day at Shea unveiled the name next to the numbers. The name followed the team to Citi Field, fittingly.

# 81 Read the Mets

This book would be incomplete without a listing of Mets mustreads. (Books are listed chronologically by year first published; sites are alphabetical.) Decorum forbids me from including any of the recent projects I have worked on, but *Mets Essential, Mets by the Numbers, Shea Good-Bye, The Miracle Has Landed*, and the *Mets Annual* magazine could be considered, in the immortal words of the late Bob Murphy, "Beautiful additions to your baseball library." And now we read...

## Mets Books

*Can't Anyone Here Play This Game?* by Jimmy Breslin. Chronicling the first year of the moribund Mets, it may be the best book ever written on a first-year team and may be the most entertaining book on the franchise.

*The New York Mets* by Leonard Koppett. From the dedication it's apparent that this will be an excellent book. Koppett, the late Mets beat writer from *The New York Times*, is one of the all-time greats. The only unfortunate thing is it only goes through 1969 (or 1973, depending on the edition). He was at least spared having to analyze the nightmare that followed.

*Screwball* by Tug McGraw and Joseph Durso. This 1974 book takes you into the insane "Ya Gotta Believe" season that was swirling down the toilet, reversed course, and just missed soiling the Oakland A's dynasty. Tug was in the middle of it all, and 1969, too. The world is a sadder place without him.

*If at First* by Keith Hernandez and Mark Bryan. I loved this book long before I worked with Keith on *Shea Good-Bye*. This is Keith at his most candid.

*The New York Mets: Twenty-Five Years of Baseball Magic* by Jack Lang and Mark Simon. This is the Mets bible. Jack Lang knew everything that ever happened to the Mets, and sometimes even had a hand in it. I wish he'd updated this 1986 book before his passing in early 2007.

*The Complete Year-by-Year NY Mets Fan's Almanac* by Duncan Bock and John Jordan. Not a sexy book, but it has great detail on the first 30 seasons in club history (through 1991). I've kept this close by for every Mets project I've worked on and, unlike many of the squads included within its pages, this book has never let me down.

*The Worst Team Money Could Buy* by Bob Klapisch and John Harper. This sheds too much light on an era I wish could stay buried forever, but it taught me two very important life lessons: becoming a beat reporter was not the route to happiness and doing so would forever tarnish my attachment to the team. The writers—and the horrid '92 Mets—led me to take another path. And saved me from getting bleached by Bret Saberhagen.

*The Bad Guys Won* by Jeff Pearlman. I overlooked the book at first in 2004 because I was so ready to move on from '86. Pearlman is a good writer, though, and he uses perspective to shed insight into a year that Mets fans think they know everything about. They don't. Pearlman does.

*The Ticket Out* by Michael Sokolove. This isn't really about the Mets. It is about one Met, Darryl Strawberry—where he came from and how he loused up his life so completely. Expertly written, it documents the lives of many members of the Crenshaw High team in Los Angeles.

*Pedro, Carlos, and Omar* by Adam Rubin. The *Daily News* beat writer ably handled the task of giving immediate perspective to a major transition in every aspect of franchise thinking, evaluation, and personnel.

Recent favorites: *Mets Fan* and *The Last Days of Shea* by Dana Brand; *Faith and Fear in Flushing* by Greg W. Prince; *The Complete Game* by Ron Darling; and the resissue of Stanley Cohen's *A Magic Summer*.

## Websites

**cranepoolforum.com:** Any site named after the longest tenured Met that weaves insightful comments from numerous sources and is responsible for the revitalization of the Schaefer Player of the Game Award is a site worth perusing.

**faithandfearinflushing.com:** Faith and Fear in Flushing is the de facto site when I need insight on a Mets game from four hours ago or four decades past. Greg Prince and Jason Fry are pro's pros, and I'm convinced that there's nothing that's ever happened to the Mets that one or both of them don't know and can't spin into an interesting yarn.

**loge13.com:** This is just outstanding. There's plenty of Mets stuff there, but I've also sat mesmerized, watching video of the goings-on at Shea without the blue and orange: snippets of Beatles songs from the 1965 concert, a '71 Grand Funk jam at Shea (shirts off, mutton-chops on), and watching The Who say farewell for the first time.

**mbtn.net:** I didn't say I wouldn't mention Mets by the Numbers website. Jon Springer's creation had me hooked before we ever tried to make it into a book. As someone who's long used Mets uniform numbers to memorize everything from phone numbers to passwords, it was like I stumbled on a secret society. It's not so secret anymore.

**meetthematts.com:** The name got my attention, but this is, as they claim, "Good Met fun." Two guys named Matt with shaved heads and shades cavort around the world, talking Mets, doing zany stunts, and wearing those flimsy blue jackets you used to be required to rent at the Diamond Club. Great Mets-themed improv.

**metsblog.com:** Matthew Cerrone does a great job in collecting all Mets information as it comes in and putting it in one place. He also provides analysis, interviews, and perspective in a timely manner. We can never get enough.

**metsgeek.com:** You mean there may be other people besides me who spent sunny summer days in their room as kids willing Roy Lee Jackson to get out Mike Schmidt in Strat-O-Matic? Anyway, the Mets genealogy—tracing how far back transactions for current players can be linked—is itself worth getting geeked up over. And there's plenty more.

**newyork.mets.mlb.com:** Yes, it's the company line, but it's the company you're reading this for. Plus it features longtime *Newsday* newshound Marty Noble, not to mention info on tickets, rainouts, policies, and other things that are hard to find elsewhere. It's also where you have to register for those hard-to-get ticket lotteries.

**nyfuturestars.com:** I don't know as much about the club's minor leaguers as I should (that's a habit developed when Steve Phillips traded every potential prospect for washed-up veteran relievers). This site tells you plenty about the guys on the farm as well as the guys in The Show.

**ultimatemets.com:** The Ultimate Mets Database lives up to its name. This stats-driven site has unbelievable breakdowns like individual season-by-season and game-by-game info. Need every Mets transaction ever? Bing! The most home runs by a Met in the 1970s? It's John Milner, our late, great "Hammer." Want to find out the club's all-time record against the Dodgers? You may not like the results of that one. There is no better place to do Mets research or fritter away time at work.

Besides baseball-reference.com and retrosheet.org, I also find myself at: centerfieldmaz.com, intheblack.com, metsfanbook.com, metspolice.com, metsreport.com, metswalkoffs.com, mikesmets.com, tedquarters.com, theeddiekranepoolsociety.blogspot.com, and a site that analyzed the first edition of this book like a series of term papers: yankees2000.com/y2k/.

# 82 Go to a Mets Road Game

Personally, I think you get a better feeling for a non–New York ballpark if you don't see the Mets play there because when the Mets are playing you concentrate more on the game than the ballpark experience. That said, I've made many road trips following the Mets and it's something that really has to be done at least once.

Trying to be fair to the home of the Mets won't stop me from telling it like it is at the ballparks the Mets have visited (including interleague play) since 1962. I missed all the parks torn down before 1975 and have yet to go inside several of the nicer new parks, including Petco, Comerica, and Safeco (sounds like a list of investment opportunities rather than ballparks). On the other end, I have never been to a few maligned ballparks like Tropicana and I missed Veterans Stadium and Fulton County Stadium purposely. I've been to the Metrodome for a Vikings game but never felt compelled to return to see the Twins.

Enough, already. Let's go to the ballpark. Lists are in order of goodness (and lousiness).

## The Best (The Short List)

**Tiger Stadium, Detroit:** The Mets only played there one series and were swept, but Tiger was simply as good a place for baseball as I've ever seen.

**Wrigley Field, Chicago:** Cubs fans can be rough, but a Friday afternoon game at Wrigley is one of the greatest guilty pleasures man has created. Even people who don't like baseball—if such people exist—make sure they get to Wrigley. Best NL ballpark since 1916.

**Fenway Park, Boston:** Enough has been said about this place, and the fans have kind of gone around the bend, but a bad seat there is better than a good seat in a lot of places. Stay gold, Fenway.

**Camden Yards, Baltimore:** Worth the hype. It's a shame the owner has turned it into a ghost town. If Baltimore is satisfied with ballpark perfection, and the Orioles don't demand a new stadium in another 20 years, this could be a multigenerational jewel.

**Kauffman Stadium, Kansas City:** Buried on the edge of Missouri, this is Dodger Stadium without the parking hassles or seventh-inning exits. This forward-thinking park was designed 35 years ago to be smaller than its contemporaries (with its neatly clipped decks) and prettier (with its signature fountains). I saw it before the recent renovations, but I'm hoping it hasn't changed for the worse. Visit K.C.'s Negro League Museum, too.

**Pac-Whatchamacallit Park, San Francisco:** There was plenty of whining about Candlestick (see "Worst Parks"), but you can't complain about this place. While it's more expensive than New York (that is, after all, where the Giants came from), it's worth a trip across the country for a single afternoon. If only the phone company would stop changing its name.

**Dodger Stadium, Los Angeles:** Once you get over the fact that this team was stolen from Brooklyn, it's quite a nice ballpark that wears its age extremely well. Dodger Stadium is something L.A. got right and a gem. Let's hope it stays that way.

**Minute Maid Park, Houston:** Wanted to hate it with the semi-dome, Tal's Hill, cheap homers, Enron, and all, but it's just a great place to watch a game. And in Texas that A/C and roof come in quite handy.

**PNC Park, Pittsburgh:** The better of Pennsylvania's two nice ballparks, this is what a retro park should feel like and play like. Yet while Honus Wagner, Willie Stargell, and Roberto Clemente all have massive statues, Ralph Kiner got a statue of just his hands and a bat at the bottom of the concourse in left field. You can see a lot of PNC in the details at Citi Field.

**County Stadium, Milwaukee:** A lot like Shea only with a Midwestern hospitality you'd never find in New York. Between the Braves, the Brewers, the brats, the bleachers, and Bernie's slide, that park had so much cool going for it—Milwaukee was, after all, the Fonz's hometown—so it was tragic that nerd owner/commissioner Bud Selig blew the place up. Miller Park has the charm of an airplane hangar.

# Fan's VIEW — Double Duty

### Another Take (Me Out to the Ballgame)

While I've been to 32 ballparks, there's still plenty more I haven't seen. As easy as it seems to make judgments about a park by watching on television, the only way to really know is to go. So I went to a couple of ballpark connoisseurs whose stories appear in other parts of this book to offer critiques of a few places the Mets have played. This is where all their business travel—with nights free for baseball—finally pays off.

Paul Lovetere (PL) has seen all 30 major league teams play a home game. Dan Carubia (DC) saw his first Mets road game in 1964 and when I called him in 2007, he was on his way to Petco Park to see the Mets and Padres. (A one-time usher at Shea, he now works at Joe Bruno Stadium, the Class-A ballpark in Troy, New York.)

**Coors Field, Denver:** The Rockies—the mountains—sitting in the mile-high purple row, buffalo burgers…nice. (PL) Big outfield, a lot of range to roam. Around the ballpark everything is built up, a great place to hang out before a game. (DC)

**Petco Park, San Diego:** The stadium was built to fit in with the warehouse in left field, which couldn't be torn down because it's a historical landmark. You can watch the game from the warehouse patio with a view of the bridge connecting San Diego to Coronado Island. There's a big sandbox for kids in right-center. In right field you can sit over the visiting bullpen, close enough that we became friendly with Guy Conti, then the Mets' bullpen coach. (DC)

**Safeco Field, Seattle:** The exposed-iron-beams look that's prevalent in the new parks works fantasticly with the surrounding neighborhood on the edge of an industrial area. Great, great views from the upper-left field concourse of Puget Sound and the ferries with commuters going back and forth. I like that when the retractable roof is closed, the sides remain open to the weather. You feel the chill in the air in the spring and October. (PL)

**Connie Mack Stadium, Philadelphia:** It reminded me a lot of Ebbets Field because left field had covered upper and lower stands. It's the first ballpark I remember seeing the Mets in their away uniforms.

Our seats were close enough to see inside the dugout and hear the sounds of the game. Really cool being there. (DC)

**Yankee Stadium (1923–1973):** My first game, age six. I remember the enormous flagpole and tombstone in center in play. ("Wow, Babe Ruth and Lou Gehrig are buried there.") In '71 it was old, faded painted seats with the verde green oxidized façade, not white like they made it later. (PL) With the low stands down each line, the fence couldn't have been four feet high. You sat in the first row in those seats and it was like being on the field. After the game you walked through the outfield, past the monuments, and out under the bleachers onto River Avenue. If you got there early you could go to the window exchange and for an extra 75¢ go to the other side by walking through the Yankees' bullpen. (DC)

**Jacobs Field, Cleveland:** Easy entrance into my seat from the turnstile in right field. No stairs, escalators, or ramps, just walk in and straight to the seats. I went during the height of the sellout string in the late 1990s. The crowd was really into it and that added to the atmosphere. (PL) Left field was the most interesting part because of the high wall with bleacher seats. (DC)

**Turner Field, Atlanta:** Hate the team but the stadium is great. They did an incredible job reconfiguring it from the site of the opening/closing ceremonies for the 1996 Olympics. You would never know it wasn't originally built for baseball. (PL) Lots of things to walk around and see there; the interactive games are fun. (DC)

**Busch Stadium, St. Louis (1966–2005):** They made the best of a bad situation. It has less of the held-captive feel to it than others built back then. The sea of red is impressive in the collegiate way. (PL). For an old park it was pretty cool because you were on top of the players. Even way out in center field—I never saw that angle because Shea doesn't have that—you were still close enough to tell they were throwing curveballs or sliders. (DC)

**Veterans Stadium, Philadelphia:** Like the others built in the early '70s it was the same: artificial turf and walk in a perfect circle without knowing what part of the field you're located in. Look out to the field from the concourse in the upper deck and all you see is the other side of the upper deck. (PL) No ambiance and you didn't feel close to the players. It was a place where you went to watch the game and didn't think about the ballpark. (DC)

## The Worst

**McAfee Coliseum, Oakland:** Notice this is the corporate version of the stadium, not the cavernous park that swallowed the Mets' dreams of the 1973 world championship. The monolith of empty seats Al Davis demanded as ransom for the Raiders is a crime; it made it easier to hit home runs and is just damned ugly. As Gertrude Stein said of Oakland, "There is no there there."

**Three Rivers Stadium, Pittsburgh:** The Mets were spanked there often, but this place made Shea seem like a palace. I'm sure it was fine for Steelers games.

**RFK Stadium, Washington:** Built shortly before Shea, but you can see the differences a couple years made in design. You can be sitting in southwestern Virginia and still be in the lower deck staring at security in the press level staring at you. While it was pitcher-friendly, RFK's is a much better place for concerts, football, and soccer than baseball.

**Candlestick Park, San Francisco:** Again reminiscent of Shea, but the wind currents here were far worse and the fans constantly complained about the cold. (They were right!) Saw the Mets there at night in 1988 and I had to bribe our crew to stay to the end, even though I'd brought blankets, sleeping bags, and jackets...in August. Went for a day game a few years later and it was gorgeous. 3-Com Park may have been the only corporate name worse than its current handle as home of the 49ers: Monster Park.

**Sun Life Stadium, Miami:** It's great that it's so deep to center—more parks should try this—but it's like there's a state law forbidding anyone from saying that the Marlins play there. Another law states the name has to change every year. The franchise deserves better, so they will move into a brand-new ballpark to be built on the site of the old Orange Bowl in 2012.

# 83 The Road Is Long

The last two years the Mets have traveled to new parks in D.C. and the Bronx, making it 53 parks the team has visited (including the postseason). That includes brief stops in Mexico, Puerto Rico, and Japan. The following list includes all these parks, but it does not count the Polo Grounds, Shea Stadium, or Citi Field. County Stadium is listed under both the Braves and the Brewers.

To keep from wasting everyone's time by going through the litany of changing corporate names that have been forced on the public—unless, of course, a company plans on sending some naming rights fees this way—the list only includes the name on the park when the Mets first played there. Cities are listed if it is different than the current host city.

**National League**
Astros: Colt Stadium, Astrodome, Enron Field
Braves: County Stadium (Milwaukee), Fulton County Stadium, Turner Field
Brewers: County Stadium, Miller Park
Cardinals: Busch Stadium (I) previously known as Sportsman's Park, Busch Stadium (II), Busch Stadium (III)
Cubs: Wrigley Field, Tokyo Dome (Japan)
Diamondbacks: Bank One Ballpark
Dodgers: Dodger Stadium
Expos/Nationals: Parc Jarry (Montreal), Olympic Stadium (Montreal), Estadio Hiram Bithorn (San Juan), Robert F. Kennedy Stadium, Nationals Park
Giants: Candlestick Park, Pac Bell Park

Marlins: Joe Robbie Stadium

Padres: San Diego Stadium, Estadio Monterrey (Mexico), Petco Park

Pirates: Forbes Field, Three Rivers Stadium, PNC Park

Phillies: Connie Mack Stadium, Veterans Stadium, Citizens Bank Ballpark

Reds: Crosley Field, Riverfront Stadium, Great American Ball Park

Rockies: Mile High Stadium, Coors Field

**American League**

A's: Oakland Coliseum

Angels: Edison International Field

Blue Jays: SkyDome

Devil Rays: Tropicana Field

Indians: Jacobs Field

Mariners: Safeco Field

Orioles: Memorial Stadium (World Series only), Camden Yards

Rangers: Ballpark in Arlington

## Tiger Stadium Tames Mets

Tiger Stadium may rate high on the ballparks list with fans lucky enough to have seen games there, but the Mets weren't exactly fans of Detroit's old ballyard. During the 87 years the stadium existed (1912–1999), the Mets played there once. It was a series to forget. In 1997, the first year of interleague play, the Tigers walloped the Mets by a combined score of 31–13 in a three-game sweep. The Dodgers, Reds, and Cardinals scored about the same number of runs against the '97 Mets…and they played the Mets 11 times apiece. The Mets did not play in Detroit again for a decade, thanks to the vagaries of the interleague schedule and the shifting of Detroit from the AL East to the AL Central. Detroit won two of three against the Mets in Comerica Park in 2007. The Mets swept the Tigers in their only visit to Shea in 2004.

Red Sox: Fenway Park
Royals: Kauffman Stadium
Tigers: Tiger Stadium, Comerica Park
Twins: Hubert H. Humphrey Metrodome
White Sox: Comiskey Park (II)
Yankees: Yankee Stadium, Yankee Stadium Redux

# 84 Battles Loved and Lost, Then Forgotten

The realignment of divisions in 1994 kept the Mets in the National League East, but several rivals were whisked away to the Central Division. The adoption of the unbalanced schedule in 2001—plus the continuation of interleague play—made sure the Mets played some old foes as few as six times per year. Here's what you're missing.

## Mets–Cubs

In 1962 the clubs combined to finish 99–223 and 103 games out of first. The Mets were the worst expansion team ever (40–120) and the Cubs were a disgrace in the laughable "College of Coaches." All that had changed by 1969 when they battled tooth and nail for the first NL East title. The Mets won while the Cubs collapsed, creating animosity that elder Chicagoans—led by Ron Santo—have held onto through all these years. The Mets clinched the 1973 and 1986 NL East titles against Chicago, but New York finished second to the Cubs in the East in 1984 and 1989. The most contentious season since the division shift was 1998, when the Cubs took the wild-card while the Mets folded in the closing week of the season.

## Mets–Pirates

The Mets and Bucs were quite the rivals through the first 30 years of their shared existence. The Pirates were the first team the Mets ever played at the Polo Grounds and at Shea Stadium (the Bucs won both). Pittsburgh was also the first team the Mets ever beat (April 23, 1962). That was the only time in nine tries the fledgling Mets won at Forbes Field that year; they were also 1–8 against Pittsburgh at home. Even in 1969 the Mets had trouble with the Pirates; they were just 4–5 against the Bucs at Shea and were no-hit by Bob Moose on September 20. A crazy carom in 1973 off a Pirate's poke helped the Mets move past Pittsburgh for the NL East crown, but the Bucs otherwise ruled the rivalry. Pittsburgh won nine division titles to the four the Mets accrued while they shared the NL East (1969–1993). Willie Stargell hit more home runs against the Mets (60) than any other slugger in history and launched the first homer at Shea in 1964. The Mets hold the slightest edge at home (174–171–1) while the Bucs have dominated at their three homes (186–152–1).

## Mets–Cardinals

This one runs hot and cold. The Mets played their first-ever game in St. Louis and clinched their first-ever division title at home against the Cardinals. While the rivalry hasn't always meant a lot, at other times it has been life and death in two passionate baseball cities. The Mets finished a close and frustrating second to the Cardinals in both 1985 and 1987, causing much cursing of Whitey Herzog around New York. The Mets followed both times with dominating seasons, going 8–1 in St. Louis in 1986 (throwing the Cards into capitulation mode in April) and rolling to their first undefeated record against the Cards at Shea in 1988 (9–0). The clubs were separated into different divisions in 1994, but they've twice met in the postseason. The first resulted in a five-game Mets rout for the 2000 pennant. The next went to the Cardinals in devastating fashion in the 2006 NLCS. Advantage: St. Louis.

**Mets–Expos**

Technically, this rivalry still exists because the Washington Nationals are still in the NL East, but there is a big difference between going across the border and going down to D.C. It all began for the Expos at Shea Stadium on April 8, 1969, when they won the first game of their existence 11–10. Their last game as Montreal also occurred at Shea on October 3, 2004, with buddy Endy Chavez making the last out. The Mets had loads of trouble in Montreal, going 135–152. The rivalry has favored the Mets since the relocation to Washington, but the Nats played spoiler to devastating effect in 2007 and 2008; the Mets has their first losing mark in D.C. in 2009.

> **TRIVIA**
> **Question**
>
> **Who has the most career World Series hits as a Met?**
>
> Trivia answers on page 256

# 85. A Missed Shot in the (Alvin) Dark

Looking back, it seems that Casey Stengel could have run the Mets for as long as he wanted. The truth was, with the three other expansion teams showing signs of progress and the Mets still stumbling mightily, the natives were getting restless.

The Mets were 40 games under .500 at the start of August 1964, the same record they'd had a year earlier. The draw of brand-new

Shea Stadium could only last so long without a team worth watching. And there were doubts that the 74-year-old Stengel could do enough to speed the progress of the young players essential to the team's future. Joan Payson, being an old New York Giants fan and stockholder, liked the one-time Giants star—and now Giants manager—Alvin Dark.

Dark had led the Giants to the 1962 World Series, where they lost to the Yankees in seven games. Despite two down years in San Francisco, both the Mets and Yankees, who had already privately decided not to bring back Yogi Berra, had their eyes on Dark.

But Dark, an avowed Christian very vocal about his beliefs, made comments contrary to the doctrine of "treat thy neighbor as thyself." Interviews in *Newsday* about the state of the Giants revealed that Dark had doubts about the intelligence and desire of the many African American and Hispanic players on his team. The comments of the Louisiana-bred manager, coming at the time of the Civil Rights Act, riots in Harlem, and violence in the South, did not play well in New York. Even when Dark contritely explained during his next trip to New York that he held no such beliefs—backed by statements from old friends, including Jackie Robinson—his future in this town was nonexistent.

As Leonard Koppett, who covered the Mets for *The New York Times*, reported in his history of the team: "The mere accusation, and the impossibility of ever putting it to rest conclusively among those who would be naturally suspicious (after all, Dark was a Southerner, and whatever he was, he certainly wasn't a liberal), was enough to knock him out of the box."

The Yankees couldn't touch Dark either, although Berra would still be fired after winning the pennant and then join the Mets. (That same scenario had landed Stengel with the Mets to begin with.) Casey would remain with the Mets despite averaging 113 losses his first three years. It would take a broken hip to push out the

Ol' Perfessor. His successor wouldn't be Dark, who would return to the majors and win a world championship with the Oakland A's a decade later, or even Berra, but third-party candidate Wes Westrum.

It was for the best. Did New York need a manager who questioned future Hall of Famers Willie Mays, Orlando Cepeda, Willie McCovey, and Juan Marichal? The Mets had enough problems.

# 86 Mets Wives: Anna Other Thing

Not to digress into the tabloid and infotainment world, but the wives of several Mets have kept fans entertained over the years. Family Day photos from bygone yearbooks and numerous charity functions offered glimpses of the ballplayers' better halves, who took charge of many aspects of family life while their husbands traveled the country and concentrated on the daily work of being Mets.

Nancy Seaver was front and center when Tom pitched, cameras focused on her as she watched nervously. Golfing legend Nancy Lopez was on hand for husband Ray Knight's crowning moment in baseball in October 1986. Ruth Ryan was blamed by GM Bob Scheffing for getting Nolan traded from New York, and her presence with Nancy Seaver in a fateful sentence by vengeful columnist Dick Young became the final straw in the trade that launched a thousand tears: "Nolan Ryan is getting more money than Tom Seaver and that galls Tom because Nancy Seaver and Ruth Seaver are very friendly and Tom has long treated Nolan Ryan like a little brother."

No Met spouse, however, has caused a stir like Anna Benson. She made more news for *not* posing in *Playboy* than Mike Piazza's wife Alicia Rickter did for having been a 1995 centerfold.

*Despite the team's statements to the contrary, many believe Kris Benson's wife Anna helped orchestrate her husband's trade to the Baltimore Orioles in 2006.* Photo courtesy of AP/Wide World Photos.

A one-time stripper, professional poker player, and wife of pitcher Kris Benson, Anna was never shy about being quoted. Her revealing red dress at the team's 2005 Christmas party had the boys on hand thinking about more than electric trains and video games. Low-cut would also describe her comments about new Met Carlos Delgado's stance on "God Bless America" and GM Omar Minaya's dealing for more players of Latin descent than she liked. The Bensons soon found themselves in Baltimore, but Anna continued blasting the Mets. It turned out to be a great deal, sending out a high-priced veteran/headache for young starter John Maine and reliever Jorge Julio, whose name Anna transposed in her diatribe. The Mets traded Julio for Orlando Hernandez. Kris Benson went 11–12 in 2006, missed 2007 with rotator cuff surgery, and has bounced around since. Mets Christmas parties will never be the same.

# 87 April 17, 1964: First Day at Big Shea

Let's turn this over to someone who was actually there on April 17, 1964—here's Dan Carubia from Valencia, New York:

Who would guess that on this day, I would wake up to a new world? I was 17 and both my parents knew I was skipping school with my good friend Louie Prochaska to go to Opening Day at the brand new ballpark in Flushing, Queens. We met in front of Westfall's Restaurant on the corner of Atlantic and 111th Street in Richmond Hill, Queens. We waited for the Q37 Green Line bus to Kew Gardens, where we would go down into the subway and take the E or F train to Roosevelt Avenue. Then we would go upstairs and hook up with the Number 7 elevated trains that would take us to the ballpark.

We still got to Shea in less time than going up to the Polo Grounds in Manhattan, where we'd seen the Mets the previous two years. Sleek new light-blue cars were on the 7 line in preparation for the crowds that were to come for the World's Fair and the new Shea Stadium. The train's cars were new; we could smell the freshness of the new seats even though my nose was almost buried in a guy's armpit as we held onto the center pole.

We both knew that after the 111th-street station, Willets Point/Shea Stadium would be next. This was a time to stretch our necks to the left and see the completed stadium with its blue and orange squares that hung from cables on all sides of the stadium. Then, if we quickly looked to our right as we crossed the bridge over the Grand

Central Parkway, we were able to look straight at the 1964 World's Fair opposite Shea.

As the cars came to a halt at our stop, we exited down the stairs and muddled our way onto the wooden ramp that would lead us right to the gates that would soon open for the very first time. As we walked down that ramp, we could view most of the playing field. Some people were just standing there waiting to view the game from this location. As we started to walk to the designated gate listed on our tickets, we heard three familiar words: "Let's Go Mets." That cheer wasn't new; it had started in the cavernous Polo Grounds by fans like Louie and me during the 1962 season. It had made the trip, too.

Finally, the gates to Shea rolled up and we made a beeline straight to the ticket takers, who, in their new uniforms, ripped our tickets in two. We were now in Shea for the very first time and heard those familiar calls of "Hey! Lineup, program, scorecard, Mets yearbook!"

It was hard to fathom the large semicircle stadium with the biggest scoreboard I have ever seen. On top of the scoreboard was a large square screen that had the Mets' logo in place. The logo, we heard, would lift up to show the player's face once he came to bat. The green grass was trimmed and ready to be played on, there were the multi-colored seats of the four different sections, with no poles and no obstructed views!

The escalators were crowded with fans unsure of where to go. This caused some panic as people stopped at each level to see exactly where they were going and backed the "Let's Go Mets" fans coming up the escalators. We knew where we were going: right to the top deck, Section 29, on the first-base side.

# The World's Fair

There was a time that the World's Fair was, in the vernacular of the day, pretty neat. The 1904 World's Fair in St. Louis was so big they tossed in the Olympics. The New York fair in 1939 showed us television for the first time. Montreal's 1967 fair gave the world the name Expos.

The 1964 event started off by cheesing off the world, and that's not counting the "World's Largest Cheese" that Wisconsin later brought to Queens. Robert Moses, who turned neighborhoods into parkways, built Flushing Meadows out of a garbage dump a generation earlier, and helped nudge the Dodgers and Giants out of town by insisting any new stadium only go where he wanted it, went to Paris to get sanctioning from the World's Fair muckety mucks despite his event being held too close to fairs in Seattle and Canada. The French said no. That meant few Europeans would come and Canada, the Soviet Union, and Australia would not participate. Yet plenty of smaller countries did take part, and exhibits like "Futurama," Belgian waffles, and Michelangelo's Pieta—not necessarily in that order—kept people happy. And despite not having the best foreign draw, they had the best thing in the world to bring Americans to Queens: Shea Stadium.

The Mets did their part by wearing a patch on their uniforms featuring the Unisphere, the symbol of the 1964–1965 World's Fair. The Mets lost 221 times during the run of the fair. The foreigners who wandered over to see the woeful club hardly knew the difference. For the nationals, the Mets were at least better than looking at that big cheese (not Robert Moses).

Despite alien plots in the area via *Men in Black* and the marching of time, the fair is still there. While several of the exhibits found other uses—like the maddeningly upbeat "It's a Small World" ride in Disneyland and the pavilion that moved to California and became a church—the largest structures, Unisphere included, still remain in Flushing Corona Park. You can visit the park and see the Queens Museum of Art, New York Hall of Science, have a picnic, watch cricket, or just take in the sights. Drive to a sold-out Mets game late and you will see it all again, because you'll end up parking in the park's nether regions.

As we got off the escalators, we turned right and walked down the inner corridor to our section. Arriving at our section, we made the left, walked into a small tunnel-like entrance that took us out to the aisle where steps led us up the rows to our seats. The view and the height took my breath away. It seemed to me that this top deck at new Shea was higher than the top deck at Yankee Stadium and way higher than the two decks at the Polo Grounds. We just stood in the entranceway, food in hand, taking in a sight that we had never seen before. We viewed part of Jamaica Bay, the junkyards in back of the parking lot in right-center field, the top of the Whitestone Bridge, and the buildings of Flushing, with a sign attached to one of the buildings that said, "Serval Zippers." But the weird part of standing in the aisle in the upper deck was seeing the fly-bys of planes on their way to LaGuardia Airport. In some cases these planes were the same height as us.

We viewed the many different colors of the clothing in the stands, the bunting ringing each deck, the marching band now in place in center field, and the large floral piece that was all alone on a stand near home plate. Lindsey Nelson introduced William Shea and dedicated the horseshoe wreath to the man responsible for bringing National League baseball back to New York after a five-year absence. Nelson announced the entire roster of the Pirates and Mets and both teams lined up on the foul lines in front of their dugouts. You could tell the favorite players of the "Let's Go Mets" fans—guys like little Al Jackson, Frank Thomas, Jesse Gonder, and Jim Hickman (if only he could hit a curve)—by the loud cheers that they received. The crowd rose, and the band on the field played our national anthem.

Once that was completed, the starting pitchers, Bob Friend for Pittsburgh and Jack Fisher for the Mets, warming up on the circles at either side of home plate, were ready to go. The umpires met with the managers, Danny Murtaugh and Casey Stengel, to go over the ground rules for the stadium for the first time. A roar went up from the near-capacity crowd as our Mets took the field.

After one inning there was no score. Willie Stargell led off the second. Even from afar, this guy was humongous, a big left-handed hitter with a long, looping swing. On his first at-bat at Shea, he hit a fat pitch by Fisher on a rope, straight into the right-field lower stands, the ball staying no more then 10 to 15 feet off of the ground and gone before Stargell was halfway to first base. That was the first hit, first home run, and first run at Shea. My first thought was: "New park, same team…only a year older."

The history of that game is now gone with the wind, with only faded memories of the day's events nestled in the minds of those who attended or watched on TV. The crowd stayed until the last out, a 4–3 loss. We had come to see, as did most of the 50,000 "Let's Go Mets" fans, a Mets victory. But Louie and I saw something different in this loss—we saw hope. Though they were now 0–3, the Mets played good baseball, and the guys hustled, especially Ron Hunt. He was one of our own, along with Ed Kranepool, who came up to the Mets last year from the minor leagues.

We figured we just needed more time and patience. You see, it was a brand new world here at Shea, and Louie and I were part of it. Mets baseball at Shea had just begun.

# 88 Shea Good-Bye: The Ceremony

How do you say good-bye? For many Mets fans, Shea Stadium pre-dated them. For those born before the opening of Shea in 1964, it was like a family that moved into the neighborhood and then became the embodiment of the area, changing with the times yet remaining in one place—good times and bad. Unlike the Brooklyn Dodgers and New York Giants, whose departures helped usher the Mets into existence, this team wasn't going anywhere. They were just moving across the street, but in this case the old address had to go.

Many people didn't like Shea. That group included hitters, opposing teams, management, and the media, along with a large number of fans. It was an old, dingy, leaky, sometimes smelly slab of concrete where the ball didn't carry, visibility was substandard, planes few over incessantly, and the concessions were considered the worst in baseball. Just as Shea Stadium's newness had trumped the older ballparks wheezing toward the end of their days in the 1960s, new parks built in the 1990s had rendered Shea's multi-use concept obsolete. It took almost a decade longer than planned to get the municipal backing, but the announcement of a new stadium in Flushing was made in January 2006 as part of a New York 2012 Olympic bid everyone knew wouldn't be successful. That April, the Olympic plans officially dead and with no need for a stadium that could be converted to 80,000 seats, the Mets announced a cozy baseball-only stadium with seating for 42,000. Ground was offi-cially broken that November with the stadium named after a bank—thanks to a 20-year, $400 million deal with Citi. Shea's days were numbered.

There was more to worry about in 2007 than obsessing over Shea Stadium, but once the '08 season began the word "final" was on everything, including a patch on the uniform sleeve. The season started with the addition of "Shea" to the retired numbers row. And as with the closing of other recent stadiums, a countdown was held before each game and the number of games left reduced by one. For every Mets great like Ed Charles and former Shea organist Jane Jarvis, there were Lincoln Mercury dealers (about 10 in all) and hosts of local programming getting the honor. Yet even as the drama on the field boiled over and Shea's life dwindled to a precious few days, it was obvious that everything was window dressing for the final day.

Former Mets arrived by the carload on September 28, dodging raindrops as the final game was delayed for an hour. Unlike most stadium closings—including the one at Yankee Stadium a week earlier—Shea's ceremony would be held after the game. And it wasn't just a meaningless finale. The Mets had to beat Florida to tie the Brewers for the wild card and a possible extra day—or even days!—at Shea (the Mets had won the coin toss in case of a one-game playoff). Whoever was scripting the ending to this 44-year epic missed something. The Mets lost, Milwaukee won, and there would be no more games at Shea. Now, on with the show...

A few thousand people left immediately after the game in disgust. Fans chanted at the celebrating Marlins—the second straight year they'd eliminated the Mets on the last day—to "get off the field." Mr. Met was booed as he pulled down the final number on the center-field scoreboard. Workers meticulously measured the exact placement of cardboard cutouts on the field that served no purpose. Fans sat looking straight ahead wondering why they spent so much time, money, effort, and emotion on something that consistently came up short, save for a few glorious exceptions. Then, uncharacteristically, the Mets showed them why.

First came the kin of the departed Mets, the families of Gil Hodges, Tommie Agee, Bob Murphy, longtime employee Jim Plummer, and many more. Classy. Then the stars kept coming, double barrel, from each bullpen: Jack Fisher, Ron Hunt, Al Jackson, Frank Thomas, Jim McAndrew, Ed Charles, Art Shamsky, Wayne Garrett, George Theodore, Dave Kingman, Felix Millan, Craig Swan, Doug Flynn, John Stearns, George Foster, Tim Teufel, Todd Zeile, Ron Swoboda, Lee Mazzilli, Wally Backman, Ron Darling, Sid Fernandez, Howard Johnson, Bobby Ojeda, Robin Ventura, Al Leiter, Ed Kranepool, Cleon Jones, Buddy Harrelson, Jesse Orosco, Edgardo Alfonzo, John Franco, Rusty Staub, Lenny Dykstra, Gary Carter, Jerry Koosman, Yogi Berra, Keith Hernandez, Darryl Strawberry, Dwight Gooden, Willie Mays, Mike Piazza, and Tom Seaver.

From my point of view, with the entrance of the seemingly for-gotten Kingman (my first favorite Met) and Swan (who started the first Mets game I ever attended), I forgot the Mets had even played a game that day. I was back in 1975, 1983, 1986…dipping and darting between memories as the eras mixed and coalesced. People around me were yelling, crying, laughing all at once. There may not have been a moment where I understood what Shea had been all about more than right then…and then the players lined up along the foul lines and started moving toward home plate.

The unexpectedly frail Willie Mays, making people feel alter-nately young and old, gingerly bent down and touched the plate with his hand. You could feel the whole place gulp. Anyone who thought this sequence hokey immediately changed their tune. Each player did his own thing. Harrelson danced across the plate, Cleon mimicked the pose from his '69 clinching catch, Hernandez got into his batting stance, and a thunderous ovation greeted the trou-bled Gooden that said both "Thanks" and "We're pulling for you." Then came the final pitch from Tom Seaver to Mike Piazza that sig-naled the end of Shea Stadium as a venue. The pair walked slowly toward the open gate in center field amid "What a Wonderful World" by Louis Armstrong, a longtime Queens resident buried in Flushing, just as Shea would soon be.

Pitcher and catcher walked through the center-field gate and pulled it shut. There were fireworks briefly and this baseball version of *The Last Waltz* was over. The ceremony was nearly perfect, its timing ironic, but in the Metsian world of constant trauma, the consoling mixture of melancholy and nostalgia couldn't have come at a better moment for a fan base losing its home base. And with the festivities concluded, for the first time in anyone's memory, the Shea ushers did not push the crowd out of the building. They stood and watched like everyone else. Now what?

Fans visited different levels of the stadium one last time, or went to take in the view at a favorite seat, or just sat where they were. The sun had set and evening enveloped the area; the book was closed on the season (89 wins) and the stadium (1,856 wins, 1,709 losses, five ties), and there would be adding to Shea's 39 postseason games (26 wins).

Some fans would return in the weeks to come, to what was no longer a ballpark but a construction site. Shea was taken apart piece by piece and sold off or turned into scrap or rubble. The last section was pulled down on February 19, 2009, in front of a small crowd on a cold, gray morning. Most will remember the place on warmer, happier days.

The location of the bases and pitching rubber at Shea are still marked in the left-field parking lot at the new park. The dimensions are perfect for a game of catch.

# 89 Citi Field

The first season of Citi Field made it hard to quantify where the Mets' new home ranks in the overall Metropolitans experience. The critics had their way with the team and the stadium in their maiden voyage. At a time when teams in bandbox parks were reaching the World Series, how could the Mets build such a pitcher-dominant park? Why isn't there more Mets stuff in Citi Field? Why can't you see the whole field from many of the seats? Why is the line for Shake Shack so long? Yes, complaining about the Mets reached a new high in 2009. Sure, the Mets lost 92 games. But hey, it was a 17-game improvement over the first year at Shea Stadium.

Citi Field is a beautiful park. The gourmet food is plentiful, reasonably affordable, and available to all regardless of seat location. There are actually a number of free amusements for children in the center-field concourse. (Though it's difficult for parents standing in line with the kiddies to even follow the game back there—how about a couple more well-placed screens, guys?) There are some 100 different types of Mets hats available at the various stores, Alyssa Milano's own boutique, and a store for Jackie Robinson (in addition to a rotunda). It's a good thing the stadium is named after a bank because you might need a small loan to sit in most of the seats surrounding the field.

The average ticket price at Citi Field in 2009 was $37, almost half what it cost for the average ticket at new Yankee Stadium. But with the Yankees winning a World Series—and sweeping the Mets at Citi during the season—the crosstown comparisons end there. The highest-priced seat in the first year at Citi Field topped out at $495; the cheapest was $11 (though figuring out how much to pay for a ticket can change weekly and even nightly with the variable-pricing structure that charges more for higher-profile teams and for games played during the summer months).

Shea held 57,000 fans and sold a record 4,042,045 tickets in 2008, averaging more than 51,000 per home date during the stadium's final year. That's about 7,000 more than Citi holds with standing room packed to the rafters. There are seats for 42,000, with the Mets averaging 38,941 for a total of 3,154,262, seventh-best in the major leagues. Yet Citi operated at 92.7 percent capacity, 10 percent higher than the Dodgers, whose 3.7 million fans in their larger venue was the best in baseball. The question, with a recession and the '09 Mets beset by injuries and freefalling in the standings, is this: you built it, but will they come?

Price reductions—announced while the '09 season was still on—will help. And visiting Citi Field is just as convenient as Shea was via mass transit. With fewer bodies fitting into the ballpark, there are fewer cars fighting for parking spaces (about 5,500 spots in three lots—though those arriving early often opt for the free alternative under the rumble and shade of the Whitestone Expressway).

What will bring fans to Citi isn't the shrimp po' boy—not that it isn't delicious—it's the quality of the product on the field. The Mets didn't spend a lot of time thinking about their history when putting together initial décor inside the park, but they did take it into account in a much more important matter: they built Citi with pitchers in mind. Left field immediately catches the eye, with a wall that tapers in height from 12- to 15-feet high, making its 384-foot marker into a "Do Not Enter" sign for balls not absolutely crushed (and even those shots won't go out in early season night games). Center field is 408 feet away, though it feels farther. At 415 feet, a poke to right-center is reserved for the likes of Ryan Howard alone. Right-center, David Wright's favored power alley, has turned into a graveyard for him at 378 feet. The right-field line, at 330 feet, is the only spot shorter than Shea.

The height of the fences are a bit of an issue, too, with seven height changes. The catty-cornered wall above the "Mo Zone" in right field is just plain silly. But sillier still would be to move the fences in. Opposing sluggers don't like Citi Field already, and if the Mets build a good pitching staff, teams coming to New York will hate it even more. Think of cavernous Busch Stadium and how it played tricks with the Mets in the 1980s. As for its dimensions scaring off free agents, Jason Bay answered that question by signing on for four years in 2010 ($66 million helped him see the light).

With Shea Stadium gone, the nostalgic part of the Mets experience exists only in the mind now, but with Year Two brings more orange-and-blue artifacts and reminders of glories past. A year-overdue Mets museum at Citi Field is designed to create some flashbacks and keep down the grumbling while fans await the next museum-quality Mets season.

# 90 Al Leiter

Alois Terry Leiter grew up a Mets fan in Toms River, New Jersey, but some fans hold it against him for beginning and ending his career as a Yankee and then taking a job with the YES Network. Well, that does sound bad, yet his numerous achievements as a Met were accomplished despite the lefty's seeming inability to retire a batter on less than five pitches. He won in double figures in each of his seven Mets seasons, leading the team in wins five times, ERA four times, and even complete games once—1998, his first year. It was his October efforts, however, that fans should remember most: his 142-pitch odyssey in which he ended up the tragic hero in the 2000 World Series Game 5 loss to the Yankees, and the magnificent two-hit shutout he tossed in Cincinnati in the 1999 one-game playoff that ended an 11-year postseason drought in Queens.

Leiter earned two World Series rings with one-time expansion teams—neither club was the Mets. He won with the 1993 Blue Jays and the 1997 Marlins, but he pitched much better in the postseason as a Met despite not winning a game; Leiter was victimized by three Armando Benitez blown saves. He had an identical 2.87 ERA in the Division Series and World Series for the Mets—he had more difficulty in the NLCS, though his only loss was a 1–0 heartbreaker to Tom Glavine in 1999. It was as if the baseball gods enjoyed tormenting animated Al, who seemed to spend an hour each start holding his glove over his face to try to mask his emotions.

Traded by the Marlins to the Mets for 21-year-old A.J. Burnett and two other minor leaguers just before spring training in 1998, Leiter instantly became the Mets' ace. He went 17–6 his first year, though he missed time with knee problems. Leiter, whose career was on hold for five years due to arm problems, was relatively healthy for most of his time as a Met, allowing him to join the upper echelon of Mets pitchers in wins (95), losses (67), starts (213), innings (1,360), strikeouts (1,106), and, of course, walks (546). Leiter had a great move to first base and picked off 28 runners as a Met, by far the most in team history. He won 162 times overall, logged a 3.80 ERA, and threw a no-hitter as a Marlin in 1996. He received the Roberto Clemente Award for his community involvement in 2000. Give him a hand.

# 91 David Cone

If Al Leiter's feet are held to the fire by Mets fans for his involvement with the Yankees, David Cone seems to get a free pass. Cone won four world championships as a Yankee, including the 2000 World Series, when he quelled the Mets' best chance to tie Game 4 by coming out of the bullpen to retire Mike Piazza. Like Leiter, he pitched a no-hitter in another team's uniform, but Cone took it to another degree, throwing a perfect game in the Bronx and then falling to his knees in disbelief after the last out. Cone tossed his final major league game as a Met, however, ending an itinerant career that saw him pitch for three other American League teams.

The first was Kansas City, where the Royals didn't realize what they had in their local star (Cone was drafted in the third round in 1981 out of K.C.'s Rockhurst High). The Royals used him solely in relief late in 1986 and then dealt him to the Mets just before the 1987 season. The trade—for Rick Anderson, Mauro Gozzo, and Ed Hearn—remains one of the most lopsided deals in Mets history. Cone continued in the bullpen at Shea, but moved into the rotation because of injuries before he too was hurt while trying to bunt. In 1988, the right-hander again didn't move into the rotation until May, but he allowed a total of just four earned runs over his first six starts and rarely pitched in relief again during his 17-year career. That season, the fun-loving Cone went 20–3 with a league-best .870 winning percentage while placing second in ERA (2.22) and third in the Cy Young voting to shutout machine Orel Hershiser. Hershiser subdued the favored Mets in the '88 NLCS, but it was Cone's complete game in Los Angeles that forced the fated seventh game.

Cone led the National League in strikeouts in 1990 and 1991, ending the latter season with a 19-strikeout performance in Philadelphia. He would have won the K crown the next year as well, racking up 214 to go with 13 wins—including four shutouts in a month—but his NL tenure ended August 27. "The Worst Team Money Could Buy" traded Cone to the Blue Jays for the stretch run. The Mets got overhyped Ryan Thompson and under-appreciated Jeff Kent, who would go on to greater things once he left New York; Cone wound up with a World Series ring that fall. He returned to Kansas City and won the Cy Young Award in 1994 despite his heavy involvement in union negotiations as the strike shut down the season in August. When play resumed in 1995, the Royals saw enough red in their financial future to again trade the hometown boy, this time to Toronto. But those were not the same

Jays he'd known in '93, and they cut bait midseason and traded him to the division rival Yankees.

For all the rings and fanfare in the Bronx, Cone was better in almost every category during his Queens tenure. Coney the Met won 81 times, completed 34 games, had a 3.13 ERA, and fanned 1,172, doing so in far fewer innings (1,209⅓) than the four names higher on the all-time Mets K list. He fell shy of 200 wins in his career, but when he walked off the field for the last time in 2003—returning after a year's retirement—it was at Shea Stadium, where he'd given it his best shot.

# 92 Johan Santana

There's one simple reason Johan Santana is so far back in this book: time. Santana came to the Mets in what by all accounts is one of the most one-sided deals in club history. The Mets had the Twins over a barrel in January 2008 since Minnesota was looking to deal their ace and the Yankees and Red Sox were content not to let each other get him. The Mets won out, sending three minor league pitchers and outfield prospect Carlos Gomez to Minnesota. Yet the Twins still won 16 more games than the Mets over the first two years of the deal, even with Santana winning 29 games for New York and the prospective pitching trio winning none in Minnesota.

The Mets weren't the first team to get Santana at a bargain. Signed out of rural Venezuela by the Astros in 1995, the Marlins took him in the Rule 5 draft and immediately sent him to the Twins for a minor leaguer and cash. His transition from reliever to ace starter was gradual, but in his first season starting exclusively in 2004, Santana won 20, led the league in ERA, strikeouts, and

## Swan Song

Craig Swan is a Mets pitcher who is often overlooked because he did not get a lot of wins due to the lousy teams he was on. Yet Swannie is one of four Mets to win an ERA title. The others are:

- Tom Seaver, 1970 (2.82)
- Tom Seaver, 1971 (1.76)
- Tom Seaver, 1973 (2.08)
- Dwight Gooden, 1985 (1.53)
- Johan Santana, 2008 (2.53)

Swan's 1978 NL-best 2.43 ERA, however, did not translate into even one vote for the Cy Young Award because the 96-loss Mets couldn't even get him 10 wins (Swan was 9–6). A touted prospect out of Arizona State, the '78 season was actually his first winning season in a major league career that began in 1973. Injuries derailed Swan throughout his 11 seasons at Shea. He had extended stays on the disabled list for his right elbow, shoulder, and rotator cuff, plus a broken rib in 1981 after catcher Ron Hodges drilled him trying to throw out Montreal leadoff man Tim Raines in a game that Swan, naturally, wound up losing.

By the time the Mets were finally building a good team in 1984, Swan didn't have much left. Nor did he have a lot to show for 11 seasons with the Mets in terms of wins and losses: 59–71. Swan remains in the club's all-time top 10 in starts (184), complete games (25), innings (1,229⅓), and strikeouts (671); ironically, his 3.72 ERA does not crack the top 20.

WHIP (walks and hits per nine innings). Santana earned the AL Cy Young in '04 and again in '06, while helping Minnesota reach the postseason four times.

In his first year as a Met, Santana did everything humanly possible to will the Mets into the playoffs, but the bullpen did in Santana—and the club. The pen blew seven Johan leads and probably cost him the Cy Young as well. His 2008 season, leading the league in starts (34), innings (234⅓), and ERA (2.53), ranks among the five best Mets seasons ever. Though his 16 wins look puny compared to the finest years of Tom Seaver and Dwight Gooden, Santana's final '08 performance—a complete game on three days' rest to help the Mets pull into a wild card tie—instead turned out to be the franchise's last win at Shea Stadium.

Santana was superb out of the gate in 2009, though this time it was his offense and defense that sabotaged him (with a blown save tossed in). He had an ERA of 0.71 through his first seven starts yet only a 4–2 mark. Johan was good but not great after that; though pitching with an elbow that required surgery in September and beholden to a punchless lineup of fill-ins, he still managed 13 wins and went at least seven innings in 16 of his 25 starts. The only question mark with Santana is his health—and if the Mets can put together a team worthy of such an ace.

# 93 Dave Kingman

In their first 13 seasons of existence, the Mets had players who could hit the ball hard—and far on occasion—but no one who could hit titanic home runs like the man known as "Sky King," "Kong," or, as Bob Murphy liked to call him, David Arthur Kingman. He landed balls in the Shea Stadium parking lot, hit a house in Chicago with such a thud that the homeowner thought a caller was knocking, and launched a ball so far in an exhibition game it put a bee in George Steinbrenner's bonnet about the Mets that has never left.

While golfing in Arizona in the winter of 1975, former Mets GM Bob Scheffing learned that the Giants were strapped for cash and were willing to part with Kingman. The first overall draft pick in 1970 as a pitcher out of USC, Kingman converted to full-time slugger. Averaging 24 home runs his first three years in San Francisco, he was also good for about 130 strikeouts and never batted higher than .225. After sending the Giants $150,000, the Mets had a slugger in his prime for the first time since 1962. A giant of a Met at 6'6", the free-swinging Kingman broke Frank Thomas's inaugural-season club record with 36 homers, including a still unbroken Mets mark of 13 home runs in July 1975—his 31 RBIs that month were also a club record at the time. Though the press didn't like the surly slugger, Mets fans loved him. He played both corner outfield positions, first base, and, remarkably, third base—starting 12 games at the hot corner and committing only three errors (a paltry number considering how shaky he was at his accustomed positions). Kingman even led the speed-challenged Mets with seven steals.

The next year Kong kicked it up a notch. He reached 20 home runs in early June and had 30 at the All-Star break. The starting right fielder in the All-Star Game, Kingman's home-run pace threatened Hack Wilson's National League record of 56—and with a little luck, Roger Maris's 61. His luck ran out on July 19. Diving after a Phil Niekro flyball, Kingman tore ligaments in his thumb and missed six weeks. He didn't even claim the NL home-run crown, losing out by one to Mike Schmidt—though Kong did break his own club record with 37.

Kingman held out for a bigger contract, returned, complained, and was traded the same night as Tom Seaver in June 1977. He played for four teams that season before signing with the Cubs. In 1979 he launched 48 home runs—including three in a loss visiting Shea—and batted .288, 50 points higher than in any Mets season. He returned to the Mets amid campy "Kingman Fallout Zone" parking lot signs in 1981 and fanned 105 times in a shortened 103-game season. He won the first home-run crown by a Met in 1982—and batted .204. The arrival of Keith Hernandez in mid-1983 left Kingman without a position, and the all-time home-run leader for the franchise (154) and Shea Stadium (88)—he later settled to fourth in both categories—went to Oakland as a designated hitter. He amassed exactly 100 home runs in three seasons with the A's…and was not offered a major league contract. He retired with 442 home runs, for a while the highest total by anyone not in the Hall of Fame.

# 94 Lee Mazzilli

Brooklyn-born Lee Mazzilli, the ambidextrous son of welterweight fighter Libero Mazzilli, was drafted in the first round of the pennant-winning year of 1973…and then he rarely got a whiff of fifth place. In the midst of a 99-loss season and the smallest attendance at Shea Stadium over a full season (788,905), Maz was hitting in the .330s in 1979 when he was named an All-Star. In what would be the only two All-Star plate appearances of his career, Mazzilli homered batting left-handed to tie the game in the eighth and then walked with the bases loaded batting right-handed against Yankee Ron Guidry to force in the go-ahead run in the ninth. A few weeks later, the basket-catching center fielder was shifted to first base after the Mets traded Willie Montanez.

In line with the cockeyed Mets thinking of that era, Mazzilli, a neophyte at the position, played first base in 1980 while Mike Jorgensen, a one-time Mets prospect and very capable first baseman, manned right field; Joel Youngblood, who had a great arm but had trouble tracking the ball, was in center. When Joe Torre switched these players back to their natural positions in the beginning of June, the Mets suddenly came as close to contention as Maz had seen in his first four years as a Mets regular. Mazzilli returned to first base during a span when the Mets lost 18 of 19.

## Minor Mets

In the past decade, the Mets, like a lot of organizations, have put more minor league teams closer to their franchise base. In 2009, the Mets added Buffalo as their top minor league team, the same city where the Mets had their Triple A team from 1963 to 1965. But Buffalo is actually almost as far from Flushing as Norfolk, Virginia, the Triple A home to the Mets for 37 years. The Mets were edged out of the Tidewater region—birthplace of David Wright and many other talented ballplayers—in 2007 by the Orioles, who wanted their top affiliate in their part of the country.

The Mets' Double A home in upstate Binghamton is somewhat closer. Class A Brooklyn—Coney Island, actually—is closer still, but the travel time is longer than you might think. Here are the Mets affiliates as of 2010 from top farm club to lowest rung, with approximate mileage to home base in Flushing. Keep in mind that the Gulf Coast Mets play in the same Florida facility as St. Lucie—the spring training home for the big-league Mets.

- Buffalo Bisons (NY), Triple A: 400 miles. Affiliate since 2009.
- Binghamton Mets (NY), Double A: 190 miles. Affiliate since 1992.
- St. Lucie Mets (FL), Long Season A: 1,170 miles. Affiliate since 1988.
- Savannah Sand Gnats (GA), Class A: 820 miles. Affiliate since 2007.
- Brooklyn Cyclones (NY), Short Season A: 25 miles. Affiliate since 2001.
- Kingsport Mets (TN), Class A (Rookie): 630 miles. Affiliate since 1980.
- Gulf Coast League Mets (FL), Class A (Rookie): 1,170 miles. Affiliate since 1991.
- Santo Domingo Mets (Dominican): Class A (Rookie): 1,550 miles. Affiliate since 1993.
- Venezuelan Mets (Carabobo, VZ): Class A (Rookie): 2,140 miles. Affiliate since 2000.

Despite moving back and forth in the field, Maz had his finest season at the plate, hitting 16 home runs, knocking in 76, and stealing 41 bases. The next year he fell off the map.

On April 1, 1982, Mazzilli was traded to Texas in return for minor league pitchers Ron Darling and Walt Terrell. By the time the Mets had a good team, Maz was playing for the Pirates, who were repeatedly pummeled by the New Yorkers like the Bucs used to whip Maz's Mets. Pittsburgh released Mazzilli in July 1986 and he was scooped up by the Mets, the runaway leaders in the NL East. Maz batted .276 over 39 games with the Mets, and then came through with pinch-hit singles that started game-tying rallies in Games 6 and 7 of the World Series. Mazzilli hit .400 against Boston and was the Met with the most first-hand experience of the bad times to savor the climactic finish.

Mazzilli hit a career-high .306 in part-time duty in 1987, but he didn't get above .200 the next two years. He was released by the Mets in July 1989 and ended his career in the playoffs with the Blue Jays. Maz rejoined Torre as a Yankees coach and managed the Orioles in 2004–05. Top five in steals (152) and pinch-hits (38) in Mets history, he returned to the fold to work in the team's network studio. The last game at Shea Stadium was Maz's final game on SNY.

# 95 The Mr. Met Dash

Warning: severe patience required. This is for people with kids under 12 or those willing to take nieces, nephews, or neighborhood kids to a game. It's something they may or may not do at the new stadium, but the Mets have allowed kids to run on the field on selected weekend afternoons for more than 15 years. It's a wonderful thing. That said, there's a few things you need to do.

You need to leave the game early and head toward the center-field entrance. Bring a radio to follow the action and hope the game is one-sided…and quick. Also bring something for the kids and yourself to eat or drink or do. The waiting area is in the sun, so bring a hat and sunscreen. You'll queue up outside the stadium in a line that snakes all the way to the 7 train. You'll work your way into the stadium and there'll be photo opportunities galore as kids slam into the wall while making pretend catches (it's padded). There is a rope that keeps you from leaving the warning track and going onto the field.

Keep an eye on your kid! In my three-year-old son's Shea Dash debut, he ducked under the rope and ran Billy Wagner–style toward the infield and I pursued where Rusty, Kong, and Straw once trod. If I'd stopped to get a photo, I probably would have rightfully been reprimanded or ejected, so I just dashed out and got my son maybe 100 feet before he reached second base. Didn't get the picture, but it is an image I'll never forget.

Once you make it safely to the infield, the kids run free from first to home. If they're reluctant to run, the team reps may let you lead them around the bases. If you have a parent/guardian/friend tag team, station one parent near home plate or third base to get a good photo. From the first-base side there are always people walking in front of you, and that results in some bad pictures (trust me). Enjoy your dash. (There's no seconds for any reason!)

Congratulations. For your patience, you've just spent more time on the field in Flushing than some heralded Mets prospects. As for the experience, a little kid may not have much memory of having seen a great player like Albert Pujols visit the Mets, but running across the diamond is forever.

# 96 Broadway Joe and the Jets

The Jets are going on their second stadium since Shea, but Joe Namath's greatness forever belongs in Flushing. Drafted out of Alabama by both the NFL's St. Louis Cardinals and the AFL's Jets in

1965, Joe Willie chose the bright lights of New York, even if the upstart league's destiny had not yet been written. Namath finished the story. His $427,000 contract was unheard of, as was the 50,000 per game Shea attendance for the previously ho-hum Jets. His signing helped push the rival leagues to make peace. So one could say that Namath (plus the AFL's NBC contract) led to the creation of the Super Bowl, and his 1969 guarantee solidified it as a must-see event.

Namath said he'd beat the Baltimore Colts and he did, thanks to a stingy defense and smashmouth running back Matt Snell. Despite ravaged knees and the Shea wind tunnel, Namath found Don Maynard and a few others often enough to lead his league in passing yardage three times. Madison Avenue turned Namath into a pitcher, using him to sell everything from shaving cream to pantyhose.

In 1977, Broadway Joe went to Los Angeles and Tom Terrific went to Cincinnati. The Jets without Namath were slightly more entertaining than the Mets without Seaver, but neither team won much without a star attraction. During Namath's time, even losses could be exciting, like the day O.J. Simpson became the game's first 2,000-yard rusher at snowy Shea in 1973. Shea was busy then. The Yankees and Giants joined the Mets and Jets there for 173 games in 1975, but then Shea went back to just the Mets and Jets. And starting in 1984, following years of quibbling over the Shea schedule, Flushing belonged solely to the Mets. The next year Namath was enshrined into the Pro Football Hall of Fame.

# 97 The Beatles

Like Joe Namath, the Beatles live on entwined in the Mets experience. The Beatles forever changed the rock concert with their show at Shea on August 15, 1965. No one was complaining about soul-less multiuse stadia that night. No one could hear a thing, either.

The Beatles couldn't hear their specially equipped amplifiers, and the 55,600 were screaming so loud that's all anyone in the crowd could hear (think of Lee Mazzilli Poster Day and amplify it by, say, 55,000). But hey, this was the Beatles. In person!

While the Mets were in Houston shutting out the Astros 3–0, Shea was shaking with the first stadium rock show in history. Fans weren't allowed on the field, and the uncovered stage at second base looked tiny from the outer reaches of the stadium. The crowd tried to pay attention through the warm-up acts: the King Curtis Band, Cannibal and the Headhunters, Brenda Holloway, the Young Rascals, and Sounds Incorporated.

And with anticipation at its fever pitch, out stepped the top showman of the day, Ed Sullivan, who'd had the Fab Four on his show the previous year and turned America into full-fledged Beatles country. Wearing a Mets-blue tie and handkerchief, Sullivan made the announcement:

"Ladies and gentleman, honored by their country, decorated by their queen, and loved here in America, here are the Beatles…Here they come."

Out of the visiting dugout they came in their tan Nehru jackets, wearing badges from the Wells Fargo armored car that had delivered them, and carrying their guitars as they crossed into fair territory toward the stage. A sound like a million cicada bugs enveloped Shea at the sight of John, Paul, George, and Ringo.

Here's that night's lineup:

Twist and Shout

She's a Woman

I Feel Fine

Dizzy Miss Lizzy

Ticket to Ride

Everybody's Trying to Be My Baby

Can't Buy Me Love
Baby's in Black
I Wanna Be Your Man
A Hard Day's Night
Help!
I'm Down

*The Beatles twisted and shouted in front of more than 50,000 fans at Shea Stadium in 1965 and 1966.*

That's it. A little over 30 minutes and done. But the scene was unforgettable: girls in dresses climbing the screen behind home plate, others crying their eyes out, moms frantically handing out tissues like it was a triage station, and young men appreciatively bopping their heads. The policemen had it the toughest, keeping fans away from the band and chasing down stray fans who ran the barricades and ignored the Shea scoreboard's plea: "For safety sake, please stay in your seats." The cops wished they were anywhere else in the world that night, surrounded by people who couldn't imagine being anywhere else.

## R-O-C-K in the U.S., Shea

After that first Beatles concert everything else seems like a letdown, but the show must go on. Since the Beatles christened Shea as a landmark rock venue, some other pretty big rock bands shook Shea. Turn up your amps...

Grand Funk Railroad (1971)
The Who (1982)
Simon and Garfunkel (1983)
The Police (1983)
The Rolling Stones (1989)
Bruce Springsteen (2003)
Billy Joel (2008)

Let's not forget the Festival for Peace held on August 6, 1970. An event to raise funds for anti-war candidates, it featured one of the last major performances by Janis Joplin, who died less than two months later. Also on the Shea bill were Paul Simon, Creedence Clearwater Revival, Steppenwolf, Miles Davis, and The James Gang.

Shea also found religion with Billy Graham (1970), the Jesus '79 Interfaith Rally, and the first U.S. visit by Pope John Paul II in 1979. The place has also witnessed soccer, cricket, boxing, roller derby, and wrestling. The New York Jets hosted the first postseason game in Shea Stadium history in December 1968—a 27–23 win over the Raiders for the AFL title—some 10 months before the Mets captured a world championship on the same earth.

The hype from that show and tour, a documentary, *The Beatles at Shea Stadium*, plus a record $304,000 box-office take ($160,000 going to the main act), led to another Shea show on what wound up being their last tour. Just over a year later, on August 23, 1966 (while the Mets were in Chicago, having won that Tuesday afternoon), the Beatles returned amid similar screaming but slightly less hysteria. Forty-two years later, former Beatle Paul McCartney appeared with Billy Joel at Shea's final concert and closed it out as a rock venue with "Let It Be." He would play the first show at Citi Field in 2009, breaking in the place with "Drive My Car."

# 98 Banner Day

One thing it doesn't seem likely Citi Field will ever see is Banner Day. Younger fans may only vaguely have heard about this tradition, but Banner Day was a celebration of the creative, allowing fans to explain the unexplainable—why they cared so much about a sports team— and parade around the field holding a bed sheet. It's been a decade since Banner Day went the way of the dodo bird, but the concept of fans carrying banners dated to the fledgling days of the team.

Casey Stengel was the patron saint of Banner Day, with an assist from the beat writers who helped convince staid team president George Weiss that confiscating banners was as silly as anyone expecting the expansion Mets to be good. While Yankee Stadium actively confiscated homemade banners (never more so than during the first Mayor's Trophy Game against the Mets in 1963), the Mets encouraged the homemade signs and even set up a day in their honor at the Polo Grounds. From those laughably bad teams to the not-funny-but-absolutely-horrible clubs of the late 1970s,

## Banner Headlines

"Eamus Metropoli." (Let's go Mets in Latin)

"To error is human, to forgive is a Met fan." (1965 grand prize winner)

"Pat Zachry, now in the sixth year of his sophomore jinx."

"Ralph Kiner is God."

"Free Sergio!" (On numerous 1987 banners referring to Michael Sergio, who served time for parachuting onto the field in Game 6 of the 1986 World Series…carrying a banner, of course.)

the stream of banners seemed endless as fans marched in from the center-field gate. The Mets even took them cross country, flying "Sign Man" Karl Ehrhardt to Oakland to hold up his placards—as Casey called them—against the A's in the 1973 World Series. Alas, the signs had little power beyond the city limits.

The end of the scheduled double-header in the 1980s was really the death knell for Banner Day. The Mets gamely tried to keep the tradition going by being one of the few teams to schedule a double-header, but even Mets players found the hour-plus wait between games irritating. Visitors found it even more so because Sunday was always a getaway day.

## TRIVIA
### Question

Who was the first Met to collect a hit in a regular-season game at Citi Field?

Trivia answers on page 256

The Mets inevitably made Banner Day a pregame festivity before a single Sunday contest in August, but who wanted to show up hours before the game and parade in front of a near-empty stadium knowing that there was little chance of a prize? (Prizes had long been given out to a handful of entries, with a player often included in the judges' panel.) Thousands still came each year with banners in tow. In 1991 the Mets even had two Banner Days. One was added in April for fans to express their feelings (mostly positive) about the recently concluded Gulf War. The 1994 season saw no Banner Day—thanks to the strike—but it resumed the next two seasons. When the 1997 promotional schedule appeared, however, Banner Day wasn't listed.

With blogs, MySpace, Facebook, Twitter, and many other electronic ways to boast about or lament one's favorite things, the concept of Banner Day seems outdated. Yet people still bring signs to the game and hold them up for all to see. Here's hoping someone will always think to do that and that the team always embraces it.

# 99 Giveaway Day

The Mets have long given out good stuff to their fans. Some promotions—like Fireworks or Meringue nights—you can't take with you, but literally tons of items have been pressed into the hands of fans entering the ballpark on most weekends during the season. Much of the booty is divided into adults-only and kids-only giveaways (occasional promotions have been doled out based on the sex of the recipient). In recent years kids have tended to get the better items, such as the ridiculously popular Beanie Babies or Bobbleheads (although the Ralph Kiner and Bob Murphy Bobblehead was for adults; the Ralph side looked a lot like Lindsey Nelson, but that was fitting). The team also has giveaways for the first 25,000 fans of all ages. Here's a few of the more interesting giveaways and the eras when they were doled out.

## Kids
Wiffle Ball Bat and Balls: 2000s
Russian Tea Dolls: 2003

# Fan's VIEW

## Liam Butler
## (Bats: Left, Throws: Right)

### The New New Breed

The greatest moments in Mets history are forged in stone. They are spelled out in detail in this book, but what about the future? What does it look like to the next generation? Does it matter as much to them?

Liam Butler was born with a Metscentric—and Jetscentric—father, but the kid accepted it with arms wide open, displaying optimism that older fans have seen worn away as decades run together. Since attending his first game during the dark days of the Art Howe era, Liam was lucky enough to see two milestones at Shea Stadium in 2006. The first was Pedro Martinez going for his 200th career victory.

"I was excited because it was the first time I was going to see Pedro pitch," he said. "He's been pitching for a while and he's getting old." He laughed; he's young, he can laugh. "We stayed the whole game. There were these guys near us holding up signs. One would hold up a two, the other a zero, and the other a zero." Needless to say, Pedro made sure their efforts weren't in vain.

His next game was the occasion of Carlos Delgado's 400th career home run. "Carlos Delgado…he's good," Liam said, confirming the fact by wearing a "21" Mets shirt. "I thought his [total] was higher because he's been around so long…. When he hit the home run, everyone yelled like heck and my eardrums hurt really bad."

He watched to the bitter end of Game 7 of the 2006 NLCS on TV from his home in Orange, Connecticut (near New Haven). "I felt sad," he said, then immediately shifted gears. "Actually, I felt pretty good once the Cardinals won the World Series because they are the closest to the Yankees to winning the World Series, but it's going to take a while." Since this interview when Liam was eight, the Yankees are now 27–10 over the Cardinals in titles. Sigh.

Can the Mets ever equal that mark? Liam's a realist: "The Mets have maybe a 2 percent chance." He's good at math. "It would take 20-something years to get to that."

Liam's already working on his own book on the team: *Mets in the Past*. It'll be an even bigger seller if he is successor to Jose Reyes as shortstop. You tell him he can't.

Hot Wheels Cars: 1990s–2000s
Baseball Mitts: 1992
Batting Helmets: 1965–2008 (intermittent)

**Adult**
Kiner/Murphy Bobbleheads: 2003
Negro League Caps: 1990s
Sunglasses: 1990s
Pitchers (including 4 tumblers): 1988
Flip Flops: 1984

Even with Citi Field brand-spanking-new in 2009, the Mets had some good giveaway booty in the form of Johan Santana drawstring bags, Father's Day blankets, Citi Field replicas, kids' lunchboxes, bobbleheads, batting helmets, and commemorative 1969 shirts for the 40th anniversary of the first Mets champion.

# 100 The Home Run Apple

Love it or hate it, the legacy of Shea Stadium is a shiny red fiberglass apple the size of a truck. The Citi Field version is not your father's home run apple, which was campy enough to look like something Adam West battled along with the Riddler in the 1960s TV show *Batman*. But even those predisposed to dislike the home run apple on principle have to smile because when the apple goes up, a Met has just hit a home run. What's not to like?

The original apple dates from 1981, when it debuted in Year Two of the Nelson Doubleday–Fred Wilpon ownership. Year One had featured the removal of Shea Stadium's signature blue and orange exterior metal panels and the replacement of the original wooden chairs with durable plastic seats colored orange, blue, green, and red (in ascending order by deck). The Mets made history by being the first team to hire an ad agency; pitchman Jerry Della Femina took a mighty cut, slapping a slogan on the ostensibly bare exterior of Shea: "The Magic Is Back." The magic wasn't back but the Mets were trying, which was a start after three straight star-stripping, soul-crushing, last-place finishes under team president Linda deRoulet, daughter of the club's beloved original owner, Joan Payson. The new owners paid the highest sale price in baseball history: $21.1 million (a sum that three decades later the team pays *annually* to pitcher Johan Santana). The cost was high and the '80 Mets, whose flirtation with contention came crashing down with an 11–38 slide, stayed out of the cellar for the first time in three years thanks to the 98-loss Cubs. There was nowhere to go but up.

Slugger Dave Kingman was back for his second tour as a Met in 1981, an attempt to boost the paltry 61 home runs the team collected the previous year. Along with hope of more homers, the Mets introduced a new way to celebrate the long ball. The giant top hat behind the center-field fence was nine feet tall and, according to the *Daily News*, weighed in at exactly 582 pounds. The red apple was housed in a black hat that said "Mets Magic" (later changed to "Home Run"). It wasn't the exploding scoreboard at Chicago's Comiskey Park, but you had to admit it was original.

And the '81 Mets hit…57 home runs. In their defense, baseball's first prolonged strike wiped out almost a third of that year's schedule and split the season in two. Overall, Mets home runs were up 17 percent and Kong had 22 in his return, tied for third in the National League with George Foster, who would come to the Mets from Cincinnati in 1982. Although the team's fortunes would take a couple more years to shake out, the power outage was history.

Fast-forward 28 years to another apple and another drought. Bigger (16' x 18'), heavier (4,800 pounds), and more polished (the old one looked like fruit that had been dropped a few times), the new apple rose just 49 times via the home run in its inaugural 2009 season. It even malfunctioned following 16 days of midsummer idleness. On July 12, light-hitting catcher Brian Schneider took ex-Met David Weathers deep in the home seventh, breaking the club's 80-inning homerless streak and putting the apple into game action for the first time since June 26. Two batters later, pinch-hitter Fernando Tatis homered off the same Reds pitcher, the first time in more than two months that two Mets had circled the bases in the same inning. (Not surprisingly, Cincinnati traded Weathers a few weeks later.) As Tatis trotted around the bases, however, the apple stayed inside the hat. Fans started chanting, "Apple! Apple!" Finally, when the Mets were retired for the inning, the apple went up to uproarious applause.

Fortunately, fans don't have to wait for a home run to see the apple's hydraulic ascent: before games and during the seventh-inning stretch the apple also rises—not to be confused with Ernest Hemingway's *The Sun Also Rises*. A survey conducted by the Mets found that 89 percent of fans wanted a home run apple at the new ballpark. As the Mets made arrangements with a Minnesota company to construct the new apple, an online movement—"Save the Apple"—collected nearly 9,000 signatures on a petition urging the Mets not to trash the original apple or sell it to a private collector. The old apple moved a few hundred feet to just inside the center-field entrance to Citi Field, sitting for portraits and viewable from the fittingly renamed Shea Bridge. The apple lives...and so do the Mets.

# Trivia Answers

**Page 10:** Joe Torre. The Cardinals' first baseman's 6–4–3 grounder completed rookie Gary Gentry's shutout and capped a comeback from 10 games out on August 13. This nail-in-the-Cubbies'-coffin on September 24 marked the last home game on the Mets' schedule, but it was the first of three times Shea would be torn apart in three weeks.

**Page 36:** Jerry Koosman, Tom Seaver's old friend, beat Tom Terrific at Riverfront Stadium, 4–2, on July 13, 1978. It was his last win of the year and of Kooz's Mets career. Seaver had won his first career game against the Mets at Koosman's expense at Shea Stadium in 1977.

**Page 62:** Benny Ayala on August 27, 1974. Mike Fitzgerald (September 13, 1983), Kaz Matsui (April 6, 2004), and Mike Jacobs (August 21, 2005) later followed by homering in their first major league at-bats while wearing a Mets uniform.

**Page 90:** The 1969 Mets won 41 times by one run (out of 64 such games). The close-but-no-cigar 1985 and 1998 teams were the only squads to come within single digits of 41, which is also Tom Seaver's retired uniform number.

**Page 104:** Mike Bascik. Bascik, a lefty with a 4–4 mark as a Met with 13 homers allowed in 73⅓ innings in 2002–2003, was with the Washington Nationals when his full-count fastball was drilled by Barry Bonds in the fifth inning to break Hank Aaron's home run total in San Francisco on August 7, 2007. Mets fan Matt Murphy caught the ball and held onto it amid a pounding from the rogue gallery.

**Page 114:** 1985. The 9–9 mark of Sid Fernandez was as bad as things got for Mets pitchers on that year's 98-win club.

**Page 150:** Rookie Jon Matlack allowed a double to Roberto Clemente in the fourth inning on September 29, 1972. Clemente was hit for his next time up—by Bill Mazeroski—and never batted again in a regular-season game. Clemente went 4-for-17 against Cincinnati in that year's NLCS. He was killed in a plane crash en route to aid earthquake victims in Nicaragua on December 31 that year.

**Page 174:** Frank Viola. The Mets sent five pitchers to the Twins for the previous year's AL Cy Young winner on July 31, 1989. He had a record of 38–32, including a 20-win season in 1990, in two-plus seasons as a Met. The Twins won the World Series in 1991.

**Page 219:** Jerry Grote. He had 12 hits while catching all 12 World Series games for the Mets in 1969 and 1973. He batted 49 times all told (another club mark), so his World Series average was a Grote-esque .249.

**Page 250:** David Wright doubled in the first inning against San Diego's Walter Silva on April 13, 2009. Wright later hit the first home run by a Met at Citi Field in the fifth to tie the game, though the Mets lost 6–5.

# Notes

### Standing the World on Its Ear
"What's .500?..." Koppett, Leonard, *The New York Mets,* New York: Collier Books, 1974.

### Tom Seaver
"He's the kind of man you'd..." baseball-almanac.com/quotes.

"If you don't think baseball is a big deal..." Jordan, Pat, *The Suitors of Spring,* New York: Dodd, Mead & Company, 1973.

### Messy Jesse's Sweet 16 in Houston
"I thought Jesse needed a little pumping up..." Marty Noble, "Orosco to Throw Out First Pitch to Carter," MLB.com, March 20, 2006.

### Dykstra Nails It
"Lenny Dykstra, the man they call 'Nails'..." Bob Murphy (1986 call), 40th Anniversary Commemorative CD, Sony/WFAN, 2002.

### All-Star Announcing Trio
"No network can give me..." Nelson, Lindsey with Al Hirshberg, *Backstage at the Mets,* New York: Viking Press, 1966.

"If Casey Stengel were alive" and "Two thirds of the earth..." Wayne Corbett, "Ralph Kiner," bioproj.sabr.org.

### The Seaver Deal
"Both are very good at what they do..." Bill Madden, "The True Story of the Midnight Massacre," *New York Daily News,* July 21, 2007.

"When he sat with reporters..." and "Seaver's voice broke off..." Lang, Jack and Peter Simon, *The New York Mets: Twenty-Five Years of Baseball Magic,* New York: Henry Holt and Company, 1986.

### Keith Hernandez
"The Siberia of baseball..." Hernandez, Keith and Mark Bryan, *If at First,* New York: McGraw-Hill Book Company, 1986.

"They told me it was going to be minimal lines..." Jerry Crowe, "Hernandez Spits It Out about his Role on Seinfeld," *Los Angeles Times,* July 23, 2007.

### Casey Stengel
"It's a great honor for me..." Koppett, Leonard, *The New York Mets,* New York: Collier Books, 1974.

"If any of the writers come looking for me…" Lang, Jack and Peter Simon, *The New York Mets: Twenty-Five Years of Baseball Magic,* New York: Henry Holt & Company, 1986.

## Stengel-ese Decoded

"I want to say that the Mets fans…" Nelson, Lindsey with Al Hirshberg, *Backstage at the Mets,* New York: Viking Press, 1966.

## Tug McGraw

"Ninety percent of it…" "Baseball Web Quote of the Day," quote.webcircle.com.

## Benny's Blast

"A high flyball…" Gary Cohen (2000 call), 40ᵗʰ Anniversary Commemorative CD, Sony/WFAN, 2002.

## Joan Payson

"PLEASE…" and "That was about…" Breslin, Jimmy. *Can't Anybody Here Play This Game,* New York: Viking Press, 1963.

## The Original Original Mets

"I want to thank all these generous owners…" Breslin, Jimmy. *Can't Anybody Here Play This Game,* New York: Viking Press, 1963.

## The Team to Beat

"We have so much talent…," "Sometimes when you're a team…," and "I think at times we get…" John Koblin, "Gutsy Mr. Metsy," *The New York Observer,* October 1, 2007.

## To Cheer Again

"It didn't bother me, losing that game…" Shaun Powell, "Must Not Forget That Special Night at Shea," *Newsday,* September 11, 2007.

## Fallen Stars: Doc and Straw

"When he wanted to be…" Sokolove, Michael, *The Ticket Out,* New York: Simon & Schuster, 2004.

## The New York Press

"[Bill] Shea, in his work to bring the team to New York…" and "Joyful irreverence." Koppett, Leonard, *The New York Mets,* New York: Collier Books, 1974.

## Sidd Finch, Figment

"He's a pitcher, part yogi…" George Plimpton, "The Curious Case of Sidd Finch," *Sports Illustrated,* April 1, 1985.

## Gary Carter
"By the time they finish with him…" Kalinsky, George, *The New York Mets: A Photographic History,* New York: Macmillan, 1995.

## Tommie Agee
"The wind brought the ball back…" Tommie Agee (1969 interview), 40th Anniversary Commemorative CD, Sony/WFAN, 2002.

## Swoboda Happens
"Swoboda…" and "We had no preconceptions…" Cohen, Stanley, *A Magic Summer: The '69 Mets,* San Diego: Harcourt Brace Javonovich, 1988.

## Seventh Heaven and Hell
"He struck him out!…" Bob Murphy (1986 call), 40th Anniversary Commemorative CD, Sony/WFAN, 2002.

## Carlos Beltran
"We've become irrelevant…" Gary Smith, "The Story of O," *Sports Illustrated,* June 18, 2007.

## Bud Harrelson
"A moment of insanity." *New York Times,* July 31, 1991.

## Jon Matlack
"That was a staff that knew…" Ray Lauenstein, "Interview with Jon Matlack," athletesadvisor.com.

## First to the Plate and First Out the Gate
"Most Valuable Player on the worst team ever? Just how did they mean that?" Koppett, Leonard, *The New York Mets,* New York: Collier Books, 1974.

## Closing Arguments
*The Book: Playing the Percentages in Baseball,* Tango, Tom M., Mitchel G. Lichtman, and Andrew E. Dolphin, Potomac Books, 2007.

## Marvelous Marv: M.E.T. To Be
"Hey, you're stealing my fans." Paskin, Janet, *Tales from the 1962 New York Mets,* Champaign, IL: Sports Publishing, 2004.

## The Polo Grounds
"That smug borough…," "manicured greensward…," and "It will be a sad day…" Robert Lipsyte, "An Image in Concrete," *New York Times,* July 7, 1963.

## Lost in Translation

Information on Mets players' careers in Japan can be found at japanesebaseball. com/players/index.jsp.

## 1964 All-Star Game

"I said, 'I'm going to hit the first pitch...' " Larry Stone, "Callison's Crowning Glory," *Seattle Times,* July 3, 2001.

## Cast of Characters

"I like to call it colorful..." and "People used to think I was showing them up..." Roger Rubin, *New York Daily News,* July 26, 2007

## A Missed Shot in the (Alvin) Dark

"The mere accusation, and the impossibility of ever putting it to rest..." Koppett, Leonard, *The New York Mets,* New York: Collier Books, 1974.

## Mets Wives: Anna Other Thing

"Nolan Ryan is getting more money than Tom Seaver and that galls Tom..." Bock, Duncan and John Jordan, *The Complete Year-by-Year N.Y. Mets Fan's Almanac,* New York: Crown Publishers, 1992.

## The Beatles

"Ladies and gentleman..." and song list, from loge13.com and maccafan.net.